About this book

Recent years have witnessed a growing litany of stock exchange implosions, flights of capital, currency collapses, investment scams, tax evasion, and now terrorists hiding their funds in offshore havens. They are part of a veritable epidemic of financial crises – from Mexico, through Southeast Asia, Russia, Brazil and then Argentina. The point has been reached where the rich industrial countries, led by the United States, have had to respond. This book examines the G7's attempts over the past decade to re-establish rules and a degree of order in the world financial system through the creation of the Financial Stability Forum and the G20, which they are calling the New International Financial Architecture. Susanne Soederberg asks:

• Why has the New International Financial Architecture emerged?
• At whose initiative?
• What does it involve?
• What are the underlying power relations?
• Who is benefiting?
• Will it really work?

What emerges is that the US remains wedded to financial liberalization because it is in the interests of transnational corporations and the American government itself to retain their structural power in the global economy. The US is using its political and economic muscle to compel the rest of the world, and notably the emerging markets in the South and elsewhere, to expose their economies to the un-regulated demands of international (mainly Western) finance.

This book provides a real understanding of the structural dynamics of this deliberately constructed domination of finance, and the latest developments in the global economy. The author argues, however, that this tinkering with the capitalist system will not achieve either sustained economic growth or stability in financial markets, let alone enhance the capability of developing countries to tackle the problems of mass poverty and social injustice.

About the author

Susanne Soederberg is Associate Professor in Development Studies and holder of the Canada Research Chair at Queen's University, Kingston, Ontario. She is the author of a forthcoming book, *Deconstructing Global Governance: Empire, Class, and the New Common Sense of Managing Globalization in the South* (London: Pluto Press/ Ann Arbor: University of Michigan Press).

The Politics of the New International Financial Architecture

Reimposing Neoliberal Domination in the Global South

Susanne Soederberg

ZED BOOKS
London & New York

The Politics of the New International Financial Architecture was first published
in 2004 by Zed Books Ltd, 7 Cynthia Street, London N1 9JF, UK, and
Room 400, 175 Fifth Avenue, New York, NY 10010, USA
www.zedbooks.co.uk

Designed and typeset in Monotype Bembo by Illuminati, Grosmont
Cover designed by Andrew Corbett
Printed and bound in the EU by Biddles Ltd, King's Lynn

Distributed in the USA exclusively by Palgrave, a division of
St Martin's Press, LLC, 175 Fifth Avenue, New York, NY 10010

A catalogue record for this book is available from the British Library

Library of Congress Cataloging-in-Publication Data available

ISBN 1 84277 378 x (Hb)
ISBN 1 84277 379 8 (Pb)

Contents

List of Tables

Abbreviations

AMF	Asian Monetary Fund
BEMs	Big emerging markets
BIS	Bank for International Settlements
CAC	Capital account convertibility
CACs	Collective Action Clauses
CETES	Certificados de la Tesorería de la Federación
CSOs	Civil society organizations
DWSR	Dollar Wall Street Regime
ECLAC	UN Economic Commission on Latin American and the Caribbean
EPI	Export promotion industrialization
FDI	Foreign direct investment
FfD	Financing for Development
FPI	Foreign Portfolio Investment
FSF	Financial Stability Forum
FTAA	Free Trade Area of the Americas
G7	Group of Seven
G20	Group of Twenty
GAB	General Arrangement to Borrow
GATS	General Agreement on Trade in Services

GATT	General Agreement on Tariffs and Trade
GDP	Gross Domestic Product
GNP	Gross National Product
HIPCs	Highly Indebted Poor Countries
IFI	International financial institution
ILO	International Labour Organization
IMF	International Monetary Fund
IPE	International Political Economy
ISI	Import Substitution Industrialization
LTCM	Long Term Credit Management
MAI	Multilateral Agreement on Investments
NAB	New Arrangement to Borrow
NAFTA	North American Free Trade Agreement
Nepad	New Economic Partnership for African Development
NIFA	New International Financial Architecture
OECD	Organisation for Economic Cooperation and Development
PRGF	Poverty Reduction and Growth Facility
PRSPs	Poverty Reduction Strategy Papers
ROSC	Report on the Observances of Standards and Codes
SAPs	Structural adjustment policies
SGRs	Second Generation Reforms
URR	Unremunerated reserve requirement
WTO	World Trade Organization

For Marcus

I

Transcending the 'Common Sense' of the New International Financial Architecture

The Asian financial collapse of 1997–98 caught the international financial community by surprise. It also opened the floodgates to a torrent of criticism about the viability of the dominant policy stance that free capital mobility facilitates sustained economic growth in the South. Relatedly, transnational policy organizations, such as the Bank for International Settlements, G7, International Monetary Fund (IMF), International Organization of Securities Commissions (IOSCO), also came under attack. In particular, their ad hoc and erratic forms of regulation and supervision over financial markets were criticized as inadequate for not only providing warning of the imminent crisis, but also for encouraging increased capital volatility in the global political economy.[1] In response to this mounting censure, international policymakers, under the auspices of G7 summits – most notably the Halifax Summit of 1995 and the Cologne Summit of 1999 – attempted to create a new multilateral governance structure that would ostensibly strengthen the existing international financial system through the reduction of volatility. The establishment of new international standards and regulatory institutions resulting from these closed, high-level meetings has been officially referred to as the New International Financial Architecture (hereafter NIFA).

There are three prominent features of the NIFA: the Group of Twenty (G20), the Financial Stability Forum (FSF), and a set of international standards and codes referred to as the Reports on the Observances of Standards and Codes (ROSCs). Although these institutions will be discussed in more detail in the following chapters, it is useful to outline their roles here briefly. The G20 brings together for the first time the G7, a representative from the European Union, the IMF and its newly established International Monetary and Financial Committee (IMFC), the World Bank, and what the G7 refers to as 'systematically important' emerging market economies: Argentina, Australia, Brazil, China, India, Indonesia, Mexico, Saudi Arabia, South Africa, South Korea and Turkey.[2] The FSF, on the other hand, seeks to provide regular meetings of national authorities responsible for financial stability from G7 countries. Included in the forum are Hong Kong and Singapore, the World Bank, the IMF, the Bank for International Settlements, and OECD, alongside international regulatory and supervisory groups plus central bank experts in order to enhance discussions about financial supervision and surveillance. The main objective of the FSF is to achieve systemic stability by ensuring that all countries, especially those that are seen by the G7 as the main source of instability – namely, emerging market economies – adopt the rules and standards of the global capital markets and G7 countries through adherence to pro-market principles, which essentially implies the least amount of government interference in the financial system as possible. At the core of this stabilization strategy lie the ROSCs (see Chapter 4), which encompass twelve areas that are targeted at regulating private and public sectors in the South – for example, anti-money laundering and countering the finance of terrorism, transparency, corporate governance, securities, insurance, payment systems, and so forth. The various modules that comprise the ROSCs are policed by a complex of intergovernmental organizations such as the IMF, OECD, the World Bank, and private international organizations, which include, inter alia, the IOSCO, and the International Association of Insurance Supervisors (IAIS).

In its simplest form, the main contention of this book is that the NIFA is more than an intricate network of institutions and actors striving to work towards the stability of the global financial system. I argue that the NIFA is a class-based strategy targeted at re-creating existing power relations in the global political economy – most notably transnational financial capitals and the United States – by ensuring that both public and private sectors in the South comply with the neoliberal rules of free capital mobility. Specifically, the NIFA seeks to reproduce and institutionalize two important

'common sense' assumptions. First, and foremost, financial liberalization is posited as a desirable policy because, like trade liberalization,
it leads to economic growth and stability. Second, and related to
this neoclassical assumption, debtor countries should be exposed
more directly to the exigencies of transnational finance so that they
may be forced to undertake market-based solutions to their current
economic and political problems. At the end of this Chapter, I sum-
marize the major tenets of this argument and show how the various
chapters incrementally support these propositions.

To build this argument, the main purpose of the current chapter is
to provide an analytical sketch-map through which we may widen
and deepen the mainstream understanding of the NIFA as a network of institutions and norms, but also deconstruct of the above-
mentioned common-sense assumptions underpinning the NIFA. For
Antonio Gramsci the notion of common sense (or the 'philosophy
of the multitude') is significant because it is a site for political
contestation and struggle.[3] As Mark Rupert reminds us, common
sense is

> not univocal and coherent, but an amalgam of historically effective ideolo-
> gies, scientific doctrines and social mythologies. This historical 'sedimen-
> tation' of popular common sense 'is not something rigid and immobile,
> but is continually transforming itself, enriching itself with scientific ideas
> and with philosophical opinions which have entered ordinary life. [It] is
> the folklore of philosophy...' As such, it is 'fragmentary, incoherent and
> inconsequential, in conformity with the social and cultural position of
> those masses whose philosophy it is'.[4]

Seen from the above perspective the analytical exercise of deconstructing common sense is inextricably linked to political
concerns. Following this line of reasoning, this chapter suggests that
two preliminary steps must be undertaken in order to deconstruct
the common sense of the NIFA. First, we discuss the need to conceptualize the NIFA in a more critical light. Therefore we begin
our discussion by identifying various gaps in the existing literature
and introduce the main argument of this book. Second, we outline
an analytical frame that will allow us to make sense of the blueprint
of the NIFA as a complex and contradictory class-led strategy. This
involves engaging in critical theorizations of the NIFA by moving
beyond its structural boundaries so that we may examine and explain

for whom the edifice was built and for what purpose. After elaborating on this conceptual lens, the chapter revisits the main argument of the book and outlines how the argument will be developed in the remaining five chapters.

Unexplored Areas of the New Building

Broadly speaking, two main approaches to the NIFA have dominated the literature. Without wishing to homogenize these two strands, we observe that the first approach draws more heavily on economics and the latter employs what some have termed 'orthodox' international political economy.[5] With respect to the former, economic-centred analyses gloss over historical, political and ideological factors, and thereby offer incomplete explanations of the origins and the relations of power regarding the NIFA.[6] Largely due to their acceptance of the existing economic system as a given (or natural occurrence), economic-centric approaches are not concerned with explaining change. Because these approaches subscribe to the assumption of the inherent rationality of economic actors, these theorists see an analysis of power as unimportant. Susan Strange captures this 'deliberate myopia' inherent to many economic analyses:

> anything that upsets or goes against economic theory is apt to be referred to as an 'exogenous factor' – often as an 'exogenous shock', especially shocking to economists unprepared by nature to expect power factors to intervene, whether from governments or operators in the market. And behaviour that is not constrained with the premises of economic theory then, of course, becomes condescendingly and disapprovingly referred to as 'irrational', however sensible it may seem to the ordinary person.[7]

On the other hand, students of international political economy have tended to focus on the institutional landscape of the NIFA (the FSF, the ROSCs and the G20). While these writers are interested in studying the relationships between political and economic actors, their analyses start from the premiss that the dominance of finance is a fait accompli, and thus must be accepted not contested. Likewise they ignore the important linkages among the NIFA, global capitalism, US hegemony and, relatedly, class domination.[8] Both approaches share at least two areas of insouciance. The first is geopolitical. Most scholars attempt to make sense of the NIFA from the perspective of the North, thus largely disregarding the economic, political and ideological importance of the global South to the continued expansion and stability of the G7 countries. This concurrently elides the role played by the ruling classes in the South, and their complex interactions with transnational capital. It is helpful to pause here for a moment in order to clarify what is understood by the term 'the South' in this book. As our discussions of Mexico (Chapter 2), Chile and Malaysia (Chapter 4) reveal, this book focuses on the category of emerging markets or middle-income countries.[9] There are two reasons for this. First, this group of countries has been the largest recipient of short-term, highly volatile, financial flows, and thus the unfortunate host to multiple crises.[10] Second, over the past decade, the United States has increasingly and overtly expressed its interest in fostering ties with 'systemically important' emerging markets. As Jeffrey Garten, the former Under Secretary of Commerce for International Trade, observes:

> In 10 'Big Emerging Markets' (BEMs): China (including Taiwan and Hong Kong), India, Indonesia, Brazil, Mexico, Turkey, South Korea, South Africa, Poland, and Argentina. Those countries alone contain nearly one-half of the world's population, have the most rapidly growing economies in the world, and have governments currently committed to the trade-led growth and cooperation with the United States.... America's domestic economic success will depend on deepening engagement in the 10 Big Emerging Markets.[11]

That said, the relevance of the emerging markets for the US and transnational capital does not negate the importance of the rest of the South, or what Samir Amin gloomily, albeit realistically, views as the marginal and excluded states. While the focus of this book does not directly touch upon these last two categories, this does in no way suggests that the attempts by the US and transnational capitals to construct and legitimate neoliberal domination do not apply to the rest of the South. Our discussion of the NIFA vis-à-vis emerging markets has immediate ramifications for the rest of the South for at least two reasons. For one thing, there are important lessons to be drawn from capital account liberalization and the middle-income countries – most of which are now deemed to be 'submerging markets'.[12] For another, and as Chapter 6 will recount in more detail

with its discussion of the Financing for Development (FfD) conference in Monterrey, Mexico, in March 2002, the imperative of free
capital mobility is becoming a cornerstone of the emerging global
development agenda. This is seen not only in the pronouncements
of the international financial institutions (IFIs), but also within the
plans of regional ruling elites. An recent example of this is the
economic blueprint for African renewal known as the Nepad (New
Economic Partnership for African Development). It must therefore
be taken seriously and challenged.

A second lacuna concerning the literature on the NIFA is the
unwillingness to engage theoretically with the role and power of
the United States vis-à-vis the global capitalist system. The primary
reason for this neglect is that the two above-mentioned strands of
analysis, which dominate the study of the NIFA, are largely based
in frameworks that are essentially problem-solving as opposed to
critical. A short digression is appropriate at this point in order to
elaborate on this important distinction. As Robert Cox suggested,
problem-solving theories assume that the basic elements of the
international system are not subject to fundamental transformation. Therein, with regard to the NIFA, for problem-solvers it is
the action, structures and processes within the parameters of this
new building that are the object of study. The analytical focus is
demarcated by the institutional components of the new edifice. It is
within this bounded framework that these theorists seek to observe
and explain action, without questioning the limits of the system. As
such, questions of who benefits and why from the construction of
the NIFA remain unanswered.

In contrast to problem-solving theories, critical perspectives move
beyond the confines of the existing institutional structure of the
NIFA in order to identify and explain its origins and developmental potential. 'While problem solving theory assumes functional coherence of existing phenomena, critical theory seeks out the sources
of contradiction and conflict in these entities and evaluates their
potential to change into different patterns.'[13] What sets this book
apart from existing analyses of the NIFA is not simply its focus on a
multi-levelled analysis of national and international spaces of political
activity, but also its attempts to make sense of this phenomenon by
understanding the fundamental contradiction from which this new

edifice emerged. As such, the discussion explores why the NIFA emerged and in whose interests it functions. As Robert Cox notes, anyone who 'abhor[s] the social and political implications of the [neoliberal-led] globalization project must study its contradictions in order to work for its eventual replacement'.[14]

The two key objectives of this book are to address these gaps in the literature on the NIFA and to shed more light on the contradictions underpinning the NIFA. To achieve this goal I identify three broad and overlapping moments that mark the larger contradiction from which the NIFA arose: (1) the relation between the US and free capital mobility; (2) the crisis of global capitalism, and; (3) the tensions created by capital account liberalization in the South. Before elaborating on each factor in turn, two provisos should be noted. First, the three moments of this triad are neither objects nor things but instead represent historically developing forms of human struggle and conflict. Second, the separation between these three social relations is solely for analytical purposes. In reality, the relations between the US, the South, and the crisis of global capitalism are far more complex and interdependent than this heuristic device allows. Nonetheless the three tentacles that comprise the frame for understanding are a useful way in which to begin going beyond common-sense explanations endemic in problem-solving approaches to the NIFA. This is so because these three factors help us to recognize political decisions involved in constructing the NIFA, and thus enable us to identify the source(s) of power of this conflict-led class-based strategy, as opposed to treating it as a neutral institutional response to some sort of breakdown or distortion in the international system of finance.[15]

It is to the most powerful social forces of the financial structure in the global political economy and their contradictions that the discussion now turns.

The United States and Free Capital Mobility

This section suggests that there is an important relationship between financial liberalization and the structural power of the United States in the post-Bretton Woods era (1971 to the present). Drawing on Susan Strange, we can say that structural power describes the power to shape and determine the structures of the global political economy within which other states, their political institutions, and their economic enterprises have to operate.[16] Since the demise of the Bretton Woods system (1944–1971), the shift to freely floating exchange rates and the eradication of capital controls, the US has attempted to overcome its increasingly uncompetitive position in the world economy, and therein maintain its structural power, through its ability to decide the price of the world's trading and reserve currency freely – that is, the paper dollar standard or dollar seigniorage.[17] This in turn has allowed the United States to exercise its structural power over other states, especially those in the South, by influencing international monetary and credit arrangements in the global economy.[18] The importance of US structural power vis-à-vis the South has taken the expression of what I term 'imposed US leadership'. This latter term is developed in Chapter 3, when we begin to examine more closely the power relationships surrounding the NIFA. For our current purposes, however, we need only begin to problematize US structural power in the wider global political economy.

Seen from the above perspective, the upshot of the US-led campaign for capital market liberalization has had the unintended consequence of both constraining and enabling US power in the South. The relationship between the creator of the competition strategy based on capital liberalization and the exponential growth of financial markets may be likened to Mary Shelley's celebrated novel *Frankenstein*. As in the narrative, the main protagonist (Dr Frankenstein) and his creation (the monster) have a symbiotic relationship, marked by mutually beneficial and mutually destructive tendencies. On the one hand the relationship is mutually beneficial because as the international financial markets grow in size and power, so does the US economy, which absorbs the majority of these flows.[19] This seemingly symbiotic relationship between the US and free capital mobility is captured in what Peter Gowan has referred to as the Dollar Wall Street Regime (DWSR). According to Gowan, the US

> does not face the same balance of payments constraints that other countries face. It can spend far more abroad than it earns there. Thus, it can set up expensive military bases without a foreign exchange constraint; its transnational corporations can buy up other companies abroad or

engage in other forms of foreign direct investment without a payments constraint; its money-capitalists can send out large flows of funds into portfolio investments [stocks and bonds].[20]

Similar to the rapport between Dr Frankenstein and his monster, a constraining feature also characterizes the relationship between the insatiable greed of Wall Street and Washington's ongoing obsession with financial liberalization. Through his exploits, the monster gains increasing power over his creator. The concentration and centralization of wealth within the financial system are a case in point. Notwithstanding that about 83 per cent of the approximately $3 trillion of daily foreign exchange trading involves the US dollar, or that about 59 per cent of world foreign exchange reserves were held in US dollars, the American government bond market remains the largest financial market of its kind in the world.

At the centre of the market are 38 major investment and commercial banks who are certified as primary dealers by the Federal Reserve Bank of New York – the choice of inner circle with which the Fed [Federal Reserve Bank of the US] conducts it official monetary business. At the end of 1992, according to a New York Fed survey, traders turned over an amount equal to a year's GDP in about three weeks.[21]

This highlights the increasing dependency of the US economy on the constant inflow of capital as well as on continued international adherence to the imperative of free capital mobility. Likewise, this implies the mounting vulnerability of the US vis-à-vis the growing power of transnationally oriented financial capital, a weakness that is re-addressed below.

The Frankenstein factor has distinct resonance in the South. Through the past fifteen years of imposing the imperative of free capital mobility in the Southern hemisphere, the neoliberal-led Washington consensus has increased exponentially the power of international financial markets not only over states but also over the most powerful of them all: the United States. As a consequence, the viability of American structural power has become ever more dependent on the health and stability of global financial markets, in which large American financial institutions are significant actors. In the words of the former Secretary of the Treasury Department, Robert Rubin, in reaction to Indonesia's economic woes in 1997,

'Financial stability around the world is critical to the national security and economic interest of the United States.'[22] Nevertheless, with every debacle brought on by the currency or financial speculation, the neoclassical premises upon which the Washington consensus rests – especially the equation between free capital mobility and rational-led economic 'progress' – become increasingly difficult to legitimate in the South. To return to our metaphor: with each murder the monster commits, the relationship between the monster and its creator teeters toward self-destruction.

This situation further aggravates the non-hegemonic nature of US structural power. Since the breakdown of the Bretton Woods system, US structural power has been non-hegemonic in nature, implying, in the Gramscian sense, that it lacks intellectual and moral leadership. As such, with each financial debacle in the South, US structural power, predicated on the DWSR, undergoes what Gramsci refers to as a 'crisis of authority'. Gramsci has also referred to this as a 'general crisis of the state' or 'crisis of hegemony'. These concepts describe a situation in which the

> ruling class has lost its consensus, i.e., is no longer 'leading' but only 'dominant', exercising coercive force alone, this means precisely that the great masses have become detached from their traditional ideologies, and no longer believe what they used to believe previously, etc.[23]

Nonetheless, the contradiction between the mutually destructive and beneficial relations between the monster and his creator must be conceptualized within the social relations of global capitalism. It is to the contemporary expressions of these relations that we now turn.

The Crisis of Global Capitalism and the Dollar Wall Street Regime

The basis of the Dollar Wall Street Regime and the underlying Frankenstein factor is not to be found solely within the 'limits' of the international financial system. To remain within these confines would imply not only engaging in problem-solving theory but also engendering a partial understanding of the underlying contradictions to which the NIFA is an integral response. Put differently, the structural power of the US vis-à-vis international finance and the Frankenstein factor are not simply products of political choices made by powerful classes and policymakers; they are equally tempered by the inherent contradictions within the ongoing crisis of global capitalism. Indeed, while most observers would agree that the most distinguishing feature of the world economy is the growth of power of finance over the so-called 'real economy' (production and trade), few scholars find it necessary to go beyond the appearance that finance has somehow become delinked from the world of production and distribution, and, relatedly, to question why there has been an enormous shift of capital into money since the early 1970s. In our attempts to deconstruct the NIFA it is important to ask why this apparent separation exists, in order to grasp how the dominance of finance is reproduced, as well as by whom and for whom.

The dominance of finance is readily seen in the sheer volume of transactions in the global financial markets, which have reached an estimated $1.5 trillion a day. To put this in perspective:

> 30 years ago about 90 per cent of foreign exchange transactions were related to the real economy (trade and long-term investment), by now well over 90 per cent of a vastly greater sum consists of short-term flows, about 80 per cent less than a week in duration, often much shorter, speculating against currencies or exchange rate fluctuations.[24]

What has led to the dominance of finance over production? Although technological innovation and government deregulation have played a role in integrating financial markets, they are far from the underlying reasons in explaining the root of this change. Most Marxists view the dominance of finance as a moment of the larger crisis of global capitalism, which some have referred to as a crisis of overaccumulation.[25]

Broadly, this crisis refers to a major barrier in capital valorization wherein investment in the productive sphere is no longer a profitable exercise. From this vantage point, the growth of finance must be located in the inability of production to provide enough profit for capital. As John Holloway notes, 'Capital assumes the liquid form of money and flows throughout the world in search of profit. Instead of embodying itself in the bricks and mortar, machinery and workers of productive investment, it flows in search of speculative, often very short-term means of expansion.'[26] By investing in stocks, bonds and foreign-exchange derivatives, individuals are not escaping the productive sphere but are instead 'buying and selling claims on future value created in future productive activity. They are not handing over funds for that productive activity; they are claiming future royalties from it.'[27] Put another way, although finance may appear to be disarticulated from the real economy through its continued dominance over production, finance is very much an integral moment of wider capitalist social relations and the ongoing crisis of capitalism.

The start of the most recent phase of crisis in global capitalism during the late 1960s is believed to have brought about the demise of the Bretton Woods system in 1971. This crisis has been identified by some as a crisis of Fordist forms of capital accumulation, which some define as a regime of accumulation involving specific forms of capitalist production based on mass production of goods as well as social consumption norms.[28] The fall of this regime of accumulation was marked by a general deterioration of economic conditions at the world level, marked by high inflation, high unemployment and increasingly high debt loads in both public and private sectors. Broadly speaking, this crisis is predominately characterized by shorter boom–bust cycles and growing debt burdens in both private and public sectors across national spaces.

According to Harry Magdoff et al., one of the main causes of the 'slowdown is that the rate of investment tends to exceed the growth of final demand'. To illustrate, the manufacturing sector in China, which is one of the hot growth centres of the global economy, is operating at approximately 40 per cent excess capacity, while the worldwide automobile industry has 30 per cent overcapacity.[29] Thus, despite the constant references to the growing productivity of the US, this does not always translate into faster profit growth. Let us concentrate on how this crisis manifests itself in the centre of global capitalism: the United States. For example, although America's productivity rate in the non-farm business sector rose at an annual rate of 8.6 per cent – the fastest growth rate in about nineteen years, firms are left with

> massive amounts of unused capacity and unsold inventory. And, in spite of massive attempts by companies to trim costs, usually by laying off workers, sales have not kept up with the pace of output. Further invest-

ment is then impeded because corporations are reluctant to invest in the face of substantial excess capacity – sometimes referred to as 'capital overhang'.[30]

According to these authors, from the 1980s onwards, the growth of the US economy was due to the increasing use of private debt. Writing in the context of the United States, Magdoff et al. observe that '[b]y 2002, outstanding private debt is two and one quarter times GDP, while total outstanding debt – private plus government – approaches three times the GDP. The productive (e.g., manufacturing) economy is now completely dependent upon, and overshadowed by, a mountain of debt.' The levels of indebtedness of the average American have also increased, which seems to suggest that the economic boom of the mid-1990s to 2001 was fuelled by increased consumption levels induced more by low interest and taxation rates than by higher income levels. Concurrently, Richard D. Wolff suggests that 'US families increased their personal indebtedness beyond anything ever experienced in any other place or time.... US consumer debt rose from $1.4 trillion in 1980 to $6.5 trillion in 2000. Housing (mortgage) debt, automobile debt, and credit card debt all rose faster than income, profits, and even stock prices.'[31] Mirroring Wolff's claims, a study by a Washington-based think-tank, the Economic Policy Institute, concludes, 'By 2001, total household debt exceeded total household disposable income by an all-time high of nearly 10 per cent. Much of the run-up in debt occurred over the economic boom, as the ratio of debt to personal disposable income rose from 87.7 per cent in 1992 up to 109.0 per cent in 2001.'[32] Extremely low interest rates in the US over the past few years have smoothed the way for the higher debt burden of the average American. In fact in November 2002 the Federal Reserve Bank slashed interest rates to 1.25 per cent – 'their lowest level since July 1961'.[33] Aside from leading to speculative activities vis-à-vis corporate share prices – witnessed, for example, in the Enron debacle – the upshot of easy credit in bad economic times has led to a spate of foreclosures on mortgages. According to the Mortgage Bankers Association of America, 'creditors across the country began foreclosing on 134,885 mortgaged homes, or about 4 in every 1,000 – the highest rate in the 30 years that the association has been monitoring mortgages'.[34]

Consumers and corporations are not alone in their growing dependence on credit to sustain their daily operations; governments
have also resorted to debt financing. The US Commerce Department
recently reported that the annual deficit for 2002 reached a record
$435 billion, which amounts to a 21 per cent increase over the 2001
level.[35] Moreover, the steady accumulation of these twin deficits
has meant a consistent rise of US net foreign debt. For instance,
the debt rose 67.5 per cent in 2000 to $1.843 trillion from $1.1
trillion in 1999.[36] At the end of March 2002, federal borrowing in
the United States approached $5.95 trillion, the legal ceiling, and,
according to US Treasury Secretary Paul O'Neill, surpassed it by 1
April 2002. In the hope of avoiding a federal default, President Bush
asked Congress to raise the limit by $750 billion, which will cover
borrowing into 2004. It should be stressed that the US government
is able to engage in such profligate behaviour, where other states
would have been severely reprimanded by the IMF and international
creditors, because of the powers afforded it by the DWSR.

Yet it is within this ever-increasing debt-led accumulation regime
that the Achilles heel of the DWSR begins to be felt. To feed its
persistent trade and budget deficits the US economy and government require a constant stream of capital inflows. According to the
IMF, the US will be required to borrow about $2 billion from
abroad to feed its current account, or, which is the same thing, trade
deficit. The IMF goes on to note that 'this situation poses one of the
biggest risks to the world economy'.[7] The US government's decision to enter into deeper debt levels is not merely a domestic affair,
however. For one thing, because the US dollar is the world's trading
and reserve currency, the dollar is widely held outside American
territory. 'Over half of all dollar bills in circulation are held outside
America's borders, and almost half of America's Treasury bonds are
held as reserves by foreign central banks.'[38] Moreover, because the
strength of the dollar does not reflect the competitiveness of US
exports, but instead a vast influx of capital flows, the invincibility of
the dollar, as well as the US economy, is highly dependent on the
ability to constantly suck in large amounts of capital. Yet, as noted
above, the Frankenstein factor aggravates this precarious situation.
Susan Strange cautioned against these abuses of power almost a
decade ago, when she argued that

the state of the US dollar is the most paradoxical and potentially danger-ous aspect of the whole global financial structure. Here is the leading country of the world market economy, without whose say-so no reform or change has ever been made since 1943, acting in exactly the opposite way to that of a responsible hegemon, borrowing from the system instead of lending to it, so that it is actually now a bigger debtor than any of the developing countries, and consequently hooked on the horns of the dilemma of two deficits: its trade deficit and its budget deficit.[39]

We will return to this contradiction later on in the chapter. For now, let us focus on the effects of the DWSR and crisis of global capitalism vis-à-vis the South. Given that the NIFA emerged as a response to the spate of financial crashes in emerging markets over the past decade, it is useful to take a closer look at how these two relations of the triad converge with the final feature: capital account liberalization in the South.

The Dollar Wall Street Regime, Open Capital Accounts and the South: An Unsustainable Trinity?

Tension between openness and national self-determination

Neoliberal orthodoxy holds that financial liberalization leads to the same economic benefits as free trade in goods and service. Recent history suggests otherwise. The evidence from the crises in Mexico, Argentina, Brazil, Turkey, Indonesia, South Korea, Thailand and Russia has made it very clear that capital account convertibility (CAC) has not improved the overall economic landscape of these countries. On the contrary, free cross-border flows of private capital, particularly in the form of foreign portfolio investment and short-term capital, have led to at least two problems for the South.[40] First, there appears to be a greater vulnerability of the economy to risk, financial volatility and crisis. Second, there is a growing imposition of restrictions on policy autonomy (or national self-determination), which may result in increased economic problems and higher levels of political repression in the South.[41] Taken together, both points converge on what Strange refers to as the core problematic of international political economy: 'the tension between the principle of national self-determination and the principle of openness in the world economy'.[42] We explore these tensions in depth in the cases of Mexico, Chile and Malaysia in Chapters 2 and 4. However, here we continue to outline some of the global dimensions of this tension as it relates to the contradictions of US structural power and transnational finance. As such, we will now explore each of the two points in turn.

First, as governments of emerging markets embrace foreign portfolio investment (FPI, embracing stock and bond purchases) as a source of financing, their exposure to the risks of capital flight increases. As mentioned above, the Asian crisis has clearly demonstrated that even sound economic fundamentals (e.g. low inflation, high savings rates, falling unemployment numbers) are no guarantee that highly mobile capital will not choose to flee en masse in adverse circumstances. Despite the robust macroeconomic equilibria and high rate of domestic savings, for instance, these 'miracle economies' buckled under the quick exit of foreign funds. Indeed, the changing nature of financial flows to emerging markets have made it increasingly difficult to protect the domestic economy against the devastating effects of contagion and capital flight. Raghavan notes that a

> shift of 1 per cent in equity holdings by an institutional investor in one of the G-7 countries away from domestic equity would be slightly more than a 1 per cent share of total market capitalization, but would constitute the equivalent of 27 per cent of market capitalization in emerging Asian economies, and over 66 per cent of Latin American equity markets.[43]

On the second and related point, to attract creditors continually, most of which stem from highly mobile sources of foreign capital, governments of emerging markets must send positive signals to investors about their credibility and market-friendliness, such as degrees of capital mobility, labour and production costs, and political stability.[44] Thus the need continuously to signal creditworthiness to global financial markets has not only limited the scope of the policy autonomy of states in emerging markets, but has generated stark tension between the policymakers' accountability to the needs of transnational capitals and to those of the people it governs.[45] In this way, to attract this crucial source of public financing, governments are pressured to enter into a 'pact with the devil' whereby market credibility assumes a central position in policymaking in such areas as exchange and interest rates as well as tight fiscal policies. The latter can begin to conflict or even take precedence over other domestic concerns, especially the needs of subordinate segments of the population, such as the working class, the urban and rural poor.

The corollary of the above is the growing structural power of transnational financial capitals, such as institutional investors (hedge, pension and mutual funds), vis-à-vis the states in the South. Geoffrey Underhill summarizes the tensions between these two social forces in the following manner: '[the growth in capital volatility and mobility] constrains the policy-making autonomy of ... elected governments, particularly with regard to the exchange rate and monetary policy but also with respect to fiscal and social policies.' Inherent in the policy process is, therefore, a substantial 'legitimacy deficit'. This has pushed political authorities to accept a constant 'global restructuring', which can lead to destabilizing effects for the national societies.[46]

The tension described by Underhill takes a distinct expression in the South. For example, in her extensive study of the investment behaviour of money managers, Mary Ann Haley suggests that investors, attracted to those countries that rapidly implement and maintain intense economic reforms while simultaneously controlling political opposition to these measures, may continue to find liberal democracy not only unnecessary but also perhaps even contrary to their interests.[47] Above all, and especially during times of crisis, the government is required to maintain political stability. These conditions can readily lead to increased forms of coercion and other expressions of authoritarianism aimed at quelling overt manifestations of class conflict so as to attract and maintain capital inflows. The limits placed on policy autonomy and the growing priority given to transnational finance in terms of neoliberal policies can increasingly constrain the political space for the articulation of subordinate voices. This feeds into our final section on the crisis of authority in the global South.

Crisis of authority

This third factor in our larger analytical frame for deconstructing the NIFA converges on the other two factors in that it partially reflects and aggravates the 'Frankenstein factor' discussed earlier. The relation between free capital mobility in the South and transnational finance has been on the whole negative, as the greatest beneficiaries of foreign portfolio investment and other short-term forms of capital inflows have been the ruling classes. Unlike the symbiotic relations between the US and free capital mobility, this relationship does not strengthen the power of the South vis-à-vis the rest of the world. Instead, through greater exposure to financial volatility, capital account liberalization has served to widen income polarization even further in emerging markets. Moreover, this third relation exacerbates the Frankenstein factor as growing instability in the South threatens the viability of the DWSR. As we saw earlier, the continued expansion of the US depends upon the uniformity of rules across the emerging markets. If the South cannot continue to adhere to neoliberal policies, the structural power of Dr Frankenstein could be reduced, especially in light of the deepening crisis of global capitalism when expansion of financial markets to the South is essential to continue to overcome narrowing profit margins.

Continued adherence by the ruling classes in the South to neoliberal tenets has become increasingly difficult to pursue, especially given the narrowing social basis for the neoliberal project in the wake of ever-widening income inequality.[48] For example, drawing on 2002 data from the United Nations Economic Commission on Latin America and the Caribbean (ECLAC), Emir Sader notes that the number of people living below the poverty threshold in Latin America increased from 120 million in 1980 to 214 million in 2001 (43 per cent of the population), with 92.8 million in conditions of destitution (18.6 per cent).[49]

The political and social effects of the vicious cycle of crisis and bail-out over the past two decades have made the principle of free capital mobility more difficult to sustain, especially for those who pay the costs whenever short-term debt falls due and speculative bubbles implode. As such, at issue in the South is the legitimacy of neoliberal domination over subordinate class. In what follows I suggest that the Gramscian notion of 'crisis of authority' captures the eroding legitimacy of neoliberal rule in the South. As this crisis erodes the legitimacy of the ruling classes among the subordinate classes, and therefore the former are no longer considered as 'leading' through consensus, they are forced to rely increasingly on coercion and reinvention of political domination in the form of neoliberalism. This movement is at the heart of the second generation reforms (SGRs) recently put forward by the international financial institutions (discussed in Chapter 6). The ensuing struggles and policies aimed at dealing with the 'crisis of authority' involve a constant reorganization of state power and its relationship to the subordinated classes and groups to defend and maintain dominant-class hegemony whilst excluding the masses from exerting influence over political and economic institutions.[50] Gramsci termed this class-based strategy a passive revolution. The latter entails the attempt to freeze the contradictions that arise from the crisis of authority.

Two caveats need to be mentioned with regard to 'passive revolution'. First, these new power relations do not imply that consent (ideology) is entirely absent, because the relationship between coercion and consent, within the Gramscian framework, is not mutually exclusive but rather dialectical in nature. In conditions of waning consent, the coercive element that constantly armours consensus comes more to the fore.[51] Second, coercion should be understood as a form of social discipline not only in terms of physical repression but also in economic terms. By making a political decision to adopt policies such as financial liberalization, the ruling classes within the states actually permit transnational financial actors to exercise coercive power over national social formations, through, for example, investment strikes and capital flight.[52] A case in point is the growing coercive power of foreign banks in Mexico. As Mexico undergoes privatization of its banking sector, 85 per cent of its banks are owned by foreigners from Canada, Spain and the US – with the latter representing the largest takeover by US-based Citigroup. Sanctioned by the national government, these transnational capitals are permitted to decide who in Mexico gets credit and under what conditions. This form of coercion has enormous consequences for the social fabric of the country. Small and medium-sized businesses, including the peasantry and small farmers, who remain desperately short of funding since the introduction of neoliberal agriculture rationalization, are asked to pay interest at approximately 20 percentage points higher than the 8 per cent underlying rate. In the name of 'efficiency', the banks have also cut 8,000 jobs in 2001 (more on this in Chapter 2).[53]

Seen from the above angle, the limitations placed on policy leeway through adherence to capital account liberalization drastically narrow the attempts at freezing the contradiction emerging from social discontent so as to ensure the reproduction of neoliberal rule in the South. In response, many governments in emerging market countries have begun to make explicit their discontent with the neoliberal paradigm, otherwise known as the Washington consensus. Indeed, as Sader rightly observes, the economic sickness of the economies in Latin America is accompanied not only by deterioration of the social fabric but also by a growing dissatisfaction with US-led economic growth paradigms:

> [President] Clinton left his successor with a situation very different from the one he had inherited. George W. Bush faces a Latin America in its worst crisis since the 1930s. In states with fragile economies, social structures are fragmented, with many people deprived of basic human rights. In Argentina, Haiti, Uruguay, Nicaragua, Peru, Paraguay, Venezuela, Bolivia, Columbia, Ecuador: actual or potential crises are increasing.[54]

In response to the unravelling of these economies, the idea of 'delinking', or a return to a more inward-looking accumulation regime, as found in the former 'import substitution industrialization' (ISI) growth model, has enjoyed renewed popularity on the left.[55] More recently, Keynesian voices have been heard to speak of a new development agenda, which, inter alia, is based on increased policy autonomy to assist them in overcoming what the Executive Secretary of the ECLAC, José Antonio Ocampo, refers to as the state's 'legitimacy crisis'.[56] Increased autonomy is only obtainable, however, if the key source constraining domestic policymaking is either removed or substantially hindered: namely, capital account liberalization, which is seen to destabilize national economies in the South.[57] In more concrete terms, Ocampo is arguing that developing countries should maintain national autonomy in at least two critical areas: the management of capital account and the choice of exchange rate regime.[58]

Aside from the rejection of adopting capital account convertibility, another indication of the growing discontent with and progressive delegitimation of the dominant neoliberal growth model and corruption of state officials is reflected in the recent wave of left-leaning governments throughout Latin America: Hugo Chávez in Venezuela (1998), Lucio Gutierrez in Ecuador (2002) and, most impressively, the election to the presidency in Brazil of Luíz Inacio Lula da Silva (2002), a former socialist who once urged the government of Latin America's largest country to stop paying back its foreign debt. On the one hand, while these movements reveal the discontent of Latin American voters with conservative, US-approved candidates and neoliberal policies, we need to view the emergence of these leftist parties with caution.[59] It remains to be seen whether, in the global political economic environment discussed above, these leaders will implement their powerful anti-neoliberal rhetoric. This is, as always, dependent on struggles that transcend domestic boundaries. Nonetheless, the fact that an increasing number of leaders from the 'left' are coming to power after about two decades of neoliberal rule points to the growing discontent of the critical masses, and, relatedly, to a crisis of authority in the South.

On the other hand, there is a need to theorize the phenomenon of the rise of the left, and thus look past the rhetoric against neoliberalism, through the application of a historical materialist lens. In this way, we will locate the constraints and contradictions imposed by past policy decisions and the ongoing crisis of capitalism. As the cases of Mexico, Chile and Malaysia demonstrate, leftist language appropriated by political elites can be an attempt at legitimating their dominance by 'freezing contradictions' either through a re-invented form of neoliberalism – for example, 'Third Way' schemes, usually represented by a mix of neoliberal austerity policies and anti-poverty programmes[60] – rather than any serious attempt to jeopardize a mode of domination that has assisted the ruling classes in extorting more wealth than prior to the implementation of neoliberalism in the South.[61]

As noted above, the increasing difficulties involved in the passive revolutions in the South have direct bearing on the structural power of the US (DWSR). Indeed, given the increasing intensity of economic turmoil for many emerging market countries (most notably Turkey, Mexico, Argentina, Uruguay, Brazil), not to mention low-income developing countries (or what the Word Bank has dubbed

'Highly Indebted Poor Countries' or HIPCs), debtor countries of the South may opt to decouple from the world economy rather than follow the imperative of free capital mobility across all national spaces. Strange observes that after the 1980 debt crisis the ruling classes of many developing countries decided neither to trade nor to borrow from the global economy, and thereby do 'their best to be self-sufficient, autonomous and, as some argued, free'. She goes on to note:

> Anxiety to keep the debtors inside the financial structure despite their difficulties was all the greater if the debtor country was large, was a substantial importer of Western goods and was host to a large number of Western transnational corporations – none of whom were anxious to cope with a decoupled debtor country.[62]

The Argument Restated

When we rejoin the three points of the larger triad that comprises our frame for understanding, we arrive at a dynamic and complex contradiction that underpins the NIFA: as the scope of transnational financial markets expand, the conditions for continued accumulation in the South weaken. Since the levels of profitability of financial markets depend on constant deregulation and creation of more and more esoteric instruments, there has been a continual disarticulation between finance and the real economy. This leads to greater volatility in the international financial system and an increasingly interdependent world economy. The latter condition implies, among other things, the ability of crises to spread more rapidly and strike more devastatingly. Yet for financial markets to continue to grow there must be enough stability in the system to guarantee the continuation of free capital mobility across national borders. On the other hand, as the emerging market countries are forced to prise open their capital accounts as well as their current accounts, distribution tensions, increased volatility, and difficulty in signalling creditworthiness begin to mount. The need for the political ruling classes and bourgeoisie – that is, both indigenous and foreign capitals – operating in these countries to address the resulting crisis of authority has produced the demand for increased policy autonomy in non-core countries, which could easily lead to departures from the neoliberal-based rules needed to guarantee the continued expansion of the DWSR and the power of global finance. Seen from this perspective, the NIFA is an attempt to freeze this contradiction, and thus in effect represents a Gramscian passive revolution at the global level.

To sustain its dominant position in the world economy, the US must implement, legitimize and reproduce universalized principles, such as free capital mobility, through multilateral institutions in which it wields enough power to set the agenda, such as the G7, IMF, World Trade Organization (WTO) and World Bank, in order to gain the consent of key emerging markets and social forces therein. The Gramscian notion of a passive revolution may be transferred to the interstate system to deepen our understanding of the particular nature of US dominance and, by extension, the NIFA. In order to freeze the structural contradictions inherent in the contemporary global political economy, the United States faces the constant imperative to revise and fortify the existing forms of domination over the global South (the Washington consensus) whilst attempting to exclude political forces in these countries from exercising any significant influence over the IMF and World Bank. The latter is perceived as a threat as it might constrain the ability of the Washington institutions to implement and police neoliberal policies and ideology in the South. By drawing in 'systematically important' emerging markets closer to the policy objectives and underlying values of these two US-led IFIs, the US government is attempting to relegitimate neoliberal rules in the South by signalling inclusionary politics at the international level (the G20), while concurrently establishing new ones (the ROSCs). This represents an attempt to create a consensus among powerful financial actors and their regulatory institutions as well as states (the FSF) on how best to freeze the contradiction in the South without limiting the magnitude and mobility of transnational finance.

Outline of the Book

As stated at the beginning of this chapter, the main objective of this chapter is to provide an analytical sketch-map through which we may deconstruct the common-sense understanding of the NIFA.

This frame for understanding is implicit in each of the remaining chapters. At the same time, the various topics covered in the following chapters cover a variety of levels of analyses, issues and temporal spaces in order to deepen and widen our understanding of the NIFA as we engage in its deconstruction, so as to shed light on the questions: who benefits and why? To this end the book is divided into three broad sections, which cover this discussion. Chapters 2 and 3 comprise the next broad section. Drawing on Chapter 1, which has laid the conceptual groundwork for the book, Chapter 2 is concerned with establishing the concrete foundation for the discussion of the NIFA. To this end, it explores the first major financial meltdown in the South during the 1990s, namely the 1994 Mexican crisis, by attempting to go beyond the surface analyses of the Mexican political economy found in many accounts of the crisis. The chapter does so by concentrating on the historically developing contradictions within the neoliberal development project, which was a combination of IMF-led reforms after the 1982 debt crisis and initiatives undertaken by the Mexican ruling classes. The chapter examines the attempts by the US and the IMF to manage and contain the 1994 crisis. The significance of this discussion is that the policy decisions undertaken in response to the peso debacle serve as the ideological and policy scaffolding for the NIFA in 1999.

Chapter 3 examines the various crises of authority that emerged in reaction to the Asian crisis, such as the capital controls debate, the defeat of the Multilateral Agreement on Investments (MAI), the collapse of the Long Term Credit Management (LTCM) hedge fund, and the International Financial Institution Advisory Commission (or, Meltzer Commission). The chapter suggests that events are not only linked to the Frankenstein factor but also serve as a buttress for the NIFA. The chapter then goes on to theorize two institutional structures associated with the NIFA: namely, the G20 and FSF as moments of imposed US leadership. The latter represents what Gramsci refers to as 'dominant' rule, which I argue represents another procrustean bed for the global South.

The following two chapters comprise the third section of the book Chapter 4 interrogates why the IMF has conceded that certain temporary measures to limit the inflow of hot money may be beneficial in achieving some breathing space for governments. In this sense, capital controls are only to be used as a means to reach the greater end: namely, the proper (neoliberal) management of financial liberalization. Indeed, by sanctioning a particular type of capital control it is engaging in a political judgement call, which is based on certain material interests, as opposed to mere economic logic. This becomes evident when we juxtapose two different types of capital controls: the Chilean unremunerated reserve requirement, which was endorsed by the Fund, and, conversely, the IMF's rejection of the Malaysian currency control. In doing so, I suggest that the Fund's opposition to Malaysian controls stems from its perception that capital restraint on outflows threatens the imperative of free capital mobility, thereby harming both US structural power and transnational financial capitals.

Chapter 5 explores the third major institutional feature of the NIFA: the ROSCs. The main objective of this chapter is to explain how and why one particular ROSC, namely corporate governance, has become standardized, and, more importantly, to ask: whose interests are served? I suggest that, despite the claim that the international standard of corporate governance embodies 'universal principles', the definition advanced in the ROSCs intentionally draws on the Anglo-American variant. The latter, in turn, reflects the attempt by the US to freeze existing contradictions.

In Chapter 6 our attention turns not only to the wider implications of the NIFA vis-à-vis the emerging Development Agenda but to the attempt by the US and transnational capitals to legitimate imposed US leadership in the South. The chapter critically examines the United Nations Financing for Development (FfD). This was held in Monterrey, Mexico, in March 2002 with the express purpose of garnering international financial and political support for the Millennium Declaration, most notably the halving of world poverty by 2015. To this end, various multi-level consultations were held with 'equal stakeholders', ranging from the IMF and WTO to civil society organizations, in order to forge a consensus-based framework for substantially reducing world poverty. However, once the FfD's seemingly novel attempts at inclusionary and multilateral forms of negotiations are seen as a moment of the power relations and contradictions of global capitalism, this consensus takes on a more class-based hue. In taking this view, the chapter suggests that the Monterrey consensus is, in the first instance, concerned with re-producing and thus legitimating the growing power of transnational capitals. In this sense the consensus is not so much about reducing poverty as about managing and legitimating the ever-increasing polarization of capitalist social relations in the South that have been brought about by the same contradiction underpinning the NIFA.

Notes

1. Cf. Soros 1998; Underhill 1997: 19.
2. France, the United States, Britain, Germany, Japan, Italy, and Canada formed the Group of 7, or G7. The 1998 Birmingham Summit saw the inclusion of Russia to form the G8. The G7/G8 distinction arises primarily from the fact that the G7 continues to function outside the formal summits. For an excellent website dedicated to the G7/G8 and the G20 see www. G7.utoronto.ca.
3. Augelli and Murphy 1988: 17.
4. Rupert, 1997.
5. Cf. Tooze and Murphy 1991; Palan 2000.
6. See, for example, Eichengreen 1999; Eatwell and Taylor 2000; Kenen 2001; Akyüz 2002; Cartapanis and Herland 2002.
7. Strange 1994: 35.
8. See, for example, Armijo 1999, 2002; and various essays in Soederberg 2002.
9. Middle-income countries, or emerging markets, require some explication, as these designations are highly subjective. The definition used here draws heavily on the World Bank's typology, which is essentially based upon a 2000 GNI (gross national income) per capita measurement. As such, up-per middle-income countries, such as Chile and Malaysia, register a GNI ranging from $2,996 to $9,265, whereas lower income countries, such as Guatemala and Ecuador, register incomes between $756 and $2, 995. For more information, see the World Bank's website at www.worldbank.org/ data/databytopic/classgroups.htm#low_income.
10. Ocampo 2000.
11. Stremlau 1994/95: 18.
12. Altvater 2002.
13. Sinclair 1996: 5–6.
14. Cox and Sinclair 1996: 297.
15. Susan Strange refers to the financial structure as 'the sum of all the arrange-ments governing the availability of credit plus all the factors determining the terms on which currencies are exchanged for one another'. 1994: 90.
16. Strange 1994: 24–5.
17. For a detailed account of the Bretton Woods system and its breakdown, see Helleiner 1994; Strange 1994; Gowan 1999.

18. As Strange notes, 'The power to create credit implies the power to allow or deny other people [or countries] the possibility of spending today and back tomorrow, the power to let them exercise purchasing power and thus influence markets for production, and also the power to manage or mismanage the currency in which credit is denominated, thus affecting rates of exchange with credit denominated in other currencies.' Strange 1994: 90. In its most straightforward sense, credit refers to 'the means by which we are able to obtain immediate benefit of goods or services upon the promise of payment at a future date'. Available at www.creditman. co.uk/training/whatiscredit.html.

19. With apologies to Shelley 1988.

20. Gowan 1999: 25ff.

21. Henwood 1999: 41–55.

22. *New York Times*, 1 November 1997.

23. Gramsci 1992: 275–6.

24. Noam Chomsky, 'From Bretton Woods to MAI: Finance and Silence', *Le Monde Diplomatique*, January 1999.

25. Others, such as Karl Marx, use the term crisis of the overaccumulation or overproduction of capital, which denotes a situation in which finance capital dominates over productive capital because the latter fails to be attractive to capital. For Marx, this crisis stems from the inherent contradictions within capitalism; see *Capital*, Volume 3 (Marx 1991), especially Chapter 14. On the crisis of capitalism, see Bonefeld 1999; Ugarteche 2000; Brenner 1998; Clarke 1988, 1994; Holloway 1995; Magdoff et al. 2002.

26. Holloway 1995: 132.

27. Gowan 1999: 11.

28. Aglietta 1979.

29. Bello et al., 2000.

30. Magdoff et al., 2002; cf. 'Productivity Growth: To These, the Spoils', *The Economist*, 11 May 2002.

31. Wolff 2002: 121.

32. 'Economic Snapshots', downloaded on 1 August 2002 at www.epinet. org/index.html.

33. 'Size of Cut Shocks Wall Street' *Guardian Unlimited*, 6 November 2002.

34. 'Easy Credit and Hard Times Bring a Flood of Foreclosures', 24 November 2002; see www.nytimes.com/2002/11/24/national/24FORE.html?todays headlines.

35. 'US trade deficit hits record level in 2002', *Financial Times*, 20 February 2003.

36. 'US Net Foreign Debt Increased 67.5 Percent in 2000', *Asian Wall Street Journal*, 29 June–1 July 2001. Note that all prices quoted are in US dollars, unless otherwise indicated.

37. 'The O'Neill Doctrine', *The Economist*, 27 April 2002.

38. 'The Dollar and the Deficit', *The Economist*, 12 September 2002, www. economist.com/finance/displayStory.cfm?story_id=1325394.

39. Strange 1994: 115.

40. Leslie Elliot Armijo has divided the main financial investments flowing to

the South into six ideal types, so as to identify the volatility of each one (i.e. high or low). Foreign aid and foreign direct investment are the lowest, while bank loans to government and private firms are medium. According to Armijo, portfolio investments to either governments or private firms yield the highest volatility. See Armijo 1999: 23.

41. Grabel 1996; Armijo 1999.
42. Strange quoted in Tooze 1999: 220.
43. Raghavan 1998.
44. Maxfield 1996.
45. Cf. Mittleman 2000; Gill and Law 1993.
46. Underhill 1997: 19.
47. Haley 1999, 2001.
48. World Bank 2000a: 3.
49. 'Can the New Leaders Leave Neoliberalism Behind? Latin America: Critical Year for the Left', *Le Monde Diplomatique*, February 2003.
50. Showstack-Sassoon 1992; Gramsci 1992.
51. See Gramsci 1992.
52. Gill and Law 1993.
53. 'Mexican Banks Won't Lend', *The Economist*, 10 October 2002.
54. 'Can the Leaders Leave Neoliberalism Behind?'
55. See, for example, Amin 1990; Prebisch 1971; cf. Ugarteche 2000.
56. Ocampo 2002; see, for example, Grabel 1996, 1999; Griffith-Jones 1996; Rodrik 1998; Eatwell and Taylor 2000.
57. The terms 'capital account liberalization', 'capital account convertibility' and 'free capital mobility' will be used interchangeably throughout the text. All three refer to the removal of capital controls or any policy instrument that impedes the freedom of 'exchange controls on capital transactions in the balance of payments.' For a brief but excellent discussion on capital account convertibility, see Damodaran 2000.
58. Ocampo 2000: 56. It should be noted that the argument in this book is more concerned with free capital mobility than with an exchange rate regime.
59. 'Colonel on White Charger Rides to Aid of Poor', *Guardian*, 23 November 2002.
60. See, for example, Soederberg 2001b; Weber 2002; cf. Sen 1999; Giddens 2001.
61. Structural adjustment was not only beneficial in ensuring that First World creditors, largely US banks, were paid back, but also assisted the ruling classes in overcoming the manifestation of crisis capitalism through the legitimate implementation of 'externally' imposed SAPs. See Petras et al. 1997; Sklair and Robbins 2002.
61. Strange 1994: 112.
62. Cox 1987, 1993a; Gramsci 1992.

2

The Mexican Peso Crash
and the Foundations of the
New International Financial Architecture

The Mexican peso crisis was significant for several reasons. To begin with, it was the first time a developing country had experienced a massive financial meltdown. Second, and related, the actors involved in the peso debacle were also different; instead of the traditional banks loans that marked the 1982 crisis, far larger amounts of money were transferred through securities involving pension and mutual funds from the North. Third, the Mexican crash marked the collapse of a country that figured not only as an IMF pin-up economy but also as an official trading partner of a 'first-world' trading club, namely the North American Free Trade Agreement (NAFTA).[1] And, finally, the policy response to the Mexican crisis by the US government, as well as the subsequent policy shifts in the IMF, represented scaffolding in the efforts to build the NIFA. For these reasons it is important to begin our exercise of widening and deepening our understanding of the NIFA by examining historically not only the Mexican case but also the so-called Old International Financial Architecture. In doing so I contend that the 1994 crisis had its roots in the contradictions and conflicts inherent in a stringent neoliberal restructuring strategy, which heavily tempered by the policy recommendations made conditional on IMF funding after the 1982 debt crisis. Put differently, the peso crisis and subsequent attempts by the US government to subdue and manage it reflected the same contradiction that was identified in Chapter 1 as underpinning the NIFA: as the scope of the Dollar Wall Street Regime expands, the conditions for sustainable growth – or, as we

will see, in the Mexican case, even the semblance of stable growth
– in the South weaken.

Having said that, the chapter begins by providing an overview
of the Old International Financial Architecture, or what might
be considered the de facto regulatory and ideological building
that superseded the Bretton Woods system: namely, the Washington
consensus.

The Old International Financial Architecture

A contextual overview

It will be recalled from the previous chapter that the raison d'être of
the IMF under the Bretton Woods system was to help all member
states manage their exchange rates in a fixed exchange rate system
of currencies by the use of short-term loans, which in turn provided
liquidity to states with short-term cashflow problems. However, since
the delinking of the dollar–gold pegged exchange system in 1973,
currencies are not only determined by a floating exchange rate
system, but also capital controls on short-term financial flows are no
longer the norm. The question that emerges here is, why did the
IMF continue to exist, despite the collapse of the Bretton Woods
monetary and trade regime? And, more specifically, why have the
Articles of Agreement – essentially the IMF's constitutional charter –
not been ratified, on a consensual basis, to reflect the wider changes
in the global political economy? While these questions have interesting ramifications for the relationship between the US and other G7
countries, I would like to narrow the focus of this question to how
it pertains to the global South. Drawing on our discussion in the
previous chapter, we have suggested that the answer is closely tied
to the reproduction of US structural power in the global political
economy. That is to say, with the absence of an interstate consensus,
the United States flexed its powerful muscles to pursue unilaterally,
inter alia, a post-Bretton Woods development agenda for the South
in the hope of regaining some of its slowly eroding competitive
position in the world economy, particularly vis-à-vis Germany and
Japan. It should be noted that, closely related to the erosion of its
economic status, the nature of American hegemony shifted to a

non-hegemonic form of dominance, or, following Gramsci and Cox, a passive revolution (see Chapter 1). In other words, the dominant DWSR is in essence a moment of a passive revolution. As we will see below, the US strategy in the immediate post-Bretton Woods era was to allow its banks to (over)lend to sovereign states in the South. After the 1982 debt crisis, the US relied more and more heavily on the IMF as lender of last resort and as a general disciplinary force to ensure that governments in the South followed what was considered prudent policy formation in order to repay their debt or, at the very least, make interest payments on the principal loan. The latter strategy is more popularly referred to as the Washington consensus. While we recount the changing role of the Fund in the post-Bretton Woods era, it is important to keep in mind that, as a moment of the DWSR, the IMF's role in the South is equally non-hegemonic in nature.

From obsolescence to crisis manager: a brief history of the IMF

The only binding decision the more powerful shareholders of the IMF implemented during the first several years after 1971 was the 'First Surveillance Decision'. This policy, implemented in April 1977, held 'that members shall not manipulate exchange rates or the system as a whole in order to avoid adjustment or to gain a competitive advantage'.[2] But without any financial backing or political legitimacy at the inter-state level, this decision was perfunctory. As the crisis of global capitalism continued to deepen throughout the 1970s, industrial and developing countries tried desperately to keep their economies afloat by aggressively promoting their exports. This strategy included, inter alia, the manipulation of exchange rates. With its weapon of the paper dollar standard, the US was of course able to determine the external value of its currency, as discussed in the previous chapter. With the election of Ronald Reagan in 1980, and the subsequent Republican Senate, the first since 1948, a powerful policy shift towards neoliberalism as the guiding policy would not only take hold but also imply a deep-seated suspicion of the multilateral lending agencies. However, circumstances began to improve for the IMF with the 1982 balance-of-payment crisis in Mexico.

The US government quickly changed its position vis-à-vis the Fund with the advent of the debt crisis. As Kapstein recounts, 'In early 1983, the Reagan administration went to Congress to seek $8.4 billion for America's share of an IMF funding increase.'[3] In doing so, the Fund moved from obsolescence to crisis management. We examine the nature of its crisis management in more detail below. For now, however, it is important to ask, why did the Reagan administration wish to breathe new life into the Fund? Put another way, why did the US government decide to manage the stabilization of about two dozen debtor nations through the IMF? Kapstein's response is that by acting through the IMF, the subsequent Structural Adjustment Policies (SAPs), which were made conditional for any loans from the Fund to the debtor nations, would be de-politicized. In this way, Louis Pauly is correct to note that the IMF could continue to act unilaterally behind the mask of multilateralism, and thereby legitimating its structural power.[4] As mentioned in Chapter 1, the multilateral lending institutions are not neutral and independent public authorities acting above states, but rather public authorities for transmitting the interests of the ruling classes in powerful states.[5] This move is understandable due to the immense power the US wields within the IMF. For example, with a 17 per cent voting share, it is not only the largest shareholder in the IMF but also can easily veto any changes to the Fund's Charter that it perceives as going against national interests.[6] Moreover, since the US donates the majority of standby capital for the IMF and the World Bank, it wields hegemonic influence within this institution, usually at the expense of those countries that cannot afford to contribute these amounts. As we will see in Chapter 6, as private financial actors play a greater and greater role in development finance, both IFIs become incredibly important 'intermediaries' between debtor nations and international financial markets.[7]

The Washington consensus

After the debt crisis the IMF and, to a lesser extent, the World Bank sought to use their leverage to usher in new forms of capital accumulation in those countries, such as Mexico, that fell under the weight of external debt payments. More specifically, there was to be a shift from capital accumulation based on protectionism and heavy state intervention in the economy, or what is referred to as 'import substitution industrialization' (ISI), to an export promotion industrialization (EPI) model. Broadly, the ISI refers to a development strategy in which governments play an active role not only in protecting existing firms but also in establishing new industries in the South. Among the various policy tools employed by states using the ISI model were overvalued exchange rates, tariffs, import licensing and direct government investment in key industries.[8] Unlike ISI, the Fund's neoliberal-led SAPs introduced an EPI strategy that was based on the steadfast belief that all economic, political and social problems should be solved primarily through market-based processes. Neoliberalism quickly became the new orthodoxy of the IMF and World Bank, congealing into what many authors have referred to as the Washington consensus.

According to the former Senior Vice-President and Chief Economist of the World Bank, Joseph Stiglitz, there were three pillars to the Washington consensus: fiscal austerity, privatization and market liberalization (trade liberalization and financial liberalization).[9] Stiglitz goes on to note that the success of the consensus rests on its simplicity. That is to say,

> its policy recommendations could be administered by economists using little more than simple accounting frameworks. A few economic indicators – inflation, money supply growth, interest rates, as well as budget and trade deficits – could serve as the basis for a set of policy recommendations. Indeed, in some cases economists would fly into a country, look at and attempt to verify these data, and make macroeconomic recommendations for policy reforms all in the space of a couple of weeks.[10]

The policies associated with the Washington consensus not only assisted in bringing about huge and continual resources transfers from the debtor countries to the developed world, particularly the US (i.e. the DWSR); in its emphasis on privatization and deregulation it also attracted foreign capital investment to the developing countries. According to a report by the Joint Economic Committee of the US Congress, in the mid-1980s while bank profits grew steadily during the debt crisis the developing countries exposed to the SAPs moved further into debt.[11] As we will see below, the SAPs assisted in creating a greater, not lesser, economic dependency of

Third World governments on private capital markets as opposed to the less volatile bilateral aid, not to mention causing severe social dislocation leading to higher poverty rates than before the debt crises of the early 1980s. Furthermore, the decisions to implement the SAPs in Mexico were as responsible for the 1994 meltdown as were the inherent contradictions within capitalism throughout the 1980s and 1990s.

Before continuing with our analysis of Mexico, it is useful to introduce a proviso that will move our conceptualization of the links between the 'Washington consensus' and Mexico beyond mere determinism. While the very term conjures up images of conspiracy among US policymakers and capital vis-à-vis the global South, it would be an oversimplification to assume that only those living in the US, and in other industrialized countries, benefited from the liberalization of markets in the South. This perspective fails not only to view capitalist states as historical social relations but also to grasp that capital interests transcend national boundaries. This requires some explication. Like their American counterparts, powerful sections of the Mexican political ruling class (bureaucrats and politicians) were actively endorsing the implementation of SAPs as a means to overcome the declining rates of profitability of the ISI accumulation model. For instance, the neoliberal austerity packages that accompanied the IMF bail-outs aided the political ruling class in disciplining labour, particularly unionized workers, through fiscal austerity requirements, trade liberalization and deregulation strategies, which in turn helped move the country more rapidly towards export promotion industrialization. Privatization schemes, for example, allowed both Mexican and American bourgeoisies to purchase state enterprises at bargain rates. Likewise, capital liberalization, coupled with the deregulation of the Mexican stock market (the Bolsa) permitted fusion of indigenous and non-indigenous capital interests (or transnational interests) to reap the benefits of the freely moving short-term money in and out of the Mexican borders. Seen from the above perspective, the end result of the SAPs was Mexico's deeper economic assimilation within the US as structural adjustment promoted the concentration and international expansion of Mexico's indigenous, transnational capitals by connecting them with the internal reproduction of US capital.[12]

As Judith Teichmann observes, neoliberal reforms undertaken by the Mexican government served to reinforce the status quo. In fact, through the implementation of SAPs, already wealthy Mexicans were able further to centralize and concentrate their wealth.[13] Likewise the growing polarization of Latin American societies marked by growing numbers of working poor at one extreme and a new class of super-rich Latin American billionaires, who benefited from the buyout of public enterprises, at the other.[14] Put another way, the interests of transnational capital (or the bourgeoisie) within the Mexican state does not impair its power, for the political ruling classes take 'charge of the interest of the dominant [American] capital in its development within the "national" social formation, i.e., in its complex relation of internationalisation to the domestic bourgeoisie that it dominates.'[15]

Before turning to a closer examination of the political, economic and social consequences of the implementation of SAP-inspired neoliberalism in Mexico, it is useful to provide a historical sketch of the Mexican political economy prior to the 1982 debt crisis.

The Demise of Mexico's ISI

Import substitution industrialization (ISI) in Mexico was characterized by capital-intensive production, primarily for domestic consumption, and high forms of protectionism, and was heavily dependent on both technology and foreign investments.[16] The form of the bourgeois state that accompanied this ISI strategy was characterized by an authoritarian regime based on the one-party control of the Institutional Revolutionary Party (PRI), corporatism, high levels of state ownership in strategic activities in such areas as communications, petroleum and basic petrochemicals, railroad transportation, and banking. Taken as a whole, these characteristics permitted the government to act not only as regulator and employer but also as direct investor. Cheap and abundant labour and credit, subsidized goods and services, lax taxation standards, and so forth, provided the developing industrial sectors with key inputs at low and stable prices.

Owing to the nature of Mexico's highly exclusionary capital-intensive industrialization, corporatism was, and still is, an important facet of the form of political domination in Mexico. As Diane Davis explains, through corporatist structures the PRI not only separated subordinate classes from each other but also linked them to the state in ways that undermined their independent capacities for struggle against capitals or the state.[17] Mexico's corporate political system helped to provide the institutional and ideological glue for pacts between the state, capital and workers (both urban and rural). This arrangement gave voice and power to capitals by bringing them into the political sphere. It further acted to legitimize the demands of the subordinate class and thereby limit inter-class conflicts.[18]

Like the rest of the world economy, it became clear that import substitution industrialization had entered into crisis by the early 1970s. The crisis manifested itself in Mexico in precipitous drops in oil revenues, growing levels of unemployment, spiralling inflation, rising debt-to-GDP ratios, balance-of-payment problems, massive migration to the urban areas, and capital flight.[19] For the Mexican state, this meant the loss of political legitimacy and social cohesion, brought about by increased amounts of pressure to accommodate the contradictory needs of working-class and capitalist interests. Labour was demanding material concessions for the deterioration in material standards of living of the working class, demands for wage concessions and increases. It should be stressed that the more vocal sections of the working class were the relatively well-paid, unionized workers concentrated in state industrial sectors.[20] On the other hand, the bourgeoisie was demanding that the state refrain from its heavy involvement in the economy, as witnessed by the high levels of public ownership. Capitals, which saw labour as the primary impediment to profitable accumulation, lobbied hard for the elimination of state price controls; this, of course, meant the removal of a desperately needed cushion for low-income labour in a period of escalating inflation.

The Mexican government attempted to mediate these conflicting demands between labour and capitals largely by increasing public spending. By 1981, the state contracted a substantial amount of external debt, the majority of which was held in the form of short-term loans.[21] Mexico's problems were compounded by the sudden and substantial surge of capital flight, which had its roots not only in the deteriorating Mexican economic situation but also in the sudden move by the US government to hike up its interest rates. To illustrate, real interest rates in the US skyrocketed from 0.8 per cent during 1971–80 to 11.0 per cent in 1982.[22] For Mexico, high interest rates had two serious consequences. First, capital flowed north as opposed to south. Second, the interest payments on the Mexican debt increased exponentially. As is common to herd behaviour, the slow trot of capital moving out of Mexico to the US quickly turned into a stampede as investors began to lose confidence in the peso. In the summer of 1982 the Mexican government shocked the financial world by threatening default on its external debt-service payments. The 1982 crisis marked the start of the country's general reorientation from import substitution towards export promotion industrialization. The shift to the latter would be greatly facilitated by the adoption of neoliberal-led SAPs.

Having laid the historical foundation, our discussion now turns to two waves of neoliberal restructuring in Mexico after 1982. The first pertains to the initial implementation of neoliberal policy in Mexico and spans the sexenio (six-year term) of President de la Madrid from 1982 to 1988, whereas the second details a deepening of neoliberalism during the sexenio of President Salinas de Gortari from 1988 to 1994. It should be noted that this discussion is by no means exhaustive. Indeed its purpose is to highlight the contradictions associated with neoliberal restructuring in Mexico prior to the crash in 1994.

The First Wave of Neoliberalism: The de la Madrid Sexenio

After the debt crisis, the Mexican state could no longer jump-start its economy by priming either public investment or current expenditures. The penurious public purse also precluded the use of incentive programmes that necessitated government outlays (e.g. export or investment subsidies). This meant that capital investments and capital repatriation had to be stimulated by other means: luring capital inflows via the 'demonstration effect'. Alongside signalling creditworthiness through 'sound economic fundamentals' (e.g. low inflation rates, balanced budgets, stable currency), the demonstration effect implied a clear commitment by the government to an EPI strategy. Acting as international lender of last resort, the IMF re-negotiated Mexico's external debt with the first among many bail-outs.[23] In doing so the government also accepted the terms of the bail-out: namely, the adoption of market-led policies entailed in the Washington consensus.

Unlike the method employed by the G7 countries during the late 1970s and early 1980s, the IMF argued that Mexico's exchange rate system was too volatile to use money targeting to influence prices and output.[24] Instead the Fund reasoned that to ensure required levels of new foreign investment the Mexican government would have to allocate resources in accordance with global market signals, such as prices, exchange rates and incomes.[25] In truth Washington's understanding of policy reform was aimed not at restoring develop-ment, but at increasing debt service capacities through export expan-sion and import compression, so that the overextended US-based banks could be repaid.[26] In this sense neoliberalism was successful, since it produced large sustained net resource transfers from many developing countries to the developed world.[27]

Striving to be a model debtor would prove to be politically difficult. Tight fiscality, for example, weakened the already existing thin social programmes and reduced the resources for subsidies to favoured groups, particularly in urban centres. Likewise, the cosy relations between banks and businesses that were possible when real interest rates were negative gave way to more market-dominated lending. Unsurprisingly the old vested interests in the state were quite reluctant to give way to neoliberal restructuring. For example, indigenous agricultural and industrial capital interests that produced consumer durables and non-durables for the domestic market, as well as the oligopolistic sector of finance capital, all opposed this transition.[28] Likewise, since the success of debt restructuring (based on the passage to export production) presupposed a huge amount of foreign capital investment, the state has held the door wide open to transnational capitals, especially from the US. The power of these groups has increased substantially within the Mexican social relations of production and in turn in the state. At the same time, the neo-liberal policies were eroding the PRI's traditional bastions of support, such as state-subsidized unions, especially the CNC (representing the peasantry) and the CTM (representing industrial workers), on whose support the PRI was particularly dependent in pushing through its neoliberal programmes.

Seen from the above angle, President de la Madrid's economic modernization programme was an attempt to appeal to Mexico's international investors and creditors whilst practising brokerage politics domestically.[29] Clearly such a programme would be costly, both economically and politically. The government made up for lost sources of international revenue by increased domestic borrowing, primarily by issuing government treasury bonds, or CETES (Certificados de la Tesorería de la Federación). Unsurprisingly this expansion of domestic debt helped fuel an increasing annual inflation rate, which by 1987 had reached 180 per cent. The high interest rates thus necessary to attract savings meant, in turn, higher payments on the government-issued, peso-denominated CETES and a resultant increase in the public deficit. From 1982 to 1988, total foreign debt amounted to an average of 61 per cent of the GDP.[30] Despite these efforts, however, Mexico's external debt continued to grow. To encourage Mexico to continue to adhere to neoliberal restructuring, the US government offered debt restructuring assistance under the auspices of the Baker Plan, which helped restructure $48 billion of Mexico's external debt.[31]

In 1986, international banks disciplined the prodigal government by refusing to become involved in the rollover of debt packages. The unregulated global financial markets meant that the banks were able to sell Third World debt in the secondary markets for a fraction of their face value to investors. The US government, under the auspices of the IMF, stepped in to cover the remaining bank loans. The result of this was that the Mexican government's financing requirements were to be derived from official lending and global security markets. As we will see below, this is evident in the fact that the majority of capital inflows would be in the form of portfolio investment, mostly in the Mexican stock market. Thus, to help encourage desperately needed financial inflows, as well as to combat inflation, the government set extremely high interest rates. The policy was far from effective. From 1980 to 1989, the banking system modified weekly the interest rate, which rose steadily to the point of historical highs hovering around the rate of inflation itself.[32] The real winners of

Table 2.1   Major economic indicators of Mexico (US$ million)

	1980	1990	1994	1995	1996	1997	1998	1999	2000
Exports*	24,685	54,570	78,025	96,707	115,156	131,126	140,062	158,509	192,831
Imports*	35,243	63,504	107,994	98,571	117,791	138,962	156,173	173,238	211,409
Balance	−10,442	−7,451	−29,662	−1,576	−2,328	−7,454	−15,724	−14,324	-18,157

* Goods and services.

Source: World Bank 2002: 376.

this policy were not small and medium-size businesses, or the average Mexican, who could not afford to obtain credit at such high interest rates. The clear beneficiary of such a strategy was powerful transnational capital, which made immense amounts of profit from extending loans to the cash-strapped public and private sectors.

To demonstrate the government's commitment to the implementation of fiscal discipline, public investment was drastically cut. In 1988, for example, investment levels hit an all time post-WWII nadir to close to 4 per cent, which in turn greatly affected the maintenance and expansion of Mexico's infrastructure. Despite this, however, domestic debt was hovering at around 18.5 per cent of GDP in 1988 and it became necessary to signal creditworthiness by getting tougher on non-interest expenditures and government revenues. Owing to deteriorating labour–state relations, the government set out to devise several wage and price pacts in order to muster support for policies of fiscal restraint. During the late 1980s prices were regulated through a co-operation mechanism of a tripartite 'regulation-by-agreement' embedded in the Economic Solidarity Pact (PSE) and the subsequent Pact for Economic Stability and Growth (PECE), both of which were a kind of truce between labour and the government to win votes in the 1988 elections.[33]

Between 1982 and 1990 the government sold or closed 37 per cent of these enterprises as part of its economic liberalization strategy, thereby effectively losing 14 per cent of the GDP and 30 per cent of gross fixed capital formation.[34] The revenue from these sales went directly to paying Mexico's external debt, which meant primarily American banks.[35] Thus no money was flowing into social programmes or economic development. Likewise the privatizations of government-owned industries led to a wave of job cuts, which, according to one observer, reached levels of up to 400,000 positions.[36]

Despite the state's attempts to discipline its social relations to embrace the export promotion strategy, levels of capital investment, particularly foreign direct investment, were far from sufficient to help Mexico climb out of the crisis. In the recessionary period of the early 1980s, the government, with blessing from the IMF, devalued the peso to help promote Mexican exports and thus earn hard currency for debt payments. The flood of cheap Mexican exports was met with increased US protectionism.[37] To overcome this barrier, Mexico signed an agreement to become a member adhering to the regulations in the 1986 General Agreement on Tariffs and Trade (GATT).[38] The GATT, however, would do little to salvage Mexico's dismal economic situation; in the same year that Mexico signed up to the GATT, it required, in the words of the IMF, another 'unprecedented' eighteen-month standby arrangement for the amount of 1.4 billion Special Drawing Rights (SDRs).[39] In return for this loan, Mexico promised to further deregulate its trade and financial sectors. Taken together, the GATT and further IMF conditionality lay the groundwork for Mexico's imminent membership of NAFTA, which itself should be seen as a way for both the US and Mexico to overcome their diminishing levels of profit.

Moreover, partly due to its membership of the GATT, and partly because of paltry capital inflows, the government scrapped its policy of setting official prices (universal subsidization) at the beginning of 1987 in order to boost business confidence. However, this strategy failed to attract sufficient funds to keep the country abreast of its debt repayments. In 1987, the US government, under the auspices of the Brady Plan, intervened with a $45 billion debt-restructuring package.[40]

In sum, the first wave of neoliberalism served to erode the very material basis of the social pact between the state and labour, and thus also deteriorated the PRI's political basis of support. This in turn laid the seeds for the general crisis of authority of the neoliberal Mexican state. An early manifestation of this crisis was that the new anti-nationalist and pro-market stance that accompanied the 'modernization' policies of the government was becoming increasingly difficult to sell to the majority of Mexicans, who were experiencing heightened levels of human misery. Many capitalists, increasingly distressed with the economic effects of the restructuring policies, particularly their increasing exposure to higher levels of competition through the liberalization of trade, shifted their support to the right-wing, pro-business party, PAN (the party of the current President Fox). The upshot of this swing of political support away from the PRI was that in the 1988 elections the PRI took a substantial beating at the polls. As David Barkin observes, half of Mexico's registered voters abstained from the 1988 presidential contest. A majority of the other half voted the PRI out of office. Computers conveniently 'failed' on election night, and results from half the voting booths have never been made public. The PRI 'won' with 50.4 per cent, a far cry from its usual 75 per cent and up.[41]

The Second Wave of Neoliberalism in Mexico: Continental Rationalization

The incoming Salinas administration (1988–94) inherited economic stagnation and failing political legitimacy. In concrete terms, the administration was confronted with two immediate problems. The first was to secure the maintenance and attraction of capital investment by creating a favourable or 'credible' investment environment (politically stable, low corporate taxation, investment-friendly regulations). The second was that, to ensure its existence, the state had to depoliticize the growing levels of social discontent and class conflict. The government had to to address the growing 'crisis of authority' whilst signalling creditworthiness to the international financial community and the IMF.[42] This tension was overcome by ruthlessly pursuing neoliberal prescriptions in the name of 'continental rationalization', which simply means deeper economic integration with the US economy by removing even more barriers to trade and finance, so as to invite foreign capital into Mexico.

In 1990 and again in 1991, the state lifted price controls on many products and made price setting more flexible. These steps resulted in a backlash from labour, especially in light of the fact that the buying power of the minimum wage fell by some 40 per cent between 1980 and 1987. After numerous long and bitter strikes, the government eventually conceded to raising the minimum wage, albeit to only a fraction of what labour was demanding. Regardless of how unpopular these policies were, however, they seemed to be partly justified by their success: from 1987 to 1993, inflation tumbled and short-term economic growth had been achieved.

Financial liberalization, which began in the last year of the de la Madrid administration (1988), included freeing interest rates, lifting credit controls and reserve requirements on private banks, shrinking the size of public development banks, and fully reprivatizing the commercial banks.[43] In 1990, supported by the interests of financiers and international manufacturers, President Salinas sent a constitutional amendment to Congress calling for the reprivatization of all banks. This move, premissed on a commitment to low inflation rates, was part of a broad policy package designed to demonstrate the fact that Mexico was not only a safe investment site but also a preferred debtor nation. It should be noted that the government's attempt to beat down high inflation rates in order to signal creditworthiness was largely accomplished through reliance on extremely high interest rates, which, of course, had the effect of choking the economy whilst inviting speculative capital into the country. Additionally, these reprivatization schemes, especially the establishment of a universal banking system, facilitated the integration of Mexico's financial system into the US economy. The political strategy of economic integration qua deregulation also added tremendous credibility to the new exchange rate regime since it indicates that Mexico will not have to bear the burden of unexpected market shocks alone. Nevertheless, as Ilene Grabel suggests, the downside of this new financial openness is the increased likelihood of a cross-border contagion, which is particularly disturbing in a country whose economy is marked by higher speculative capital formations than foreign direct investment, and where the trend towards deteriorating current account deficits is prevalent.[44]

To get a better sense of the effects of over a decade of neo-liberal restructuring on the Mexican economy, and thereby identify its underlying contradictions and conflicts, we now turn to a brief discussion of the two main prongs of continental rationalization strategy: the maquiladorization of Mexican society and the financialization of the economy.

Maquiladorization of Mexican relations of production: poverty and deindustrialization

Despite the privatization of state enterprises and liberalization of trade flows between the US and Mexico, the fastest growing sector of latter's productive economy is the assembly plants along the US–Mexico border, also known as maquiladoras. For many, the maquiladoras symbolize the strength of the Mexican economy and are a harbinger of the success of export promotion industrialization. Maquiladoras are generally owned by foreign corporations, which assemble finished goods for the US market.[45] Today, the maquiladoras not only represent a multi-billion-dollar industry but also, constitute one of Mexico's primary sources of export income. Yet, upon closer inspection, the maquiladoras signal some important weaknesses of the Mexican economy. According to James Cypher, the maquilas 'cannot provide socially sustainable levels of employment in the context of the lowest acceptable international labour and environmental standards, and progress on the employment front can be made only through greater foreign dependence'.[46]

Kathryn Kopinak echoes these claims as she observes that the new industries in the maquiladoras offer fewer jobs than the number lost from the privatization of state-owned industry and agriculture. Research on the maquiladoras has concluded that jobs in this sector are comparatively unskilled and poorly paid, which implies not only that workers, most of whom are young women, have reduced purchasing power and thus increased economic inequality but also that the internal domestic market has shrunk with the shift towards export-led production.[47]

Who benefits from the maquiladoras? The answer is transnational capital. The maquiladoras are an effective means of overcoming narrowing margins of profitability. For example, 'the profit share rose by 1.5 per cent of GDP to 36.8 per cent in the course of President Zedillo's sexenio (1994–2000) while the wage share fell by 3.5 per cent of the GDP'.[48] According to a 1994 study by the Organization for Economic Cooperation and Development (OECD), maquiladora wages were 47 per cent of wages in non-maquiladora manufacturing. More to the point, growth in the maquiladoras appears to have had negative effects on the rest of the Mexican economy. Martin Hart-Landsberg notes that,

> Despite Mexico's rapid growth in the production of manufactured exports, the country's manufacturing value added has remained generally unchanged over the decade of the 1990s. The reason is that the government's neoliberal policies have largely hollowed out the country's domestic industrial base and the new exports are heavily and increasingly dependent on manufactured imports.[49]

An important outcome of the above situation is that many workers have shifted their status from permanent, full-time labourers protected by union representation to low-wage, contingency workers with neither union protection nor union benefits. Another problem directly related to the general crisis of capitalism is that the despite the boom of the maquiladoras and the general transformation of the Mexican economy from import substitution to export promotion industrialization, the wider strategy of continental rationalization has turned Mexico into an export platform for the United States. As such, the doubling of Mexican exports to the US has been accompanied by the tripling of imports from the US. Evidently this leads to higher levels of debt and a growing trade deficit (i.e. current account problems), particularly since Mexico is using borrowed funds to pay for its imports. In this way, the excessive net transfer of resources abroad made the economy extremely vulnerable to external shocks, particularly any deterioration in the terms of trade (see Table 2.1).

To help finance this trade deficit, the Mexican government sold CETES at very high interest rates. In 1990, President Salinas negotiated another debt restructuring package with the US, under the auspices of the Brady Plan, amounting to $37 billion. We now turn to the second prong of Mexico's continental rationalization strategy: the financialization of the economy.

Financialization in Mexico

According to neoclassical economics, capital account liberalization, at least in a perfect rational world, is necessary to attract private flows to substitute for investment and declining aid flows. Assuming that market actors are rational, financial liberalization in Mexico 'will ensure that resources flow from countries with high savings to those countries with low savings but profitable investment opportunities [such as production].'[50] In reality, however, the deregulation of the Bolsa (the Mexican stock market) meant increased room for manoeuvre for indigenous and foreign investors in at least two ways. First, foreign investors took advantage of the privatized Mexican firms by purchasing non-controlling shares. It should be stressed that the controlling shares in many large companies, such as Mexico's telephone company Telmex, remained in the hands of powerful indigenous capitals. Second, the majority of the financial flows that gushed into the country – Susan Strange notes that from 1990 to 1993 the Bolsa rose 436 per cent – speculated in share prices, were more concerned with turning a profit via speculation than investing in the real economy and thus generating new jobs. Instead of investment in the productive sphere (technology transfer, improving labour skills, and so forth), the influx of investment into Mexico's deregulating financial sphere simply involved transfer of ownership. Dillon describes the investment strategy of the financial sector in the following way: 'over the six years of Salinas's rule, speculators increased the nominal value of their portfolios by some $100 billion by buying and selling the shares of privatised firms on the Bolsa.'[51] The immediate outcome of this move was the constant rise in company shares far above the real worth of underlying assets concurrent to an overvalued peso.[52]

Moreover, while Bank privatizations have facilitated the concentration and centralization of wealth for the transnational bourgeoisie, they have proven to be detrimental to the majority of Mexicans. Over the past two years alone, privatization schemes have handed over 85 per cent of Mexico's banks to foreign investors. The problem is that these investors are reluctant to provide credit to small and medium-size businesses in Mexico, which remain desperately short of funding. If they do manage to get a loan, 'they pay interest roughly 20 percentage points higher than the 8 [per cent] under-lying rate. To secure a mortgage, individuals must put down a huge deposit.' Moreover, these foreign-controlled banks have been lead-ing a 'slash and burn' efficiency crusade throughout Mexico.[53] To fill in the lending gap, in July 2002 the World Bank agreed to loan Mexico $64.6 billion 'to strengthen Mexico's non-bank financial intermediaries, including credit unions and cooperatives, and to expand financial services to the poor, especially in rural areas, in-cluding their access to deposit services and to remittances coming from abroad'.[54]

To ensure that Mexico remains on this path of financial deregula-tion, the architects of the NAFTA sought to guarantee the adherence to neoliberal principles of free capital mobility in the legally binding provisions in the NAFTA.[55] For example,

> Article 1109 of the investment Chapter (which also applies to financial transactions through Article 1401:2) prohibits any kind of restrictions on cross-border flows of any kinds of financial dealings, including profits, inter-est, dividends and fees. NAFTA Article 2104 requires any member country with external payments problems to consult with the International Monetary Fund and adopt any measures the Fund might recommend.[56]

When taken together, trade and financial liberalization schemes not only substantially narrowed the policy leeway of the Mexican government – that is, hampered by the constant need to signal credit-worthiness – but also increased the power of transnational capitals within Mexico. For instance, each country attempts to provide the optimal credible investment environment, such as competitive inter-est rates (high), low taxation and social benefits, so as to retain and attract the highest amount of capital investment possible from the international financial markets.[57]

As in the export of goods and services, Mexico has been fight-ing a losing battle in the game of global finance. On the one hand, capital investment remains inadequate vis-à-vis the existing public expenditure in the economy. On the other hand, given the high interest rates and deregulated financial sector brought about through NAFTA, short-term capital inflows are often speculative in nature, to the detriment of Mexico's productive structure. For instance, while foreign direct investment in actual production facilities increased

by 57.6 per cent from 1989 to 1993, the presence of more mobile, short-term portfolio investment rose by more than 8,000 per
cent, accounting for 86.8 per cent of total foreign investment in
Mexico.[58] It should be stressed that one of the principal reasons
that foreign direct investment was flowing to Mexico, as well as to
other emerging markets such as Chile, Brazil, Thailand, Indonesia,
and so forth, was the relatively higher interest rates in these countries than in the recession-hit global North. As the latter tried to
stimulate its economies through low interest rates, financial markets
were attracted to the South for higher rates of return on short-term
investment. Annual rates of return in Mexico, for example, hovered
around 19 per cent between 1989 and 1994, compared to the 10.5
per cent that could be earned by investing in the stocks listed on
Standard & Poor's index.[59]

In this brief survey of the Mexican economic landscape it has
become evident that the political decisions taken by the ruling
classes to deal with high levels of debt burden whilst moving
toward an export promotion industrialization helped to create a
mode of capital accumulation that was not only highly dependent
on foreign direct and foriegn portfolio investment but had also
become increasingly vulnerable to changes in the world economy.
Relatedly, continually to attract and retain foreign investment in its
borders, the Mexican government must continually strive to signal
creditworthiness. This becomes progressively more difficult in light
of the fact that the very nature of capital accumulation in Mexico
breeds high levels of socioeconomic inequality and in turn aggravates
the already mounting 'crisis of authority' (see Chapter 1, section on
'The Dollar Wall Street Regime'). As we will see in the next section, these contradictions inherent in Mexico's neoliberal-led export
promotion industrialization resulted in a financial crisis that would
leave the majority of Mexicans worse off economically than after
the 1982 debacle.

The Peso Crisis

To continue to suck in much-needed swathes of capital inflows, the
Mexican government needed to send out stronger signals of creditworthiness. It did so by pegging the exchange rate of its peso to the

US dollar. This not only had the effect of winning more confidence for the overvalued peso, and thus further investment in the Bolsa; the decision by the Mexican government not to devalue the peso also assisted in getting the NAFTA ratified in the US Congress. The latter perceived that a peso devaluation would create a flood of Mexican imports into the US. While these decisions by the ruling classes were beneficial to the maquiladorization and financialization processes, they were detrimental to the country's trade deficit (see Table 2.1). Between 1987 and 1993 exports rose by a healthy 88 per cent, while imports rose by an even larger 247 per cent, which translated into a trade deficit of approximately $13.5 billion by 1993.[60] To finance this trade imbalance, in mid-1994 the Mexican government decided to increase its dependency on foreign capital by converting much of its CETES debt into Mexican government securities; the latter, which were called Tesobonos (Bonos de la Tesorería de la Federación), were indexed to the US dollar. When payments became due on most of Mexico's foreign exchange reserves, access to international capital markets dried up and the thin ice upon which the economy was running was shattered. At the end of 1994 the Mexican government had $28 billion worth of outstanding Tesobonos.

The growing and seemingly unsustainable trade deficit, income polarization in Mexico, and the general discontent of political exclusion led to a palpable crisis of authority of the Mexican state, and, more specifically, of neoliberal rule. A currency devaluation, which was thought by many economists to be a way to save Mexico from a crisis, was put off once again in 1994 due to the presidential election. As economic conditions continued to deteriorate, so too did the ability of the Mexican state to demonstrate political stability to its international creditors. The most famous manifestation of political instability was the uprising of the EZLN (Zapatista Army of National Liberation), which entailed a peasant revolt in the poorest Mexican state, Chiapas, on 1 January 1994, the day after the NAFTA came into effect.[61] Yet the Zapatista rebellion was not the materialization of discontent that Gramsci refers to as a 'crisis of authority'.[62]

Alongside numerous protests by the peasantry, who belong to the lowest economic echelons of Latin American societies, other expressions of the loss of ruling-class consensus in Mexico included the assassination of the PRI's presidential candidate Donaldo Colossio, of a Roman Catholic cardinal, and of a leading PRI official, Jose Francisco Ruiz Massieu, as well as a string of highly publicized kidnappings of some of the country's corporate magnates.[63] These events seemed to throw into question the political viability of Mexico as an investment site, particularly in the minds of foreign investors and creditors. One of the roots of the crisis of authority of the neoliberal state was the rising level of poverty in Mexico; for example, 'In 1992, 23.6 million lived below the poverty line; in 1994, the figure was 30 million and in 1996, 40 million.'[64]

Compounding the mounting manifestation of political discontent, it was becoming increasingly clear that the Mexican government was not able to sustain its Tesobonos. When US Federal Reserve chairman Alan Greenspan decided to increase US interest rates in order to curb inflationary pressures at home, institutional investors, including the Mexican bourgeoisie, scrambled to cash in their Tesobonos.[65] Of course this herd-like frenzy was also sparked by the evident tip-off institutional investors received on 20 December 1994 of an imminent devaluation. The latter reveals the close ties between the Mexican ruling class and the transnational bourgeoisie. Unable to defend the overvalued peso, President Zedillo (1994–2000) allowed the nation's currency to tumble on 22 December 1994. The economy went into a tailspin, and the vicious cycle began anew. When the Mexican government devalued the peso, investors immediately bolted from the country. As Moises Naim notes, 'Within two weeks of the initial devaluation, the peso lost more than 30 per cent of its value, and the Bolsa dropped almost 50 per cent in dollar terms.'[66] When payments became due on most of Mexico's foreign exchange reserves, which were borrowed heavy short-term dollar-linked debt, access to international capital markets dried up and the thin ice upon which the economy was running was shattered. By mid-1995, output was running 10 per cent *below* its level a year earlier, private capital spending had collapsed and employment had declined sharply. According to the Bank for International Settlements, these economic circumstances did not signal a favourable business environment, given that many of Mexico's multiple rolled-over bank loans were officially deemed non-viable.[67]

The effects of the peso crisis were devastating for the lower echelons of Mexican society. In 2000, after four years of economic growth, 47 million Mexicans (out of a population total of about 104 million) were in this category.[68] Although poverty figures are notoriously difficult to determine, largely due to the varying definitions of what actually constitutes poverty, the consensus seems to be that poverty rates are higher after the 1994 crisis, and ten years of neoliberal rule, than after the 1982 crisis. According to government statistics, by the end of the 1990s, poverty rates were hovering at around 54 per cent of the population.[69] As the country underwent its worst depression on record, workers, farmers and peasants experienced a drop in real wages of over 40 per cent in just one year, while the poverty level hovered at around half of the population.[70] Political discontent raged during and after the crisis, as cross-class groups mobilized against the PRI government. A case in point is the El Barzón movement, wherein the productive middle class has joined forces with farmers, peasants and workers, as well as with small and medium-size landowners to fight for the defence of land rights and better conditions on credit.[71] The continual struggle of peasants in Chiapas, El Barzón, and of countless numbers of well-connected non-governmental organizations and local community groups, for a better life through the guarantee of minimal work conditions, basic human rights, and a greater voice in the political decisions that affect their daily lives, are symptomatic of a deep-seated crisis of authority of the Mexican state.[72]

Some have interpreted the zenith of this political discontent and the demand for more democratic rule and social justice to be when Mexicans ousted the long-standing PRI, which had been in power since 1929, in favour of the election of right-leaning Vicente Fox of the National Action Party (PAN) in 2000. However, halfway through his sexenio, Fox had merely blended social-democratic rhetoric with neoliberalism. By reviving the defunct 'trickle-down theory' of the 1970s, President Fox holds that social justice can only be achieved through Mexico's deeper integration into the world market. Jorge Castañeda, Mexico's current Foreign Minister, has summed up this strategy as follows: 'there has to be a break with Zedillo's line; but not a break with market policies'.[73]

The Initial Response from Washington

The 1994 crisis mirrored its 1982 counterpart in terms of how international policymakers, particularly the IMF and the US government, understood the cause: namely, policy mismanagement on the part of the Mexican government as opposed to speculative activities on behalf of transnational finance.[74] Yet the crash differed from the debt crisis in two main ways. First, the players were different. As Susan Strange notes, 'Instead of the big transnational banking interests, the chief players in the 1990s were the more mobile, less vulnerable insurance and pension fund managers and other portfolio investors.' Second, unlike the debt crisis of the 1980s, the extent of contagion (loss of investor confidence) could spread more rapidly with more devastating effects to other indebted countries in the South, as evidenced by the so-called 'Tequila Effect'.[75] The latter was largely due to the fact that so many emerging markets were becoming increasingly dependent on short-term capital offered by these new, more powerful financial players.

When the peso collapsed, the immediate and most pressing problem facing the American government was the lack of financial resources and the absence of institutional arrangements in place to legitimize the massive bail-out of largely American investors. Following its current rules as lender of last resort, the IMF could only provide Mexico with less than $2.5 billion in credits, which was far less than what was required to deal with the crisis.[76] There were also political and ideological barriers to a speedy bail-out. US Congress was fundamentally opposed to bailing out Mexico: it not only presented a moral hazard for future dealings with its new trading partner, but Republicans were taking advantage by playing on the nationalist fears engendered by the NAFTA debates, which included the threat of mass illegal immigration and the loss of tens of thousands of American jobs dependent on exporting goods to Mexico.

To address these concerns, the Clinton administration arranged for a bail-out that would be agreeable to US Congress, and conditionality that would further entrench commitment to financial deregulation in Mexico. To this end Clinton used his executive powers to approve a $20 billion loan from the Exchange Stabilization

Fund (a sort of 'slush fund' for the US government). In the hope of appeasing the Republicans, the administration agreed that the loan would not be classified as foreign aid. Thus the Mexican government was required to pay fees, which were set to rise each time it drew on the line of credit. Furthermore, the Mexican government was required to pay interest at the same time as 91-day US Treasury bills, in addition to a considerable risk premium of 2.25 to 3.75 per cent.[77] In order to ensure continued adherence to neoliberal restructuring, the conditions placed on this bail-out, which was policed and adjudicated by the IMF, were based on the prescriptions of the Washington consensus, but entailed far-reaching conditionality. The austerity programme announced by the IMF on 9 March 1995 contained pungent medicine for the majority of Mexicans. The Mexican government, for example, was to raise value-added tax from 10 to 15 per cent and increase the price of gasoline by 35 per cent – and by an additional 0.8 per cent each month throughout the rest of the year; the price of electricity was to be raised by 20 per cent; and government spending was to be cut by 10 per cent. All of these measures fall disproportionately on the shoulders of the working poor.[78]

These measures undertaken by the IMF are ostensibly aimed at reducing Mexico's current account deficit and stabilizing the value of the peso. Yet, as we saw earlier, they appear to be more about disciplining both the Mexican state and society into accepting the 'inevitable' rule of neoliberalism. Other conditions laid out by the Fund are clearly aimed at not only reproducing the norm of free capital mobility in Mexico but also ensuring that the Mexican financial system opens up to the needs of foreign investors – measures that were rejected by Mexico during the NAFTA negotiations. There are several ways this is to be achieved under the ambit of the conditions attached to the 1995 bail-out. First, the bail-out agreement requires that Mexico turn to the international financial markets for new borrowing to roll over old debts. This further exposes the government to the discipline of private market actors – that is, by signalling creditworthiness. Second, Mexico is to undergo further financial deregulation so that foreign investors may widen their scope of speculative activities even further, particularly by privatizing its pension system and opening up its banking system. Foreign banks are thus allowed to own 100 per cent of Mexican banks, which helps explain why there is 85 per cent foreign ownership. And, third, it forces the government to deposit all oil export revenues from PEMEX, the state-owned oil and gas company, in a New York bank, where they can be seized by the US Federal Bank in the event that Mexico misses any debt payments.[79]

Seen from the above perspective, the Clinton/IMF reform package represents an attempt to freeze the contradictions that emerged from two decades of neoliberal-led restructuring. Without the reform package and pre-existing NAFTA rules, there was a very strong possibility that the already existing political (crisis of authority) and economic turmoil would have sharpened even further, leading those in power to revert to renewed protectionism and perhaps a return to bank nationalization schemes, which were implemented prior to the debt crisis in 1982, as a method of curtailing capital flight; or, even worse, to the implementation of capital controls. As William Greider suggests, 'Mexico could have imposed emergency foreign-exchange measures that would have halted or slowed down the capital flight, at least until everyone could make orderly adjustments. When some independent economists proposed this approach, Zedillo brushed it aside.'[80]

The IMF as 'Crisis Manager': Freezing Contradictions

Transformations in key international financial institutions, such as the IMF, were regarded as necessary by most policymakers and pundits in Washington, as it became increasingly clear that Mexico would not be the last financial meltdown. In the aftermath of the peso crash, the immediate challenge for Washington and the IMF was to address the absence of international structures designed to deal with future crises in such a manner as to strengthen the neoliberal common sense underpinning the imperative of free capital mobility in the South. As the managing director of the Fund, Michel Camdessus, put it, the Mexican debacle represents the 'first crisis of the 21st century'. For Camdessus, the key to economic success for Mexico, as for other emerging markets, was to ensure the continuance of private portfolio capital inflows, which are a significant source of financing for developing countries. According to Camdessus, the 'decisive factor here is market perceptions: whether the country's policies are deemed basically sound and its economic future promising. The corollary is that shifts in the market's perception of these underlying fundamentals can be quite swift, brutal, and destabilizing.'[81] With these words, Camdessus explains away the unstable political and economic basis of neoliberalism by reproducing and bolstering the claim that liberalizing capital accounts are

> an inevitable step in development and thus cannot be avoided, and ... can bring major benefits to a country's residents and government – enabling them to borrow and lend on more favourable terms and in more sophisticated markets.[82]

To this end, there were several attempts to transform the IMF into crisis manager. The latter suggests that the Fund would assume new responsibilities and powers to help avoid near-collapses of the international payment system. For instance, during the 1995 G7 Summit in Halifax, finance ministers and central bank governors of the leading members of the Fund committee agreed to establish an emergency financing facility, which would provide quicker access to IMF arrangements with conditionality, as well as larger up-front disbursements in crisis situations. The G7 countries also called for 'stronger and more effective IMF surveillance of its members'.[83] In the words of Michel Camdessus,

> I welcome, in particular, the G7's conclusion that the role of the IMF, in an environment of increased globalization, calls for a strengthening of its surveillance. I also consider important the G7's call to ensure that the IMF has sufficient resources to meet its responsibilities and appropriate financing mechanisms to operate on a scale and with the timeliness required to manage shocks effectively. [84]

The leaders of the G7 also agreed to strengthen further the Fund's primary mandate of surveillance – and therewith the intertwined goal of transparency – regarding not only members' current accounts but also the capital accounts and financial systems. To this end the 1977 Surveillance Decision was overhauled so as to manage more effectively 'unsustainable flows of private capital' in member countries.[85] In addition, the IMF was to use its new leverage to encourage countries to publish a wider range of useful economic information. The Fund's Executive Board, for example, endorsed the establishment of standards to guide member countries in the public dissemination of their economic and financial data. These standards were to consist of two tiers: The first level, which would apply to all IMF members, was referred to as the General Data Dissemination System (GDDS).[86] The Fund's Executive Board approved the GGDS in December 1997. The Special Data Dissemination Standard (SDDS) constituted the second level.[87] The SDDS, which was approved by the IMF's Executive Board in March 1996, would apply to those member countries that had or were seeking access to international capital markets.

An additional surveillance strategy was launched in the aftermath of the peso crisis. The Fund's Article IV instituted a new series of Press Information Notices (PINs); this requirement was inaugurated in May 1997. In brief, PINs are issued at the request of a member country following the conclusion of the Article IV consultation.[88] The aim of this exercise is to make the IMF's views known to the public. This amendment was motivated by the attempt to strengthen surveillance over the economic policies of member countries by increasing the transparency of the IMF's assessment of these policies. In this way the Fund's dissatisfaction with a country's progress in adhering to the Fund's principles of 'good governance' can be a very credible threat and result in capital flight or investment strikes. Even if the information doesn't become public, the IMF can use its newly found authority to withhold bail-out money in the event of difficulties (read: non-compliance).

As if this weren't enough, the IMF was busily seeking ways to revise its charter to impose the legal obligation of open capital accounts on its member states. By committing themselves to this attempt to universalise the norm of free capital mobility, under Article VIII, Sections 2, 3, and 4, of the Fund's Articles of Agreement, 'member countries agree not to impose restrictions on the making of payments and transfers for current international transactions or to engage in discriminatory currency arrangements or multiple currency practices without the approval of the IMF'. The rationality behind the move to enforce conditionality legally was clearly tied to the concerns of reproducing the imperative of free capital mobility in the South. In the Fund's own words, the 'increasing importance of international capital flows is a fact that needs to be better reflected in the laws and agreements that help bring order to the international economy and to the process by which individual countries liberalise their capital accounts.'[89] The question that arises here is, important for whom? Clearly the hot money rushing into the Mexican economy was not beneficial to the majority of people, whose standard of living fell even further after the 1994 meltdown than after the 1982 crisis.

As we will see in the next chapter, the solution premised on more, as opposed to less, financial liberalization in Mexico, albeit policed more effectively through the IMF's SDDS and GDDS programmes, did nothing more than temporarily freeze the underlying contradictions inherent in neoliberal-led growth that helped bring about the peso crisis. Indeed, real wages in Mexico remain lower than before the 1982 crisis, income inequality is higher, the social effects of the peso crisis are harrowing – mass unemployment, steady reduction in the real value of wages, and a deepening of poverty, which is estimated to affect 54 per cent of the population.[90] Seen in this light, the continued adherence by Mexico's ruling classes to neoliberalism has become increasingly difficult to pursue, at least legitimately. Although Vicente Fox is practising 'Third Way' rhetoric and poverty-targeting programmes such as Mexico's poverty reduction programmes like the PROGRESA (Programa de Educación, Salud y Alimentación), the underlying contradiction, and in turn source of poverty-creation, not only remains intact but has also been deepened through the NAFTA ratifications demanded by the US government in exchange for its bail-out. The question that arises here is, what happens when countries outside the realm of such a disciplinary legal framework as NAFTA, and not in close geopolitical proximity to the US, fall victim to speculative attacks? The answer lies in the attempts by power interests tied to the Dollar Wall Street Regime to freeze the contradictions associated with free capital mobility, which, as discussed in Chapter 1, takes the form of the NIFA. We now turn our attention to the further construction and legitimation of this edifice in the remaining four chapters.

Notes

1. For comprehensive and critical accounts of the 1980 debt crises, see Körner et al. 1984; MacEwan 1990; Altvater et al. 1991.
2. Pauly 1997: 108.
3. Kapstein 1994: 92.
4. Pauly 1997.
5. On this see Gowan 1999: 32ff.
6. The G7 countries, excluding the United States, have a combined voting power of 42.5 per cent, compared to the meagre 39 per cent of all developing countries. See the IMF website: www.imf.org.
7. For instance, given that the entirety of World Bank loans is taken from the private financial markets at preferential rates, the Bank is dependent on the US, the G7 countries and the international financial markets for the bulk of its working capital. For a critical account of the World Bank, see Cammack 2001.
8. Cardoso and Helwege 1995.
9. Stiglitz 2002: ch. 3.
10. Stiglitz 1998a.
11. Bienefeld 1993; Kapstein 1994.
12. Poulantzas 1974; cf. Panitch, 1994.
13. Teichmann 2002.
14. Teichmann 2002; Veltmeyer et al., 2000; Sklair and Robbins 2002.
15. Poulantzas 1974: 73. This is an important distinction as it views the capitalist state as a historical social relation as opposed to an object whose power can somehow be reduced by the external constraints of globalization.
16. With regard to Mexico's trading relations with the US, with a brief exception of a bilateral agreement under the Reciprocal Trade Agreements Program (to aid and profit from the US war effort) in 1942, Mexico avoided any legally binding pacts with its powerful neighbour to the North; see Hart 1990: 32ff.
17. The three official unions are: the National Peasant Confederation (CNC), the Mexican Workers' Confederation (CTM), and Popular Sector (CNOP). Both the CNC and CTM are usually represented by corrupt representatives called *Charros*, who are appointed by the politicians of the Mexican institutional revolutionary party (or PRI). The CNOP comprises middle- and upper-class Mexicans, and is relatively more powerful in terms of its influence on the PRI than either the CNC or CTM. Unlike the CNC and the CTM, members of the CNOP are formally incorporated into the official party. See Davis 1993.
18. Davis 1993: 66.
19. Inflationary increases between 1971 and 1982 were staggering: 5.2 per cent in 1971; 15.7 per cent in 1973; 21.9 per cent in 1974; 27.2 per cent in 1976; 29.8 per cent in 1980; and, 98.8 per cent in 1982. Méndez 1994.
20. According to official sources, there were 57 strikes recorded between September 1972 and August 1973. From September 1973 to August 1974 this number jumped to 452 strikes. Nevertheless, in the following two

years, the strike waves lessened, largely due to concessions and state forms of repression, to around 100 strikes per year; see Trejo 1991: 134.

21. IMF 1983: 1.
22. Helleiner 1994: 175.
23. For example, Mexico applied for and was granted additional financing by the Fund in 1986, 1989, 1990 and, of course, 1995.
24. IMF 1992.
25. Bienefeld 1993.
26. See Williamson 1990: 5ff.; IMF 1983: 2; cf. Kapstein 1994.
27. Bienefeld 1993: 4.
28. It was not until after 1988 that the so-called Bankers' Alliance agreed to the government's neoliberal strategy. See Veltmeyer et al. 1996: 140ff.; Maxfield 1990.
29. De la Madrid's 'stabilization policy' or 'Immediate Program for Economic Reordering' rested on the following ten points: (1) reduced growth in public spending; (2) protection of employment; (3) continued public investment in the most productive projects; (4) honesty and efficiency within the public sector; (5) protection of and stimulation for programmes providing basic foodstuffs for the population; (6) fiscal reforms to increase government revenues; (7) channeling of credit towards national development and efficient management of the nationalized banks; (8) 'realistic' exchange policy; (9) restructuring of the federal bureaucracy for more efficiency; and (10) constitutional reforms to reinforce the role of the state within the mixed economy. See Story 1986: 162.
30. IMF 1992; Gurría and Fadl 1995.
31. Named after US Treasury Secretary James Baker, the Baker Plan reflected the Reagan administration's solution to the $1 trillion debt crisis in the South. Baker announced his plan at the World Bank–IMF annual meeting in Seoul in October of 1985. The Plan is largely seen as a failure, as it did little to bring down the debt burdens of the debtor countries.
32. Méndez 1994: 247.
33. Álvarez and Mendoza 1993.
34. Jenkins 1992: 172.
35. Strange 1994; Kapstein 1994.
36. Dillon, 1997: 70.
37. Between 1980 and 1986, for example, Mexico faced twenty-six US countervailing duty actions, nineteen of which led to restrictive actions. For more information, see Hart, 1990.
38. Ironically, this move to liberalise its trade occurred during a time when the majority of advanced industrialized states were busy constructing protectionist barriers, IMF, 1989: 331.
39. IMF 1986: 225. According to the IMF, the SDRs, created in 1969, were considered 'an international reserve asset, to supplement members' existing reserve assets (official holdings of gold, foreign exchange and reserve positions in the IMF). The SDR is valued on the basis of a basket of key national currencies and serves as the unit of account of the IMF and a number of other international organizations.' 'Special Drawing Right: A

Factsheet', www.imf.org/external/np/exr/facts/sdr.htm.

40. Dillon 1997: 68.
41. Cockcroft, 1990: 40–43.
42. Maxfield, 1990.
43. Banco de México 1991: 89–180.
44. Grabel 1999; World Bank 1998.
45. The maquiladoras began to spring up in the 1960s – coinciding with the general crisis of global capitalism and the termination of the Bracero programme. The latter was a federal initiative that allowed migrant Mexican farm workers to enter the US on a temporary basis (1943–64). It wasn't until the 1980s that the maquilas, whose 'comparative advantage' lay in their low-cost labour, advantageous tariffs, and proximity to the US, began to gain economic importance, however.
46. Cypher 2001: 12.
47. Kopinak 1994: 150–51; Cooney, 2001.
48. Cypher 2001: 21.
49. Hart-Landsberg 2002.
50. Bretton Woods Project and Oxfam 2001: 1.
51. Dillon 1997: 71.
52. Strange 1998; Dillon 1997; Cypher 2001.
53. 'Mexican Banks Won't Lend', *The Economist*, 10 October 2002.
54. World Bank, 'World Bank Approves $64.6 Million to Improve Mexico's Financial Services to the Poor', http://web.worldbank.org/WBSITE/EXTERNAL/NEWS/..0,,contentMDK: 20052405~menuPK:34466~pagePK:34370~piPK:34424~theSitePK:4607,00.html.
55. Cf. Porter 1997.
56. Dillon, 1997: 72–3.
57. McConnell and MacPherson 1994.
58. Pastor 1999: 213.
59. Dillon 1997: 72.
60. Pastor 1999: 212.
61. In the Mexican government's attempts to neutralize and dissolve solidarity among the peasants, which was a necessary precondition for any formal bilateral trade agreement between Mexico and the US, Articles 27 and 123 of the Mexican Constitution were amended in 1992. These changes referred to the right of the Mexican state to full ownership of strategically important areas of both natural resources and infrastructure. Article 27 took the repeal of the Sistema Alimento Mexicano (SAM – Mexican food system) one step further by repealing the right to possess a holding on communal land (*ejidos*). The notion of the *ejido* as a right of the peasantry, which was won through the revolution, was now annulled. In this way peasants were now able either to rent or to sell their land holdings to the private sector.
62. Gramsci 1992: 275–6.
63. Cf. Roman and Arregui 2001.
64. Cf. Naim 1995; Cypher 2001: 32.
65. Dillon 1997; Cooney 2001.
66. Naim 1995: 5.

67. Bank for International Settlements 1996: 40ff.
68. Cypher 2001: 32.
69. Veltmeyer et al. 1996; SEDESOL 1999; de la Rocha 2001.
70. Cooney 2001: 79.
71. Greider, especially El Barzón's chapter.
72. Soederberg 2001b; Teichmann 2002.
73. Castañeda 2001: 32
74. Cf. Lustig 1995; Masson et al. 1996; Weintraub 2000.
75. Strange 1998a: 99–100.
76. Naim 1995.
77. Dillon 1997.
78. Ibid.
79. Ibid.
80. Greider, 1997: 263.
81. M. Camdessus, 'The IMF and Challenges of Globalization: The Fund's Evolving Approach to its Constant Mission: The Case of Mexico', address at the Zurich Economics Society, Zurich, Switzerland, 14 November 1995, www.imf.org/external/np/sec/mds/1995/MD5951/HTM:3.
82. IMF 1997a: 321.
83. See the virtual library of the G8 Information Centre based at the University of Toronto, www.g7.utoronto.ca/summit/1995halifax/financial/6.html.
84. IMF 1995.
85. Pauly 1997: 127.
86. For more information, see the Fund's DSDD website: http://dsbb.imf.org/gddsweb/diffbw.htm.
87. http://dsbb.imf.org/sddsindex.htm.
88. See IMF 1997a, 1997b, 1997c.
89. Cohen 2003.
90. Veltmeyer et al 1996: 139

3

The New International Financial Architecture: A New Procrustean Bed for the South?

Mexico was not to be the last of the financial meltdowns in the South. It is important to keep in mind that the next wave of crises were due not so much to policy formation, such as the inefficiency of the IMF's transparency initiatives, as to the fundamental contradiction from which the new international financial architecture emerged and continues to rest; that is, as the scope of the transnational financial markets expand, the conditions for stable economic growth in the South weaken. Seen from this perspective, the Asian debacle in the summer of 1997 was largely brought about by the confluence of three aspects of the contradiction discussed at length in Chapter 1 – the Frankenstein factor, the ongoing crisis of global capitalism, and capital account liberalization in the South – as opposed to the predictable reasons offered by the US government and the international financial institutions, which included cronyism and policy mismanagement. The upshot was solutions that called for improved institutional linkages between public and private actors so as to strengthen the existing international financial system. In 1999, the G7 launched two principal units that would complement the existing multilateral institutional landscape: the G20 and the Financial Stability Forum (FSF).[1] Largely owing to the NIFA's clandestine institutional webs and the predominance of technical language used to describe its inner functions, its capitalist nature has largely been neglected. Why the new building? Who benefits from this project? This chapter seeks to examine critically the emergence of the NIFA, but not simply by studying it as some sort of political phenomenon floating above a level playing field of globalization. Instead the chapter attempts to link the NIFA's institutional components to the wider contradiction discussed in Chapter 1.

To begin our discussion of the NIFA we will first examine the contested international political terrain regarding free capital mobility in the years immediately preceding its establishment. In this way we can deepen our understanding of the global crisis of authority facing the United States, to which the NIFA is a response. It will be recalled that Gramsci described the crisis of authority as a situation in which the ruling classes no longer enjoy consensus among the subordinate classes. Henceforth they are no longer 'leading' but 'dominant'. As suggested in the previous chapter, a crisis of authority is evident not only at the level of nation-states but also at the international level, especially with regard to the tensions between the Dollar Wall Street Regime and free capital mobility, which I referred to as the Frankenstein factor in Chapter 1. We return to this distinction in more detail later in the chapter. First, however, the following section addresses several important factors that have aggravated the crisis of authority of the US in the global political economy, particularly with regard to its ongoing attempts to guarantee the reproduction of the imperative of free capital mobility: (1) the capital controls debate; (2) the near-collapse of the Long Term Credit Management fund (LTCM); (3) the defeat of the Multilateral Agreement on Investments (MAI); and (4) the establishment of the International Financial Institutional Advisory Commission, more popularly known as the Meltzer Commission.

Contesting the Consensus: The Crisis of Authority of US Structural Power

Capital controls debate

The Asian crisis is extremely important in understanding the further developments of the crisis of authority regarding the Dollar Wall Street Regime. Because we will progress to detailed examinations of the Asian meltdown with respect to the cases of Malaysia (Chapter 4), Thailand (Chapter 6), the Asian Monetary Fund (Chapter 4), and a more general exploration of state and capital in the East Asian region (Chapter 5), we will not dwell here on the details.[2] Suffice it to say that, following the Mexican peso crisis, the Asian debacle further shook the foundations upon which neoclassicism rested. Despite the fact that these economies were revered as the 'growth tigers', won high praise from the international financial institutions up to the year of the devaluation of the Thai baht in 1997, and possessed sound fundamentals – which included budget surpluses, high savings rates, low inflation and export-oriented industries – investors were badly burnt in this play.[3] Those associated with the Washington consensus were quick to blame crony Asian capitalism for the debacle, as opposed to the reckless and excessive behaviour of speculators.[4] The IMF 'made reforms of corporate governance and related institutions a condition for its bail-outs in the region.'[5] There is far from a consensus on this issue, however.

High-profile US policymakers and economic pundits, such as former Federal Reserve chairman Paul Volcker, and the former Chief Economist of the World Bank Joseph Stiglitz, have begun to question not only the wealth-creating properties of free capital mobility, but also the lack of structural coherence for continued capital accumulation. The following quotation from the celebrated financier George Soros is representative of these concerns:

> What makes this crisis so politically unsettling and so dangerous for the global capitalist system is that the system itself is its main cause … the origin of this crisis is to be found in the mechanism that defines the essence of a globalized capitalist system: the free, competitive capital markets that keep private capital moving unceasingly around the globe in a search for the highest profits and, supposedly, the most efficient allocation of the world's investment and savings.[6]

The events in the countries hardest hit by the crisis – the so-called IMF-3: South Korea, Indonesia and Thailand – made it painfully clear that the underlying tenets of the Washington consensus were more than faulty. For instance, liberalized financial markets will not consistently price capital assets correctly in line with future supply and demand trends, and neither will the correct asset pricing of liberated capital markets provide a 'continually reliable guide to saving and investment decisions … and to the efficient allocation of their economic resources'.[7] Alexandre Lamfalussy, the former general manager of the Bank for International Settlements, shares this view when he writes that the exuberant behaviour of lenders and investors from the industrialized world played a major role in spurring on the past several crises in the emerging markets.[8] Other organic intellectuals tend to agree with this position. The highly reputed MIT economist Paul Krugman, for example, has stated that 'most economists today believe foreign exchange markets behave more like the unstable and irrational asset markets described by Keynes than the efficient markets described by modern finance theory.'[9] Jagdish Bhagwati, an eminent defender of free trade, reinforced this claim by stating that the dominance of short-term, speculative capital flows are not productive, but rather are characterized by panics and manias, which will continue to be 'a source of considerable economic difficulty'.[10]

The significance of these debates is that they represent an ideological renewal of capital controls as a necessary mechanism to reduce market volatility by seeking to curb hot money. One popular way of achieving this is by imposing a steep tax on short-term inflows, such as the Tobin tax.[11] The tax, ranging anywhere from 0.1 to 0.5 per cent, would be applied to all foreign exchange transactions as a way of reducing currency speculation, enhancing in the process the efficacy of macroeconomic policy whilst encouraging longer-term investment and raising some tax as a by-product.[12] Nevertheless, to be effective it must be implemented both uniformly and universally in conjunction with other reforms to deter speculation, such as a domestic financial transaction tax.[13] And, more fundamentally, this should occur within a new international system of stable relationships between major currencies, or what some have called a new Bretton Woods.[14] This solution drives a stake through the heart of the Washington consensus, for a new Bretton Woods system would necessitate an interstate system based on serious political and economic compromises, such as currency bands and pegging mechanisms.

Those opposed to the implementation of universal controls have argued that the Tobin tax is unfeasible due to technical and administrative barriers. Yet Tobin himself has countered this claim by arguing that

> while the implementation of the tax may appear complex, it is not any more complicated, probably much less so, than the detailed provisions

of many existing taxes.... Indeed if the standards of what is feasible employed here had been used before imposing income tax or VAT they would never have been introduced! The dominant feature in the introduction of new taxation has always been the political will rather than administrative feasibility.[15]

As Benjamin J. Cohen notes, of the possible reasons why governments may hesitate in implementing capital controls, the political opposition of the United States appears to be the most decisive.[16] Despite the fact that the burden of proof has shifted from those advocating capital controls to those in favour of capital mobility, this debate has not received much attention. However, it has not, as some writers have observed, been ignored. As we will see below, the transnational bourgeoisie and the caretakers of the global economy have been painfully aware of the concerns raised by the organic intellectuals as well as those regarding the sustainability of neoliberal-led capitalism in the South.

The imperative of free capital mobility was to receive at least two powerful blows with the scandal surrounding the near collapse of the Long Term Credit Management fund. For one thing, the debacle put into question the common-sense assumptions that financial markets are not only inherent rational but, to reach maximum efficiency, require as little state intervention (i.e. regulatory constraints) as possible. For another, the near-collapse challenged the implicit assumption that the financial system of the global North, and more specifically the arm's-length relationship between states and financial actors as found in the Anglo-American model, was far superior to Asian crony capitalism.[17] These points will become more apparent in our brief excursion into the LTCM.

The LTCM debacle

In September 1998, a US-based macro-hedge fund, the LTCM, found itself on the verge of bankruptcy. It will be useful to say a few words about hedge funds before proceeding. Put most simply, hedge funds are a type of deregulated mutual fund.[18] This implies that as long as the hedge fund has fewer than 99 members and does not involve small savers, the US Securities and Exchange

Commission (SEC) does not regulate how much leverage (borrowed money vis-à-vis its capital) is involved in their speculative activities.[19] It should be noted that while there are thousands of hedge funds, the more powerful version is the macro-hedge fund. What makes these funds so dangerous is the combination of their large degree of capital strike force (most of which is leveraged) and their strategy, which, as Adam Harmes explains, is 'to profit from changes in macroeconomic variables, such as shifts in interest rates, currencies and entire stock markets, rather than movements in the prices of individual stocks or bonds'.[20]

The LTCM received worldwide press coverage not only because of the unusual action taken by the Federal Reserve in facilitating a $3.625 billion creditor rescue but also because this bail-out came with very few strings attached in the way of reform.[21] As Ibrahim Warde recounts, in response to its near-collapse, and the potential losses of eminent investors tied to the Fund, including the chairmen of Merrill Lynch and Paine Webber, William J. McDonough, president of the Federal Reserve Bank of New York, called on the international financial community to buoy up the LTCM. In several hours, some fifteen or so American and European institutions provided several billion dollars in return for a 90 per cent share in the Fund and a promise that a supervisory board would be established.[22] Interestingly, the LTCM was not subject to further regulation, other than a supervisory board; nor was the deregulated over-the-counter (OTC) market, where the majority of the LTCM's, as well as other macro-hedge funds' betting activities, took place, subjected to government scrutiny.[23] Federal Reserve chairman Alan Greenspan justified the central bank's actions by suggesting that if action was not undertaken rapidly, 'the bankruptcy of LTCM "... could have potentially impaired the economies of many nations, including our own"'.[24]

On 16 December 1998, Barbara P. Holum, Commissioner of the Commodity Futures Trading Commission, testified before the United States Senate Committee on Agriculture, Nutrition and Forestry that, in her expert opinion, the LTCM was an isolated incident. The primary cause was not to be located in general market failure, but in an overextension of credit and bad money management. According to Holum,

[the] LTCM collapsed because of excess financial leverage. LTCM management mistakenly assumed that historical market relationships would continue indefinitely into the future. That mistake was compounded by a lapse in the prudential control over credit extended to the firm. But a debate over whether the losses were in cash or derivatives markets would miss the real point. The real cause of LTCM's losses is not the markets in which they invested, but a fallible investment strategy combined with an overextension of credit [with capital of less than US$5 billion, LTCM was able to borrow up to US$200 billion]. Concluding that the LTCM collapse dictates expanded regulation of the OTC market would misinterpret the message of the firm's failure.[25]

Holum's reasoning resonated well with Federal Reserve chairman Greenspan's rationale that investors would simply move to offshore markets, which are free from such regulations; this would have the perverse effect of reducing, rather than increasing, supervisory and regulatory oversight.[26] Strengthening the discipline of the market, not government regulation, was the message. According to the President's Working Group on Financial Markets' Report on Hedge Funds, Leverage, and the Lessons of Long-Term Capital Management, which was released in April 1999, this discipline was to be made more effective in two ways. First, there would be an improvement in risk management practices.[27] Second, there would be an attempt to increase the availability of information on the risk profiles of hedge funds and their creditors. The Working Group did not recommended any form of direct government regulation of hedge funds, as this is seen as significantly weakening market discipline by creating or exacerbating moral hazard.[28] It is important to underline that market discipline remains central to the reproduction of the Dollar Wall Street Regime (see Chapter 1) as the macro-hedge funds' command over huge amounts of financial resources gives them tremendous advantage and sway over the markets, particularly of middle-income countries. Put differently, these funds can attack currencies and stocks and cause them to depreciate sharply, more sharply than can be justified by economic fundamentals. Or, as LTCM chief and founder, John Meriwether, phrased it when he was asked whether he believes in the efficient market hypothesis: 'I MAKE them efficient.'[29]

By viewing finance as an aspect of capitalist restructuring we are able to understand that neoliberal ideology, particularly its emphasis on market discipline, is integral to the reproduction of this mode of financial regulation and its cornerstone policy of free capital mobility. Neoliberal ideology ensures that this mode of capital accumulation is viewed as common sense, instead of constructed reality by the ruling classes. Take, for instance, Greenspan's argument against re-regulatory measures vis-à-vis macro-hedge funds: if we regulate companies like LTCM, these players will simply put their money into offshore investments. Again, this resignation that the interests of transnational financial players must be catered to or else they will engage in disciplinary strategies such as investment strikes and capital flight emerges as 'common sense', implying that governments are defenceless in the face of powerful financial actors – defenceless, that is, until the speculative activities end in a crisis, and the Federal Reserve is asked to orchestrate a substantial bail-out to restore investor confidence.

In other words, the state intervenes in order to ensure the reproduction of capital accumulation. When market failure occurs, largely due to unregulated speculation by powerful financial players, governments are asked to step in and bail out the rich and powerful, as was the case in the LTCM bust. While the economic role of the state, or extension of state power, such as the IMF, is somewhat more explicit or evident during periods of crisis, the attempts by states to reproduce neoliberal common sense regarding free capital mobility at the international level has taken place in a highly clandestine manner. Against the backdrop of the Asian crash and the LTCM debacle, these tactics have become increasingly unpopular with the growing segment of the population in both the global North and the global South.

From Article IV to the MAI

In 1998, the same year that the LTCM and Asian debacles occurred, the US and other G7 countries were rigorously attempting to construct free capital mobility as a universal norm by enshrining it in several international agreements, and thereby effectively locking it into legal structures, which would fortify the overarching set of neoliberal policies embodied in the Washington consensus. Stephen Gill's term 'new constitutionalism' captures this attempt to remove or insulate substantially the new economic institutions from democratic accountability or popular scrutiny, whilst assisting in the growing concentration and centralization of transnational capital by guaranteeing the freedom of entry and exit of internationally mobile capital in different national spaces.[30] The highly secretive Multilateral Agreement on Investments (MAI) is a case in point. The objective of the MAI was to apply the neoliberal agenda of the World Trade Organization to the remaining vital economic sectors. The basic provisions of this proposal included, inter alia, the unrestricted opening of most economic sectors and natural resources to foreign ownership; fair and equal treatment of foreign firms; the removal of restrictions against the movement of capital; allowing for individual firms to sue foreign governments before an international mediation panel; full and proper compensation for expropriation. As such, the MAI attempted to guarantee unrestricted capital mobility in law. In the words of one NGO, the MAI sought to enshrine 'the right of big companies and financial institutions to go where they want, leave on their own terms, and therefore play one country against another for the most favourable "climate" for investment leading to a downwards spiral of labour and environmental standards.'[31]

The MAI was finally defeated in 1998 by a coalition of over 600 development, human rights, labour, environmental and consumer groups from around the world, with representation in over seventy countries. After the defeat of the MAI, supporters of financial liberalization, most notably the US Treasury officials and the IMF's senior staff, sought out other means by which free capital mobility across national spaces could be ensured. As noted earlier, prior to the Asian crash the Fund sought to amend its Articles of Agreement (IV) to grant itself formal (legal) power to require capital account liberalization. In other words, similar to the MAI, the Fund could force IMF member countries to remove capital controls and investment regulations. This initiative was dropped with the advent of the Asian crisis, largely due to opposition in the US Congress.

The crisis of authority regarding the US-led imperative of free capital mobility was also making itself felt at home. This was most readily observable by the refusal of the US Congress to co-operate with the Clinton administration in a $20 billion bail-out for Mexico in 1994 (see Chapter 2), and again, during the Asian crisis in 1997, when the administration attempted to transfer contributions amounting to $57 billion for South Korea, $17 billion for Thailand and $34 billion for Indonesia to the IMF, not to mention the following year when the US government handed out $16 billion to Russia and $42 billion to Brazil. With each bail-out, the US Congress has grown more sceptical of its and the IMF's *de facto* role of 'lender of last resort' and 'crisis manager'. A direct consequence of this growing disinclination to play lender of last resort to the world, Congress established the Meltzer Commission, in November 1998, as a part of legislation adding $18 billion to the US's capital contribution to the IMF.[32] It is to this largely ignored, albeit highly significant event, that our discussion now turns.

The Meltzer Commission

The task of the Meltzer Commission was to evaluate the effectiveness of seven major international institutions – the IMF, the World Bank Group, the Inter-American Development Bank, the African Development Bank, the Bank for International Settlements, and the WTO – and to suggest ways the US government should formulate policy towards them.[33] At a deeper level, the Meltzer Commission is significant for our understanding of the emergence of the new international financial institutions because it attacked a key facet of reproducing US structural power via free capital mobility in the South: namely, the international financial institutions (see Chapter 2). The Commission represented the first systematic, bipartisan review of the roles of the IFIs in the post-Bretton Woods era. Although the results of the Meltzer Commission report were not released until March 2000, the year in which Republican President George W. Bush came to power, the debates that informed the Commission preceded its formation. At the forefront of this discontent with the IFIs is that they are seen as failing in their objectives to reduce world poverty and ensure economic stability.[34] In the words of Chairman Meltzer, 'We must rid ourselves of a system that imposes changes that countries do not want and will not enforce, that brings demonstrators to the streets protesting real and imagined wrongs, and that is ineffective.'[35]

The upshot of these criticisms has been the recommendation by the Commission that the US government overhaul the IFIs, with special emphasis on a substantial reduction of their present powers, and on debt forgiveness vis-à-vis highly indebted poor countries (HIPCs).[36] Owing to the important role the IFIs play in reproducing the imperative of free capital mobility through conditionality and surveillance, it should not come as a surprise that the US government resisted these reforms. The following quotation is extrapolated from the US Treasury's response to the Meltzer Commission's recommendations:

> The IFIs are among the most effective and cost-efficient means available to advance US policy priorities worldwide. Since their inception, they have been central to addressing the major economic and development challenges of our time. They have promoted growth, stability, open markets and democratic institutions, resulting in more exports and jobs in the United States, while advancing our fundamental values throughout the world.... At the same time, and despite our shared objectives, it is fair to say that we disagree in fundamental respects with the bulk of the Commission's reform prescriptions ... [if the recommendations were be implemented they] would profoundly undermine the capacity of the IMF and the multilateral development banks ... to perform their core functions of responding effectively to financial crises and promoting durable growth and market-oriented reforms in developing countries – and would thus weaken the IFIs' capacity to promote central US interests.[37]

It will be recalled that the IMF and World Bank are not neutral and independent public authorities acting above states, but rather public authorities for transmitting the policy of states, particularly of their largest shareholder, the United States.[38] In this sense, the recent attempts of the IFIs to recast themselves as invaluable and democratic institutions are closely linked to growing criticism of their effectiveness in managing free capital mobility in the South. The production by the IMF and World Bank of copious, cross-conditional second generation reforms (SGRs), such as the Poverty Reduction Strategy Papers (PRSPs), the Comprehensive Development Framework (CDF), and the Poverty Reduction and Growth Facility (PRGF), are examples of a passive revolution that is attempting to freeze the contradictions created by two decades of top-down, economistic and growth-oriented policies. In doing so the IFIs have simply grafted rhetorical notions of 'country owner-ship', partnership and empowerment onto the structural adjustment programmes in an attempt to address the waning legitimacy of their existing neoliberal agenda, and, more fundamentally, of American interference in the South (see Chapter 6). As will become clear in the following discussion, in similar vein to the NIFA, this attempt to reinvent the SAPs serves two interrelated purposes. First, at the national level, it assists the ruling classes in overcoming their crisis of authority so that they may effectively implement neoliberal reform, embodied in the market-led policies of the Washington consensus. Second, both the second generation reforms and NIFA are about the broadening and deepening of the surveillance and disciplinary powers of the IFIs in the South. The latter is necessary in the US government's and transnational capital's quest to ensure the homoge-neity of rules and standards so that the financial deregulatory playing field becomes more level for transnational capitals in their constant need to broaden and deepen their speculative scope.

Taken together, the four aspects of the crisis of authority dis-cussed above – the capital controls debate, the LTCM debacle, the MAI defeat, and the Meltzer Commission – acted to aggravate the existing tensions between the Dollar Wall Street Regime and the imperative of free capital mobility. In order for the US to reproduce its structural power it needed to formulate policies that would act to freeze the contradictions associated with the Frankenstein factor. This leads us to the question of how US structural power is repro-duced in a multilateral interstate system that promotes, and feeds off, growing competition between other nation-states.

Freezing Contradictions:
The Anatomy of Imposed American Leadership

Giovanni Arrighi's notion of 'forced leadership' is useful in begin-ning to conceptualize the changing nature of US leadership in the post-Asian-crash global political economy:

> A dominant state exercises a hegemonic function if it leads the system of states in a desired direction and, in doing so, is perceived as pursuing a general interest. It is this kind of leadership that makes the dominant state hegemonic. But a dominant state may lead also in the sense that

it draws other states onto its own path of development. Borrowing an expression from Joseph Schumpeter ..., this second kind of leadership can be designated as 'leadership against one's own will' because, over time, it enhances competition for power rather than the power of the hegemon.[39]

While Arrighi's notion is helpful in drawing out the distinctions between hegemonic and non-hegemonic leadership, the term 'forced leadership' conjures up a degree of confusion for our purposes and is thus in need of fine-tuning on two counts. First, unlike Arrighi, I am not promoting the idea of US hegemony in terms of regional or coalitional hegemony; rather, the crisis of US hegemony is a moment of global dominance. Indeed, this reflects the nature of the Dollar Wall Street Regime, as three decades of financial liberalization have resulted in a highly interconnected and interdependent world in terms of financial flows. Second, *pace* Arrighi, it is not the assumption of non-hegemonic leadership by the US that is forced. Rather, non-hegemonic leadership involves forcing other states to follow suit. As such, 'imposed leadership' seems to be a more precise term to use in the present analysis. It follows that the Dollar Wall Street Regime is largely reproduced and regulated through coercion. The key point here is that coercion does not imply brute physical force. As Antonio Gramsci forcefully argued, hegemony entails both coercion and consensus. The two are intimately intertwined in a dialectical relation, although in a hegemonic situation consensus is more predominant than coercion, whilst the inverse is true in non-hegemonic periods.

Imposed leadership entails at least two types of coercion: (1) core–alliance coercion; and (2) core–periphery coercion. Both expressions of coercion mirror two principal understandings of Gramsci's conception of the restructuring involved in dealing with hegemony: (1) a leading fraction has the power and ability to articulate the interest of other fractions; (2) the dominant classes use their moral and intellectual leadership to establish their view of the world as all-inclusive and universal. Two caveats should be flagged at this point. First, in the current context of the US 'crisis of hegemony', these two types of coercion reflect a highly contradictory strategy of what Gramsci referred to as 'passive revolution', which by its very nature is exclusive. Second, for the purpose of this chapter, we need to extend these fractions and dominant classes to the international level. As such, the first type of coercion may be labelled core–alliance coercion. Although highly contradictory in practice, core–alliance coercion is aimed at forging agreements (formal or informal) between those interests tied to US structural power (DWSR), powerful industrialized countries, and transnational financial interests. Core–periphery coercion, on the other hand, entails the relationship between the US and the emerging market economies. Taken together, both types of coercion should be seen as class-led attempts to impose leadership through what Robert Cox refers to as transnational processes of consensus-formation among the official caretakers of the global economy, such as the IMF and the Paris Club.[40]

Core–alliance coercion may be located in the less visible and highly complex networks of the transnational bourgeoisie and political elites, which have been key players in defining the nature of international financial regulation (or the lack thereof) that has evolved around the Dollar Wall Street Regime. Since the fall of Bretton Woods, for example, there have been various international financial regulatory institutions, such as the G10 Central Bank governors, with their newly formed Basle Committee on Banking Regulations and Supervisory Practices in 1975, as well as the globally oriented International Organization of Securities Commissions, formed in 1984. Likewise, in 1994, insurance supervisors from around the world established their own association: the International Association of Insurance Supervisors (IAIS). Alongside these regulatory bodies, the Bank for International Settlements and the G10's Eurocurrency Standing Committee produced information on and analysis of global financial markets. Both these transnational forms of political authority emerged as a response to financial capitals to establish a regulatory regime to assist in the continued concentration and centralization of wealth in an interstate system characterized by increasing forms of competition for and dependency on private, short-term financial inflows. Equally, both institutions are regarded as closed policy communities of industrialized countries 'wherein an elite group works out the management of its own vital interests without wider public involvement'.[41] As we will see below, it is precisely the power of these highly clandestine global management webs and linkages that the NIFA is attempting to strengthen through tighter communicative lines and increased cooperation – as opposed to reforming them via democratization processes.

Core–periphery coercion is embodied in the so-called Washington consensus.[42] The consensus was an important feature of the Dollar Wall Street Regime, not only because it expanded markets but because it assisted in stabilizing and universalizing the norms and values of global financial capital, which in turn strengthened the position of the United States in the global economy. The orthodoxy of the consensus is based on the hypotheses of an efficient market and rational expectations; neoclassical economics assumes that progress will be brought about via free trade, free capital mobility and a non-interventionist state. This position rests on the neoliberal assumptions that globalization is an inevitable and natural progression that emanates from external forces, and that governments and societies are required to embrace globalization if they wish to share in increased prosperity.[43] These assumptions assist in reproducing the Dollar Wall Street Regime by legitimating free capital mobility and free trade as conditions arising from the market, whilst drawing attention away from the active role states are playing in ensuring that these conditions are not only met, but also reproduced.[44]

As noted in the previous chapters, the neoliberal orthodoxy of the Washington consensus was transmitted primarily through the structural adjustment programmes, which were tenaciously pursued by the international financial institutions in the global South after the debt crisis of 1982. These programmes locked Latin American, Asian and African economies into an open world market economy, so as to guarantee the freedom of entry and exit of internationally mobile capital across the globe. Countries that were willing to play the game by Washington's rules were rewarded with generous financial assistance and other forms of support.[45] The consensus should not be conceived in deterministic core–periphery terms as a blunt policy and ideological instrument that the United States forced onto the governments of the global South. Although the consensus clearly supported the Dollar Wall Street Regime, it has also, albeit unevenly, benefited the political elites and bourgeoisies of emerging market economies, which were restructuring their relations of production in order to overcome declining profit levels in the productive system. After all, 'it was not the Washington consensus idea that taught people to transform social relations; it was the material transformations of social relations which produced the power of the Washington consensus idea.'[46] Put another way, the Washington consensus is not simply political and ideological strategy; rather, it is a transnational class-based project rooted in the wider contradictions of global capitalism. In this way, contradictions in the Dollar Wall Street Regime will fundamentally affect the Washington consensus, or, more specifically, explain its altered existence in the form of the new international financial architecture. It is to this issue of inherent contradictions of US leadership that the chapter now turns.

The Continuing Contradictions of Imposed Leadership

How do we make sense of the inherent relations within the Dollar Wall Street Regime, namely the US government and global finance? As I suggested in Chapter 1, this relationship may be regarded as symbiotic yet constraining.[47] It is enabling because as the international financial markets grow in size and power, so too does the US economy. Because of its low level of domestic savings, the US is dependent on a constant stream of funds (or liquidity market) to Wall Street from abroad.[48] The mutually reinforcing elements of the insatiable greed of global finance and Washington's ongoing obsession with neoliberal practices to maintain its structural power in the world economy resulted in a constant thrust toward financial liberalization to reproduce the DWSR. Indeed, prior to the Asian crash, the Interim Committee of the IMF was attempting to revise the Fund's charter to impose a legal obligation of open capital accounts on its members.[49] Benjamin J. Cohen rightly observes that this was the high-water mark of the attempt to consecrate free market mobility as a universal norm.[50]

It is important to note that the Dollar Wall Street Regime thrives not only in periods of systemic stability but also during times of instability. As Gowan notes, it feeds off crises in the following ways. First, during times of crisis or economic downturn, funds flee towards the safe haven of the US dollar and Wall Street. Second,

SAPs encourage export-oriented industrialization so that countries can pay off their debts; this exporting into the dollar zone serves to strengthen further the centrality of the dollar. Third, the risks faced by US financial operators are widely covered by the IMF, enabling them to return to international activity more aggressively than ever. Four, the weakening of states of the South strengthens the bargaining power of the Wall Street credit institutions and decisions on the form of future financing. In response, creditors turn to forms that are safer, such as securitized debt and short-term loans rather than long-term loans.[51]

As discussed in Chapter 1, there are also constraining features in this apparent win–win aspect of the Dollar Wall Street Regime. One important limitation worth examining here concerns the global South. Given the growing interconnectedness brought about by the DWSR, its viability has become increasingly dependent on the health and stability of the financial markets, regardless of their location. As the former Secretary of the Treasury, Robert Rubin, stated in reaction to Indonesia's economic woes in 1997, 'Financial stability around the world is critical to the national security and economic interest of the United States.'[52] With each debacle in the emerging markets, the neoclassical premises upon which the Washington consensus rests – especially the equation between free capital mobility and sustained prosperity – becomes gradually more difficult to legitimate. Fundamentally speaking, for transnational capitals to continue to prosper, and relatedly the Dollar Wall Street Regime, it is crucial that the bourgeois governments in the global South are able to re-create the conditions for capital valorization, and do so in such a manner as to benefit the DWSR. Susan Strange picked up on this contradiction almost fifteen years ago when she noted that

> The sorry state of the financial system is undoubtedly aggravating the difficulties in the path of economic development for poor countries while conversely the difficulties of the deeply indebted developing countries, so long as they persist, will aggravate the instability of the banking system.[53]

As mentioned in Chapter 1, the predominant type of inflow to the South – that is, short-term, speculative in nature – have two negative and mutually reinforcing effects on governments in the

South. First, they impose constraints on policy autonomy. Eager to ensure a steady inflow of credit, bourgeois states of the South have been keen to pursue policies laid out by the IMF, whose seal of approval is the ultimate device to signal creditworthiness to the financial markets. Second, such inflows lead to increased vulnerability of the economy to risk, financial volatility and crisis.[54] Economists refer to this as the 'policy trilemma' or the 'open-economy tri-lemma', which means that governments can only pursue two of the following three goals: (1) fixed exchange rates; (2) open capital accounts; and (3) monetary policy geared toward domestic goals.[55] While this policy contradiction has been largely overcome by the setting of high interest rates in advanced industrialized countries, for emerging markets, high interest rates not only translate into short-term, volatile flows, but also, and more importantly, into the tendency to push up the external value of the currency, which could have detrimental consequences for their exports. High interest rates also translate into higher payments on internal debt. Either way, it is a Hobson's choice. Governments of emerging markets are finding themselves increasingly caught between a rock and a hard place, between sound policies and the practice of compensatory politics.

Given the high dependence on exports, a currency revaluation would be, and has proven, fatal for emerging markets. Moreover, high interest rates choke the highly indebted private sectors within these countries, and, in effect, raise the already high indigence and poverty rates. These policy constraints pose a threat both to the emerging market economies and to the Dollar Wall Street Regime. Taken together, they are political expressions of the underlying contradictions of the capital relation in the countries with emerging markets. Their importance arises from the fact that they place an incredible burden on governments, which must maintain the political and social conditions for the continuation of capital accumulation within their borders by meeting increasing social demands from the private sector and society at large. Moreover, imposed leadership demands that emerging markets overcome these policy constraints in such a manner as to support free capital mobility. The problem, at least for those interests tied to the DWSR, is that emerging markets are seeking to protect themselves from this trilemma by calling for increased policy autonomy in the areas of management of capital account and the choice of exchange rate regime.[56] The former clearly runs contrary to the interests of the DWSR. How has Washington responded? The next section focuses in on this question by probing the management of these contradictions in the form of the new international financial architecture.

A Procrustean Bed for the South?

> The problem is to see whether in the dialectic 'revolution/restoration' it is revolution or restoration which predominates; for it is certain that in the movement of history there is never any turning back, and that restorations in toto do not exist.
>
> Antonio Gramsci[57]

The shape of the new building

Although the G20 and the Financial Stability Forum are the principal institutions of the international financial architecture, it should be kept in mind that they act as annexations to the existing structure rather than forming a new edifice. Before moving on to consider the nature of the NIFA, however, it is useful to provide some further information about these two fortifying units.

In response to the various issues relating to the emerging markets financial crisis of the late 1990s, through the smokescreen of cooperation and a multilateral spirit, the G7, the United States unilaterally pushed through an agenda that would officially incorporate 'systematically important' emerging markets with the IMF and the World Bank. The stated aims of this project may be most clearly seen in the primary directive of the G7 Summit meeting in Cologne. The primary directive was the attempt to integrate emerging market economies more fully and flexibly into the global financial system by, for example, soliciting the IMF and its members to increase their transparency by publishing economic data, especially on short-term indebtedness and the state of foreign exchange reserves. Further, 'It urged the IMF to co-ordinate surveillance of the degree to which countries comply with international standards and codes of conduct. The G7 also wants greater disclosure of the degree to which private sector financial institutions are exposed to hedge funds and other highly leveraged institutions.'[58] After hearing provisional reports from such ad hoc committees as the G22 and G33, whose membership was selected under the watchful eye of the US, the G7 leaders created the G20 on 25 September 1999 in Washington DC. Unsurprisingly, the G20's membership structure reveals an important tendency in regard to the two types of coercion.

The G20 comprises not only the 'systematically important' emerging markets of Argentina, Australia, Brazil, China, India, Indonesia, Mexico, Saudi Arabia, South Africa, South Korea and Turkey, but also the G7/G8, a representative from the European Union, the IMF, the Fund's new International Monetary and Financial Committee (IMFC), the World Bank, as well as the Bank's Development Committee. Taken together, the constitution of the G20 demonstrates renewed attempts at core–periphery coercion by inviting these countries into the highly exclusive G7/G8, or, put more bluntly, by co-opting them into the rules and standards of the core–alliance coercion by ensuring official, and thus more tightly integrated, relations with the IMF and World Bank. The latter had never been attempted before the G20. The mission of this esoteric community of international financial institutions, emerging markets and core states involves meeting the G7's commitment stated at the Cologne Summit.[59] Thus, it seeks to promote consistency and coherence in the various efforts aimed at reforming and strengthening the international financial system – as defined by the IMF and the World Bank. To this end, since its inception the G20 meetings have regularly included general and regional gatherings. Furthermore the G20 is expected to coordinate the Financial Stability Forum, and the possibility was even noted that it might supplant the G7. As is the case with the G7, the G20 does not have a permanent secretariat. Instead it is based in the country of the Chair, which was initially held by the former finance minister and current prime minister of Canada, Paul Martin.

On 3 October 1998, the finance ministers and central bank governors of the G7 commissioned Hans Tietmeyer, president of the Deutsche Bundesbank, to consult with various public and private international bodies and recommend ways to enhance the cooperation among national and international supervisory bodies and the international financial institutions in order to achieve stability in the international financial system. The main recommendation of Tietmeyer's report (more formally known as the Report on International Co-operation and Co-ordination in the Area of Financial Market Supervision and Surveillance) was to establish a Financial Stability Forum. The FSF, which first convened in April 1999, was established to promote international financial stability 'by facilitating better-informed lending and investment decisions, improving market integrity, and reducing the risks of financial distress and contagion'.[60]

The Forum is a political body that reports to and is supervised jointly by the G7 leaders. Unlike the G20, however, it is a type of core–alliance coercion. In its own words,

> The *Forum* brings together on a regular basis national authorities responsible for financial stability in significant international financial centres, international financial institutions, sector-specific international groupings of regulators and supervisors, and committees of central bank experts. The FSF seeks to co-ordinate the efforts of these various bodies in order to promote international financial stability, improve the functioning of markets, and reduce systemic risk.[61]

Crucially, the initial chairman of the FSF is not from a 'strategically important' emerging market economy; but is instead the general manager of the Bank for International Settlements (BIS). Moreover, the Forum is housed in the BIS in Basel, Switzerland.

As stated on its website, the key objectives of the FSF are: (1) to evaluate the vulnerabilities in the international financial system; (2) to identify and oversee action needed to address these vulnerabilities; and (3) to improve coordination and information exchange among the various authorities responsible for financial stability.[62] To this end, the FSF meets twice a year, or as many times as is necessary to carry out its objectives. Some important developments that have emerged from these meetings are the establishment of three working groups to assess extensively and recommend policy actions regarding: (a) highly leveraged institutions; (b) capital flows; and (c) offshore financial centres. At a meeting in Singapore in March 2000, the Forum urged national authorities, international financial institutions, and international groupings and other agents referred to in the reports to consider promptly its recommendations and take the necessary actions to implement them. Together with the IAIS, the FSF has also put together and disseminated a 'Compendium of Standards'. The Compendium essentially establishes a common reference for the various standards and codes of good practice that are internationally accepted as relevant to sound, stable and well-functioning financial systems. Furthermore, the FSF has approved a Financial Supervision Training Directory, which was created jointly by the IMF, the World Bank and the Bank for International Settlements.

Making sense of the NIFA: a tale of two coercions

The new international financial architecture signals an attempt to freeze the contradictions found within global capitalism by strengthening the existing institutional structures of imposed leadership. A cursory glance at this nascent project reveals a striking similarity to the Washington consensus. For one thing, both are expressions of imposed leadership that are rooted in the Dollar Wall Street Regime. For another, both are concerned with legitimizing the power of global finance by blocking tendencies towards increased state regulation over international financial flows, as well as ensuring that governments in emerging market economies continue to adhere to the tenets of free trade and capital mobility. The NIFA accomplishes these tasks in three overlapping ways. First, it reinforces the position that increased volatility in the international financial system is due to home-grown policy error, not so much in the form of profligate governments – which have been largely 'corrected' via structural adjustment programmes – as that of corporate governance structures in emerging markets. Relatedly, this presupposes that the regulatory structures of the advanced industrialized countries need not be subjected to reform, especially the United States. Second, by shifting the blame for the crises to the emerging markets, the international financial markets are vindicated and thus also need not be subjected to reform.

The third way the conditions of global capital accumulation have been reproduced to support the status quo is through the practice of inclusionary politics. As the G7 made clear during the Cologne summit, the key objective of this interstate initiative is to integrate emerging market economies more fully and flexibly[63] into the

Dollar Wall Street Regime. This move is not an attempt to permute power between the First and Third Worlds, but rather to strengthen the existing system through such tactics as international collective surveillance. Because the new international financial architecture is constructed in the existing power relations of the interstate system, the hierarchy of power will also be reflected in the structures of the G20 and the Financial Stability Forum.

This collective effort represents a renewed attempt to construct constitutional forms of transnational consensus formation by centralizing power in clandestine regulatory institutions. As Geoffrey Underhill notes, these closed transnational communities provide ad hoc and patchy regulation and supervision of the markets, which in turn greatly facilitate the growth of capital volatility and mobility.[64] The technical orientation of these institutions tends to depoliticize highly political issues, such as hedge funds, capital flows, and offshore financial centres.[65] In essence, the Financial Stability Forum and G20 represent a larger tendency towards the construction of transnational consensus formation in regard to the institutionalization of international regulation of finance. Put another way, the new international financial architecture is an expression of core–alliance and core–periphery coercion. In the following, the chapter probes how the governments of strategically important countries of the global South continue to adhere to globalizing free capital mobility and free trade, and thereby remain 'good investment sites' for the Dollar Wall Street Regime – which is the encrypted meaning of 'systematically important' emerging markets.

Drawing other states into the path of the consensus: imposed leadership

> [T]he bourgeoisie can and will exercise its function of continuous expansionary movement; indeed, it enforces bourgeois laws as if there is only one class and only one society.
>
> Antonio Gramsci[66]

The new international financial architecture is an attempt to strike a balance between financial deregulation and stability by encouraging governments of emerging markets to impose prudent policy responses which, while not hindering the idea of free capital mobility, restrain the inflow of speculative capital and encourage more productive, long-term capital formation.[67] Top officials from the international financial institutions have promoted the case that particular capital controls (as opposed to universal controls, such as the Tobin tax) in emerging markets are desirable as temporary and second-best option – that is, next to direct liberalization allowing the magical self-corrective forces of the market to do their trick through an open capital account.[68] It must be stressed, however, that this position is not far from the orthodoxy of the Washington consensus. John Williamson notes that convention has always held that, to ensure stability during the reform process, policymakers should concentrate on liberalizing other parts of the economy before opening the capital account.[69] In this sense, particular capital controls are a useful, temporary policy instrument to achieve breathing space for corrective action, which, of course, involves the implementation of neoliberal reforms.[70] Stanley Fischer, the IMF's deputy director, supported this claim by stating that the Fund 'is prodding countries toward the importance of pursuing sound macro-economic policies … and phasing capital account liberalization appropriately – which means retaining some capital controls in the transition is virtually axiomatic now'.[71] Emerging markets should employ 'certain' types of controls so that they may undertake the necessary reforms – the adoption of First World financial and banking structures – to achieve the goal: full financial liberalization. That is to say, capital controls assist countries to make a full commitment to free market principles based on a single best approach for all countries in a global financial system where all are subject to the same rules.

Not all capital controls are welcome, however. We discuss at length the political economy of this judgement call in the cases of Chile and Malaysia in the following chapter. Despite the fact that fourteen emerging market economies have employed a variety of capital controls over the past decade, Washington has heralded Chilean capital control (1991–98) as the most successful in averting the negative side effects of an abundance of short-term financial flows, such as exchange rate appreciation and capital flight (see Chapter 4).[72] When viewed in the light of the Washington consensus, however, the reason for this endorsement was not just Chile's fastidious adherence to the principles of neoliberalism since General Pinochet so inhumanely introduced the policy and ideology in 1973, but also that, and in keeping with neoliberalism, Chile was zealously liberalizing capital outflows. On the other hand, spokespeople for the international financial markets (including George Soros) and the US government condemn states that run against free capital mobility. In stark contrast to the endorsement of Chile, the IMF passed judgement on the much shorter-lived Malaysian controls on outflows (1998–99) as a policy choice that clearly abandoned liberalization on capital accounts. Although the jury is still out regarding the effectiveness of both types of control, the US remains vehemently opposed to Malaysian controls.[73] What is more, although Malaysia modelled its controls on the Chinese model, it was not only exposed to disciplinary action by both the IMF and capital markets (investment strikes) but was also denied entry into the G20.[74] Despite its use of capital controls, the sheer geopolitical might of China guaranteed its access to the elite club of the G20.

There are at least three overlapping reasons for the rejection of the Malaysian control, all of which may be traced to the interests of the Dollar Wall Street Regime. First, controls on capital outflows restrict the liquidity needed to nourish Wall Street and the US economy.[75] This is particularly compelling in light of the fact that the Asian region has the highest savings rates in the world.[76] Second, despite the general opposition of the United States to restricting capital mobility of short-term flows, largely through its vilification of the 'Asian model', these controls pose an ideological threat to the logic of financial liberalization. To be sure, neoliberal supporters cannot deny that countries such as China and Taiwan, and later Hong Kong,[77] all of whom closed their economies to these volatile flows, escaped the direct impacts of the crisis in large part because their respective currencies were nonconvertible, preventing both inflows and outflows of hot money – but not inhibiting foreign direct investment.[78] Relatedly, the Malaysian currency controls have been rejected by the United States because they mirror a larger historical tendency in the region to invoke a form of state intervention that runs directly against the neoclassical spirit of the Washington consensus, namely a developmental state. John Zysman defines developmental states as involving non-Anglo-Saxon state regulations, strong-state technocratic dirigisme, corporatist structures – like Japan.[79] Unlike its neoliberal counterpart, this form of state intervention does not regard the role of the political as an unproductive activity and unnecessary evil to maintain economic stability.

What is more, the developmental state is closely associated with specific practices that run contrary to the new international financial architecture's attempt to implement 'good corporate governance' (e.g. separation of management and ownership) and transparency (e.g. public availability of information) in the region in order to destroy exclusive capitalist communities, which are particularly closed to foreign intrusion, like 'bamboo networks' and pyramids.[80] Because this type of state intervention and accumulation regime has been highly successful in the past, its increasing attractiveness to governments as a viable alternative to the Washington consensus – especially in light of the present economic downturn in the region – poses a powerful threat to Washington's bid to consecrate global capital mobility.[81]

The Contradictions of Imposed Leadership Revisited

These strategies undertaken by the caretakers of the global economy, in an attempt to refurbish and fortify the political and ideological scaffolding of the Dollar Wall Street Regime, reveal an overriding concern to address some salient contradictions produced by free capital mobility. Nonetheless, the new face of imposed leadership has resulted in a new contradiction. On the one hand, the power of both the DWSR and global finance has been reproduced in the process of guaranteeing the continuation of global capital accumulation, particularly financial capital. On the other hand, the maintenance of imposed leadership in the interstate system serves to intensify the competition for power, as opposed to the establishment of a hegemonic era of capital accumulation (i.e. a golden age of growth). This can take the form of interstate rivalry within the core alliance, which in effect also entails heightened forms of unevenness, leading to what the former Brazilian president Fernando Henrique Cardoso referred to as 'asymmetrical globalization'. The latter is argued to create increased distributive tensions not only between the North and the South but also within the national social formations of the global South.[82] With one hand tied behind their backs by constraints placed on them by structural adjustment programmes and the threat of capital flight and investment strike by the financial community, these governments are asked to subdue escalating levels of social conflict and demands placed upon them by labour, grassroots organizations, national business associations and the like. For example, as Leo Panitch points out, China has made enormous concessions to foreign capital to get into the World Trade Organization. As in all developing countries, the country's workers were the first to pay for these compromises.[83] China is not the exception in this regard, however.

The contradiction within imposed leadership has touched off a general 'crisis of authority' (see Chapter 1). If they are viewed in tandem, attempts to standardize the global playground for finance through the new international financial architecture seem to be the necessary counterpart to the World Trade Organization and the General Agreement on Trade in Services (GATS). The effect of these core–periphery coercive strategies has been to handcuff these governments' remaining free hand to the bedpost of the DWSR. This has enormous consequences for the ability of states to adhere to the dictates of imposed leadership. More crucially, however, in attempting to deal with the policy constraints within the current era of 'asymmetrical globalization', emerging markets appear to be moving towards a half-way Polanyian double movement, which we can understand as a form of Third Way politics. This may be observed at both regional and domestic levels in the global South.

The regional double movement is an attempt to cope with the increased competition and uneven nature of deeper integration into the world market. Of course both strategies are attempts to reproduce capital accumulation and accommodate capital valorization. The larger significance of the refusal to allow Malaysia into the G20 was not merely that it was perceived as a 'neoliberal rogue state'; rather, it was intended as a general deterrent against a regional double movement towards what Karl Polanyi referred to as a Phase II type of economic and social development (a reinvented developmental state). Polanyi describes this as a shift towards explicit state intervention not only to stabilize and regulate the markets but also to create conditions for wealth creation and efficient resource allocation tasks. Indeed, an important case in point is the establishment of a 'network of currency swap/repurchase arrangements, designed to protect member countries against the sudden withdrawal of hot money investment by Western speculators' by the Association of Southeast Asian Nations (ASEAN) +3 (i.e. the ASEAN countries plus Japan, South Korea and China). China's dual role in the G20 and ASEAN+3 will prove quite interesting.[84]

The domestic variant of the Third Way may be seen as a reaction against the Washington consensus. Specifically, it is an attempt to cope with the crisis of the state by re-embedding market society into the market economy without political empowerment or substantial material concessions. As José Antonio Ocampo writes,

> There are actually no strong arguments in favour of moving towards capital account convertibility. There is no evidence that capital mobility leads to an efficient smoothing of expenditures in developing countries through the business cycle and, on the contrary, strong evidence that in these countries the volatility of capital flows is an additional source of instability. There is also no evidence of an association between capital account liberalization and economic growth.[85]

For the executive secretary of the UN Economic Commission on Latin America and the Caribbean, Latin America as a whole is the region where reforms have gone the furthest – growth in the 1990s was on 3.2 per cent a year, far below the 5.5 per cent record set during the three decades of state-led development from the 1950s to the 1970s. Ocampo goes on to argue that these countries can only adhere to the universalization of standards and rules in finance and trade by increasing policy autonomy in terms of capital account liberalization and exchange rate regimes in order to devise a countercyclical macroeconomic policy to shield them from the devastating socioeconomic effects brought about by speculators. This in turn will assist states of the global South to reembed what Polanyi refers to as market society (the social and cultural values of society) within the market economy (neoliberal-driven growth). For example, some governments in Latin America, such as Mexico and Chile, have turned to national anti-poverty programmes to fragment grassroots struggle and co-opt disincorporated labour groups (usually found in the ever-expanding informal sector).[86] At the same time, however, these policies are designed to complement the other aspect involved in overcoming the crisis of the state: namely, repression of domestic class struggle and impinging on the freedom of association. It is clear that Third Way politics in the South do not entail a form of delinking (Amin), but rather seek different ways of achieving export competitiveness. Yet these strategies aimed at salvaging political legitimacy do have the potential to shake the foundations of the new international financial architecture. More importantly, the contradiction from which the architecture arose, that between the Dollar Wall Street Regime and asymmetrical globalization, opens up space for political protest and struggle radically to transform class relations in the emerging markets and beyond. It remains to be seen whether the velvet glove of inclusionary politics covering the 'sledgehammer' politics of the new international financial architecture will be able to impose a single set of rules to perpetuate the power of the DWSR, especially in the face of a crisis of global capitalism.

Notes

Earlier versions of Chapter 3 appeared in the *Socialist Register 2002* (London: Merlin Press), and as 'The New International Financial Architecture: A Procrustean Bed for Emerging Markets?', *Third World Quarterly*, vol. 23, no. 4, 2002, www.tandf.co.uk/journals/carfax/01436597.html. Permission to reprint here is gratefully acknowledged.

1. The ROSCs, which constitute the third main institutional feature of the new international financial architecture, will be discussed in more detail in Chapter 5.
2. Cf. Stiglitz 2002; Jomo 1998; Wade and Veneroso 1998a, 1998b; Bello 1998.
3. This has been well chronicled by many authors across the political spectrum. See, for example, Sachs 1998 and Bello 1998.
4. This was made clear in the IMF's first comprehensive review of the crisis, Lane et al. 1999.
5. 'A Survey of Asian Business: In Praise of Rules', *The Economist*, 7–13 April 2001: 3.
6. Soros 1998: 55.
7. Felix 2002; cf. Haley 1999, 2001.
8. Lamfalussy 2000.
9. Arestis and Sawyer 1999: 153.
10. Bhagwati 1998: 10.

11. Dillon 1997: 95.
12. Tobin 1978.
13. Many countries already have some form of domestic financial transaction tax, for example, Australia, Austria, Belgium, Germany, France, Hong Kong, Japan, Singapore, the United Kingdom. This tax operates like the Tobin tax, but is applied to the domestic as opposed to the international economy. See Dillon 1997: 100–102.
14. This was the conclusion of a private conference of forty-seven international financial experts called the Bretton Woods Commission, which was chaired by former Federal Reserve chair Paul Volcker. See, for example, Bretton Woods Commission 1994.
15. Arestis and Sawyer 1999: 163.
16. Cohen 2003.
17. Cf. Martin Khor, 'Hedge-fund Crisis Shatters Myths'. See www.twnside. org.sg/title/myths-cn.htm. For more elaboration on crony capitalism, see Chapter 5.
18. According to Randy Charles Epping, 'A mutual fund is a collection of bonds or stocks sold to investors as a single investment.' Mutual funds allow investors to diversity risk over a wide range of stocks and bonds 'within a single investment vehicle'. Another ostensible benefit of these types of fund is that they enable investors to operate in markets in which their information is quite limited – for example, emerging markets. See Epping 2001: 214.
19. Ibrahim Warde, 'Hedge Funds', *Le Monde Diplomatique*, November 1998.
20. Harmes 2001: 122.
21. The Financial Economist Roundtable Statement on the Long-Term Capital Management and the Report of the President's Working Group on Financial Markets, 6 October 1999, www.luc.edu/orgs/finroundtable/statement99. html.
22. Ibrahim Warde, 'LTCM, a Hedge Fund above Suspicion,' *Le Monde Diplomatique*, November 1998.
23. Over-the-counter (OTC) refers to a deregulated market of securities (stocks and bonds); that is, securities that are not traded on official (regulated) exchange markets. Instead of dealing in regulated markets (e.g. the New York Stock Exchange), brokers negotiate directly with each other over computer networks or by phone. OTC securities are risky, as they do not conform to the capital requirements of major exchanges. Derivatives (swaps, options and futures) are a key financial instrument used in OTC markets. Essentially, derivatives describe any financial instrument that derives its value from another financial instrument. Derivatives are old instruments that were traditionally used to hedge risks. Today these hedging activities are accompanied by speculative ventures – largely due to the deregulation of financial markets.
24. Warde, 'LTMC'.
25. US Committee on Agriculture, Nutrition, and Forestry, 1998. 'Testimony of Barbara P. Holum, Commissioner Commodity Futures Trading Commission before the United States Senate Committee on Agriculture, Nutrition, and

Forestry,' 16 December 1998, Washington DC, www.cftc.gov/opa/speeches/ opaholum-22.htm.

26. US Treasury Secretary's offical response to the Meltzer Commission is available at www.treas.gov/press/releases/reports/response.pdf.

27. 'Hedge Funds, Leverage, and the Lessons of Long-Term Capital Management', Report of the President's Working Group on Financial Markets, April 1999, Washington DC, www.ustreas.gov/press/releases/reports/hedgfund.pdf.

28. Moral hazard refers to 'the risk that the presence of a contract will affect on the behavior of one or more parties. The classic example is in the insurance industry, where coverage against a loss might increase the risk-taking behavior of the insured.' See www.investorwords.com/cgi-bin/getword. cgi?3117.

29. Ibrahim Warde, 'Crony Capitalism', *Le Monde Diplomatique*, November 1998.

30. Gill 1992.

31. Friends of the Earth, 19 February 1997, www.globalpolicy.org/socecon/ bwi-wto/oecd-mai.htm.

32. The all male commission included six Republicans and five Democrats. Members include: Allan Meltzer, Professor of Political Economy at Carnegie Mellon University; C. Fred Bergsten, Director of the Institute for International Economics; Charles W. Calomiris, Professor of Finance and Economics at Columbia University; W. Lee Hoskins, Chairman and CEO of Huntington National Bank; and Jeffrey Sachs, Director of the Center for International Development at Harvard.

33. As stated on its website, the 'World Bank Group consists of five closely associated institutions, all owned by member countries that carry ultimate decision-making power. As explained below, each institution plays a distinct role in the mission to fight poverty and improve living standards for people in the developing world. The term "World Bank Group" encompasses all five institutions. The term "World Bank" refers specifically to two of the five, the International Bank for Reconstruction and Development (IBRD) and the International Development Association (IDA).' The other three institutions are: the International Financial Corporation, the Multilateral Investment Guarantee Agency, and the International Centre for Settlement of Investment Disputes (ICSID). For more elaboration on these institutions, see web.worldbank.org/WBSITE/EXTERNAL/EXTABOUTUS/0, ,contentMDK :20046275~menuPK:48380~pagePK:43912~piPK:44037,00.html.

34. Mutume 2001; cf. Pender 2001.

35. Bank Information Centre 2002.

36. The controversial HIPC was initiated by the World Bank and the IMF, and agreed to by various governments in 1996. According to the World Bank, the HIPC initiative 'was the first comprehensive approach to reduce the external debt of the world's poorest, most heavily indebted countries, and represented an important step forward in placing debt relief within an overall framework of poverty reduction' – that is, the second generation reforms (SGRs). For more information, see www.worldbank.org/hipc/.

37. US Department of the Treasury Response to the IFI Advisory Commission, www.ustreas.gov/press/releases/reports/response.pdf.

38. Gowan 1999: 32ff.
39. Arrighi 1994: 29.
40. Cox 1994: 49.
41. Underhill 1997: 31.
42. For more policy-oriented discussion of the Washington Consensus, see Williamson 1990, 1993.
43. Bhagwati 1998; cf. Eichengreen 1999.
44. On the importance of the role of the state in globalization, see, for example, Panitch 2000.
45. Cohen 2003.
46. Gowan 1999: 58.
47. For an innovative and historical treatment of the DWSR, see Ikeda 2002.
48. Gowan 1999: 125–6.
49. IMF 1997: 8.
50. Cohen 2003.
51. Gowan 1999: 35ff.
52. 'Economic Stakes in Asia', *New York Times*, 1 November 1997.
53. Strange 1986: 92–5.
54. Grabel 1996: 1763.
55. Saxton 2000.
56. Ocampo 2000.
57. Gramsci 1992: 219.
58. 'The New Financial Architecture', *Financial Times*, 24 September 1999.
59. See www.g20.org.
60. Akyüz 2002: 29.
61. www.fsforum.org.
62. Ibid.
63. 'The New Financial Architecture'.
64. Underhill, 1997. See also Tony Porter, 'The G7, the Financial Stability Forum, the G-20, and the Politics of International Financial Regulation', www.library.utoronto.ca/g7/g20/g20porter/porter4.html.
65. See Tony Porter, www.g7.utoronto.ca/g7/g20/g20porter/porter7.html.
66. Carnoy 1984: 74.
67. Stiglitz 1998b, 1998/99; IMF 2000b.
68. Recently, the former chief economist of the World Bank, Joseph Stiglitz, as well as IMF officials, such as deputy managing director Stanley Fischer, have championed the use of particular capital controls in select emerging market economies. See, for example, Stiglitz 1998b; 1998/99; IMF 1998.
69. Williamson 1997.
70. Eichengreen 1999; IMF 2000b: 12.
71. IMF 1997b.
72. See, for example, Buch 1999; Ffrench-Davis 2000; Agosin 1998.
73. Cf. IMF 1999a, 1999b, 2000c, 2000d; see Chapter 4.
74. John K. Kirton, 'What is the G20?' www.g7.utoronto.ca/g20/g20whatisit.html.
75. In the words of the US Federal Reserve Chairman, Alan Greenspan: 'flood of imports into the US [is] unsustainable, for the current wealth in the US

[is] not being created through producing goods and services, but the stock market.' 'Ministers Nervous about How Long US Expansion Can Last', *Financial Times*, 24 January 2000.

76. Asian countries always had a high rate of savings vis-à-vis the rest of the world. However, in the post-Asian environment, these rates have risen considerably. Malaysia and Singapore, for example, have recorded rates hovering around 45 per cent of their respective GDP levels. Savings levels in Hong Kong registered at about 30 per cent of GDP and Japan at 27 per cent; *Taipei Times*, 9 July 2000.

77. Wade and Veneroso 1998a: 22.

78. Wade and Veneroso 1998a: 21.

79. John Zysman defines AICs *developmental* states as non-Anglo-Saxon state regulations, strong-state technocratic *dirigisme*, corporatist structures (such as France and Japan). See Zysman 1983.

80. See Chapter 5.

81. Of course, this raises the question of why China was admitted into the G20, whilst Malaysia was ostracized. For more on the possible reasons why, see Chapter 4.

82. Mahon 1999: 105.

83. Panitch 2001.

84. Tim Armstrong, 'Asia Is Going It Alone,' *Globe and Mail*, 12 February 2001.

85. Ocampo 2000: 56–7.

86. For a historical materialist analysis of the Mexican National Anti-Poverty Programme (PRONASOL), see Soederberg 2001b.

4

Unravelling Washington's Judgement Calls: The Cases of Chilean and Malaysian Capital Controls

Given the increasing vulnerability and volatility in the global financial system, capital controls have become fashionable again. As we saw in the previous chapters, the World Bank and the IMF remain firmly committed to the assumption that full capital and current account liberalization are the only means to achieve sustainable economic development. Nevertheless, in response to the growing discontent spurred on by the Asian crisis, these institutions have grudgingly accepted prudent forms of capital controls as a second-best and temporary policy mechanism for emerging markets. Alan Binder, a former vice-chairman of the US Federal Reserve Board, argued that 'the hard-core Washington consensus – which holds that international capital mobility is a blessing, full stop – needs to be tempered by a little common sense'.[1] In other words, when pursued alongside sound macroeconomic policies, country-level capital controls could stem the inflow of speculative capital and encourage more productive, long-term capital formation (foreign direct investment).[2] It should be noted that Blinder and other official proponents of capital controls are careful to temper their comments by stressing that they are not recommending the imposition of heavy-handed controls to protect the local financial sector from foreign competition. Rather, 'the suggestion is to find mechanisms that just "slow down the flow of money". The country most commonly used as the model to emulate is Chile.'[3] Many economic pundits disagree, however. Sebastian Edwards posits that Chilean capital control was not effective in reducing macroeconomic instability, whilst Barry Eichengreen et al. have found correlations between countries pursuing liberalized capital accounts (read: no capital controls) and higher rates of economic growth.[4]

Despite the lack of evidence supporting the claim that Chilean capital control is an effective strategy to manage large inflows of hot money in the South, the IMF has continued to endorse this policy, while repudiating other forms. Why? Whose interests are furthered by this judgement call? This chapter tackles these questions by probing the underlying political motives of the Fund's reluctant acceptance of the Chilean unremunerated reserve requirement (URR) (1991–98) and, conversely, its abhorrence at and rejection of Malaysian currency control (1998–99). In doing so, it suggests that the Fund's opposition to Malaysian controls stems from its perception that capital restraint on outflows threatens the imperative of capital account liberalization that the US government has attempted to transform into a universal norm over the past fifteen years and that is sanctioned within the framework of the NIFA. Thus the IMF's judgement call is not, as common sense would have us believe, an economic, and thus seemingly objective and neutral, decision but rather a highly subjective and political one that is rooted in US imposed leadership (see Chapter 3). This is so because the judgement call is tightly tied to those interests that benefit the most from free capital mobility: the Dollar Wall Street Regime (DWSR) and the transnational capital interests that are tied to it (see Chapter 1).

Two caveats should be introduced at this point. First, transnational capital interests are not exclusively American, but constitute capitals operating in the global financial structure that spans both the South as well as the North. Second, because all capitalist states comprise dominant social relations, the status of which is determined by their position within the national forms of wealth production, the Dollar Wall Street Regime, or imposed US leadership (Chapter 3), is not some sort of deterministic force or process external to the nation-states. Instead, the tensions between imposed US leadership and the states in the South should be conceived as ongoing class-based struggle over policy implementation. Seen from this perspective, the South is not simply a victim of imposed leadership, and, by extension, of the new international financial architecture. Indeed, as the Chilean and Malaysian case studies reveal, the dominant social forces within these two national social formations implemented the controls temporarily to help overcome a 'crisis of authority' brought on by free capital mobility, from which the political elites and powerful capitals historically benefited. This is not to say that there are no victims when states pursue a policy of either open or closed capital accounts. As we will see, the lower echelons of all societies, and particularly in the South, have shouldered the majority of the burdens of these policy decisions.

Before embarking on a discussion of Chilean and Malaysian capital controls, it is necessary to introduce three premises to help us critically evaluate the political motives surrounding the Fund's rulings. To this end, I begin the discussion by providing a sketch of the significance of the IMF to the global South and how the interests of the largest shareholder of the IMF, namely the United States, are tied to the imperative of free capital mobility. Second, I investigate the validity of the claim that capital account liberalization leads to increased prosperity and stability from the perspective of the emerging market economies. Third, I briefly explore Washington's reaction to the growing wave of dissent and discontent regarding its stance of free capital mobility.

The Epicentre of Structural Power in the Global Political Economy

Linkages between free capital mobility and US structural power

Since the world economy switched over to a freely floating exchange rate system in 1973, the year the Bretton Woods system was effectively dismantled by declaring the inconvertibility of the dollar–gold standard, the US has actively pursued a growth strategy based on the liberalization of speculative global financial flows. The US dollar constitutes the epicentre of this post-Bretton Woods competition strategy, or what is also known as 'dollar seigniorage'. The latter term refers to the privileged global financial position of the US, effected largely by securing the dollar's central international role and helping the country continue to manage its growing budget and trade deficits with foreign funds.[5] Dollar seigniorage is based upon the ability of the US to decide freely the price of the world's trading and reserve currency.[6] As the preceding chapters have made clear, seigniorage has allowed the US effectively to exercise structural power over the global political economy and thereby ensure the re-creation of the common-sense assumption that financial liberalization is a necessary policy to achieve competitive success in today's globalized world. Chapter 1 discussed the mutually beneficial yet equally destructive relationship between free capital mobility and US structural power in terms of what I refer to as the 'Frankenstein factor'.

It is important to stress that the growth of finance is not a natural, rational progression, but a phenomenon closely tied to the underlying crisis of global capitalism, particularly the lowering levels of profitability in the productive sector (see Chapter 1), as well as political decisions undertaken by states.[7] Through these political decisions undertaken by the US to guarantee the constant deepening and widening of financial movements, and thus higher levels of profitability, there has been not only a concentration and centralization of wealth and power of transnational finance but also a need to discipline states in the global South to implement policies that would facilitate expansion in the financial sphere and thus guarantee the competitive position of the US economy. As noted in Chapter 1, the US requires a steady inflow of funds to Wall Street from abroad to compensate for the country's low level of domestic savings, as well as to feed its trade and budget deficits. The decision by the US government to allow securitization is tied to the needs of what Gowan refers to as the Dollar Wall Street Regime (see Chapter 1). Philip Cerny argues that one of the most important factors in changing the power relations within the financial structure has been securitization, or the 'transfer of capital through the sale of stocks and bonds'.[8] For Cerny, the significance of securitization lies in its flexibility for transnational capitals:

> The capacity of institutions to avoid being burdened over long periods with specific assets and liabilities, that is their ability to trade those assets and liabilities in liquid secondary markets at a discount, has always played a role in the development of banking as well as being at the heart of stock and bond markets. But the possibility of selling literally anything – from huge 'block trades' of standardized securities to packages of small bank loans to specific customers – on the other institutions is growing vaster, and a whole range of new markets have grown up in and around traditional stock and bond markets to service this demand.[9]

The end result of securitization has been the ongoing creation of ultra-sophisticated financial products, whose primary purpose is to speculate on future prices of commodities or foreign exchange, most notably in the form of derivatives. This has allowed for smaller and smaller numbers of financial capitals to set into play numerous (and highly esoteric) types of securities based on the future value of production for a longer and longer period of time. It is well known that the foreign exchange derivatives market (buying and selling national currencies) constitutes the largest of all financial markets. However, as Gowan observes, 'the centres of this market are in the US, in London and in Canada and no less than 75 per cent of business in these centres is handled, according to an IMF study, by just ten hedge funds'.[10] Put differently, securitization, which was brought about through political decisions, has led to an explosive growth in institutional investors as well as the global value of assets managed by them. And these assets are quite significant. According to the Bank for International Settlements, in 1995 the assets managed by professional money managers in North America, Europe and Japan totalled $20.949 trillion, which exceeded the aggregate GDP for the industrial countries concerned.[11]

What does securitization mean for the South?

[The] growing appetite for liquid, transferable securities that offer diversification possibilities is a natural consequence of the rapid growth of institutional investment. But there has been a marked downward trend in the supply of such staples of pension and mutual fund portfolios as industrial-country government bonds and publicly listed equities.

As the supply of equities and government bonds decreases, Chakravarthi Raghavan suggests, markets for securitized debt, private equity, emerging-market securities and other alternative forms of investment will continue to grow as the general crisis of capitalism persists.[12] Despite the global slowdown since 2001, the greediness of capitalists will once again push up the limits of the market, as the recurrent crises over the past two decades clearly reveal. When the drive for more profits takes hold, transnational finance will move southwards once again. It should be noted, however, that this attempt to transcend the existing barriers to profitability of the financial markets would likely follow the existing uneven pattern regarding the flow of investments from the North to the South. For instance, according to the 1999 United Nations Development Programme's *Human Development Report,*

> Some 94 per cent of the portfolio and other short-term capital flows to developing and transition economies went to just 20 of them in 1996. Today only 25 developing countries have access to private markets for bonds, commercial bank loans and portfolio equity. The rest are shut out by their lack of credit rating.[13]

A central corollary of securitization, which has serious ramifications for both the South and the Dollar Wall Street Regime, is the spread of transnational debt. Following Strange, this debt not only involves multilateral and bilateral aid but also, and more importantly,

> all the forms of debt across state frontiers: all the liabilities incurred, and claims established, between institutions or individuals under one political jurisdiction, and institutions or individuals under another political jurisdiction. It would thus include assets claimed by foreign shareholders in enterprises in another country, interbank loans across frontiers, bonds issued to non-nationals both by governments and other institutions and firms, as well as credits or guarantees extended by states or multilateral organizations like the IMF or World Bank or the regional development banks in Asia, the western hemisphere or Africa.[14]

The creation of the new international financial architecture (as discussed in Chapter 3), with its intersecting network of public and private institutions is clearly an attempt to manage this growing complexity of transnational debt, but also, and paradoxically, an attempt to re-create the conditions for the expansion of this debt by ensuring that all countries adhere to the principle of capital account liberalization. The question that surfaces here is, what role does the IMF play in this equation? Before addressing this question we need to undertake two steps. First, we need to investigate the underlying source of power associated with the IMF's present role as lender of last resort. Second, we need to grasp how the Fund interprets the cause of instability within the growing complexity of transnational debt formation, particularly in terms of the role played by the management of open capital accounts. We tackle these steps in the following two sections.

The IMF as a moment of imposed US leadership:
the lender of last resort

Despite its central role in the institutional configuration of the new international financial architecture, the IMF remains without a legal mandate in the post-Bretton Woods era.[15] Seen in this light, the attempts of the IMF to package itself as a lender of last resort must be critically evaluated.[16] Which member state is promoting such a role? Why? It is not difficult to trace the structural power within the IMF to the government department that contributes the largest financial contribution: namely, the US Treasury Secretary.[17] The Fund's role as global lender of last resort is not new, however. In 1962, with the creation of the General Arrangement to Borrow (GAB), ground rules were established on when, and on what terms, the Fund could lend to member states. As Susan Strange points out, the word 'agreement' is conspicuous in its absence from the GAB in that it signals that its design was the creation of the US and France, with the Netherlands and Belgium acting as supporters to the Arrangement.[18] Over the years the GAB has been revised several times in order to increase the limit available for bailing out countries in need, particularly subsequent to the 1980 debt crises in the South. In the aftermath of the Mexican peso crisis, and the problems experienced by the Clinton administration in responding quickly to the crisis, the 1995 Halifax Summit called on the G10 and other wealthy countries to help double the existing scope of financial arrangements available to the IMF under the GAB. In November 1998 the New Arrangement to Borrow (NAB) was established, in the words of the IMF,

> to forestall or cope with an impairment of the international monetary system or to deal with an exceptional threat to the stability of that system. … The total amount of resources available to the IMF under the NAB and GAB combined is SDR 34 billion (about $45 billion), double the amount available under the GAB alone.[19]

Once we situate the New Arrangement to Borrow within our frame for understanding the new international financial architecture (Chapter 1), it becomes clear that the NAB was an attempt to reproduce the political domination of the IMF in the South. First, the NAB, like its counterpart the GAB, is based on a putative interstate consensus. Hence the lack of legal mandate attached to the NAB

and the choice of wording – 'Arrangement' not 'Agreement' –
seemed to replicate the imposed US leadership discussed in Chapter
2. Second, and relatedly, if the IMF was looking to expand its
financial resources, why not consider Japan's proposal in September
1997 to set up an Asian Monetary Fund (AMF)? As Bergsten notes,
the AMF would not only have eased the financial burden of the
IMF but also, given that Asian policymakers would have treated it as
'their own institution', have acted more efficiently in terms of crisis
response.[20] Some authors have argued that because evidence suggests
that contagion is a regional phenomenon, a regional monetary fund
that was more sensitive to the institutional and legal particularities
of East Asia would be far more effective in terms of surveillance
than a more globally oriented IMF.[21] Moreover, according to the
Asian Development Bank the estimated potential financial mobi-
lization of the AMF would have been about $100 billion – over
twice the amount the IMF raised through the NAB.[22] Regardless
of these arguments, the concept of the Asian Monetary Fund was
immediately struck down by the United States (along with China),
largely due to the threat an Asian lender of last resort would have
on American structural power in the region.[23]

The decisions to overturn the Asian Monetary Fund and to
move ahead with the New Arrangement to Borrow were attempts
by the US government and other countries threatened by increased
regional integration in East Asia, such as China and the G7 countries, to ensure that the central role of the IMF would remain intact.
Jagdish Bhagwati, an influential trade economist at MIT and ardent
free-trade supporter, seems to agree with Gowan's position regarding the power of the United States in the global political economy,
or what he refers to as the Dollar Wall Street Regime. Bhagwati
coined the term 'Wall Street Treasury Complex' to highlight the
growing power of the US:

> Wall Street has become a very powerful influence in terms of seeking markets
> everywhere. ... Just like the old days there was this 'military–industrial
> complex', nowadays there is a 'Wall Street–Treasury complex' ...Wall
> Street views are very dominant in terms of the kind of world you want
> to see. They want the ability to take capital in and out freely. So the
> IMF finally gets a role for itself, which is underpinned by maintaining
> complete freedom on the capital account.[24]

Yet this state–capital complex rests on fragile foundations: the assumption that financial liberalization will lead to prosperity and economic stability for the global South has been seriously discredited, not only by recent debacles but also by rising poverty and indigence rates in the IMF's pin-up economies: namely, emerging markets like Chile and Malaysia.

If US structural power in the global political economy is to be sustained, key instruments of its power, most notably the IMF, must somehow re-create, and thereby 're-legitimate', the common-sense assumption that free capital mobility is a necessary condition for the continued growth and expansion of these countries. But also, given the importance to debtor countries of obtaining the IMF's 'seal of approval' to signal creditworthiness to their international lenders (private financial markets), the IMF is also able to discipline emerging markets to avoid policies that run contrary to what the Fund deems prudent, such as the 'excessive capital controls' of the Malaysian experience.

The common sense of free capital mobility

The underlying logic supporting capital liberalization rests on the basic assumption that international financial markets are not only inherently rational in nature but also lead to mutual gain. Liberalized capital flows, for instance, are thought to create greater welfare benefits because foreign savings supplement the domestic resource base. As a result this leads to a larger capital stock and places the economy on a potentially higher growth path than otherwise. Free trade in capital through international borrowing and lending actually helps lower the costs of the inter-temporal misalignments that periodically arise between the patterns of production and consumption. Put differently, capital inflows permit national economies to trade imports in the present for exports in the future. Another benefit of financial liberalization may be the sharing and diversification of risks that otherwise would not be possible.[25] Furthermore, because capital markets are inherently rational, they will enter those countries that demonstrate sound regulatory practices such as balanced budgets, low inflation, market liberalization, and stable exchange rates. The basic assumption at work here may be regarded as the efficient market hypothesis (EMH). Eugene Fama devised the EMH in his Ph.D. dissertation in 1960. He claims that

> An 'efficient' market is defined as a market where there are large numbers of rational, profit-maximizers actively competing, with each trying to predict future market values of individual securities, and where important current information is almost freely available to all participants. In an efficient market, competition among the many intelligent participants leads to a situation where, at any point in time, actual prices of individual securities already reflect the effects of information based both on events that have already occurred and on events which, as of now, the market expects to take place in the future. In other words, in an efficient market at any point in time the actual price of a security will be a good estimate of its intrinsic value.[26]

According to the efficient market hypothesis, the rational financial markets act as a disciplinary force, which can punish profligate governments through investment strikes and capital flight. This position implies that the underlying cause of instability and speculation is not financial market participants but irresponsible governments that refuse to implement fiscal discipline to balance their budget deficits, that cannot properly manage monetary policy, and so forth.[27] Is this conventional wisdom correct or just convenient? Does the liberalization of cross-border transactions in capital markets lead to greater prosperity for emerging markets, if these governments learn to manage these accounts adequately? Or has financialization merely led to a situation whereby hot money can flow freely into emerging markets to exploit interest rate differentials or other speculative ventures? By shifting our attention to the emerging market economies, we gain more insight not only into who was benefiting from the liberalization of capital flows but also into why the IMF, at least in its rhetoric, began to advocate Chilean capital controls whilst chastizing the Malaysian currency control.

Contradictions of Free Capital Mobility: A View from the South

The changing nature of capital flows

As discussed in Chapter 1, the Herculean task of signalling creditworthiness to global financial players both by adhering to the

conventional wisdom of the Washington consensus and by placat-
ing social strife has proved to be increasingly difficult for states of
middle-income countries. In particular, the tension between the
principle of national self-determination and the neoliberal principle
of financial openness has led to a crisis of authority in many emerging markets. To begin to unravel the complexity regarding increased
financialization and the governability problem it is useful to grasp
the changes in the composition of capital inflows to these countries.
Financial flows have undergone at least three structural changes since
the early 1990s.[28] First, official development finance, especially its
largest component, bilateral aid, has lagged behind private flows.[29]
In consequence, states have grown more dependent on international
financial players and transnational corporate giants to fill their public
and private coffers. All economic and social policy has taken a back
seat to the goal of luring and retaining capital inflows. Populist calls
for the 'incorporation' of national social formations (or what has
been referred to as low-risk investment sites) through lax taxation
standards, maintaining a well-disciplined and cheap labour force,
political stability, as well as meeting the transportation and technological infrastructure demands of business whilst cutting already
low public spending on social services and education, has been
transformed from a concern to an obsession. Second, private capital
entering these countries is in the form of international portfolio
investments (stocks and bonds). For instance, by 1993, 74 per cent of
private foreign investment in Mexico, Brazil, Chile, Argentina and Sri
Lanka came from mutual funds and pension funds.[30] As the executive secretary of the UN Economic Commission for Latin America
and the Caribbean, José Antonio Ocampo, notes, the majority of
capital flows to the middle-income countries are not only more
short-term than they have been in the 1980s but also receive the
highest concentration of the most volatile flows.[31]

The increase in the disembedding of (highly esoteric) financial
instruments from the real economy through technological innovation and liberalization processes constitutes the third change in
financial flows. Although not divorced from the productive sphere,
the steady intensification of financialization has meant that growth
rates of turnover of financial assets are many times higher than the
growth of any indicator of the 'real' activity.[32] Put another way,

finance is no longer a means of facilitating the exchange of goods and services but has become an end in itself. Nonetheless, as we saw in Chapter 1, Gowan rightly notes that these financial transactions are not escaping the productive sphere, but are instead 'buying and selling claims on future value created in future productive activity. They are not merely handing over funds for that productive activity; they are claiming future royalties from it.'[33] While this change is clearly a global phenomenon, it cannot be denied that it is particularly pronounced in emerging markets, which, by and large, receive the highest amounts of the most volatile portfolio flows. This has immediate ramifications for the labour markets in these countries. Eager to attract necessary capital investment, for example, owners of sweatshops are pressured to up the ante by further pushing down the already meagre wage levels and inhuman working conditions. This behaviour is, of course, contrary to the professed inherent rationality of market forces that are forcibly advocated by the Fund's 'conventional wisdom', which was mentioned earlier.

Indeed, the rationality of the markets is not an uncontested view. David Felix suggests that the efficient market hypothesis does not have 'general backing from more basic theorizing about the stability of competitive market economies. Rather, the theorizing indicates that liberated financial markets are inherently prone to destabilizing dynamics that can also destabilize aggregate production, trade, and employment in such economies.'[34] Mary Ann Haley's work echoes Felix's conclusions when she argues that neither the assumption that an adequate number of investors create the most favourable conditions for competition, nor that in a 'fair and efficient market investors have access to roughly the same information and react similarly and "rationally" within the confines of profit-maximization' reflect the present reality of investment in emerging markets.[35]

Policy paradoxes in the era of financialization

The changing nature of capital flows to emerging market economies has had important political ramifications for governments, or what I refer to as a policy paradox for emerging markets. Ilene Grabel identifies at least two negative and mutually reinforcing effects that financial flows have on national policy formation in the emerging markets: (1) the imposition of constraints on policy autonomy; and (2) the creation of greater vulnerability to the economy to risk, financial volatility and crisis.[36] With regard to the first point, the need continuously to signal creditworthiness to global financial markets for much-needed capital inflows has forced governments into a 'pact with the devil' whereby market credibility assumes a central position in policymaking in such areas as exchange and interest rates as well as tight fiscality — all of which must take precedence over other domestic concerns. Keeping interest rates high, for example, lures in short-term investment ready to exploit the interest-rate differential. Although high interest rates ostensibly dampen inflationary tendencies, they also choke the economy as loans become more costly. Likewise, high interest rates push up the external value of the currency. Once this occurs governments jeopardize their export markets, which in turn threatens a major source of income. Furthermore, in order to signal creditworthiness, governments of emerging markets must maintain political and social conditions for the continuation of capital accumulation within their borders by meeting the social demands placed on the state. Yet, in current times, this compliance is not straightforward given the waning levels of broad public support for the neoliberal project in the wake of ever-widening income polarization and increased poverty rates.[37]

On the second point, the changing nature of financial flows to the global South has made it increasingly difficult to protect the domestic economy against the devastating effects of contagion and capital flight. The Asian crash comes to mind as the most vivid illustration of this observation. Despite the robust macroeconomic equilibria and high rate of domestic savings, these 'miracle economies' buckled under the quick exit of foreign funds. The pundits associated with the Washington consensus were quick to blame crony Asian capitalism for the debacle, as opposed to the reckless and excessive herd-like behaviour of electronic speculators.[38] The financial and economic crises throughout the 1990s made it patently clear that foreign exchange reserves are inadequate to protect countries from exchange rate and banking crises. Whereas reserves equal to three months' imports might have been thought inadequate when the focus was on the current account, arguably countries presently need to cover all outstanding balances of short-term liabilities or even the whole domestic money supply if there is a danger that residents might flee. Ilene Grabel also identifies another downside of this new financial openness in the increased likelihood of a cross-border contagion. Grabel suggests that during panics, investors and lenders see emerging economies in an undifferentiated fashion, thus adhering to the principle of 'guilt by association'.[39] This situation becomes particularly grave when individual banks or firms are unable to roll over their short-term debt. Similarly good macroeconomic fundamentals no longer provide a guarantee that a country will escape a financial crisis.[40] The Asian meltdown drove home the point that problems can arise when smaller countries peg or stabilize their currencies against a major national currency, such as the dollar. Largely owing to dollar seigniorage, these countries have become extremely vulnerable to the United States government's fiscal policies. A revaluation of the US dollar, for instance, could prove detrimental to developing-county institutions and firms that have borrowed through instruments denominated in foreign currencies.[41]

How have the interests tied to the Dollar Wall Street Regime responded to the destabilizing effects of the policy paradox in the South whilst legitimizing the role of the IMF as lender of last resort and the assumption of efficient market hypothesis? It is to this question that the discussion now turns.

Washington Strikes Back

The G7 Summit in June 1999 provides some insight into Washington's response to the policy paradoxes in the southern hemisphere. As we saw in the previous chapter, the primary function of this summit was to establish a new international financial architecture by calling for enhanced transparency and promoting best practice whilst meeting the basic objective of integrating 'important' emerging market economies more fully and flexibly into the global financial system. To be fair, the IMF has traditionally supported gradual adoption of capital account convertibility (free capital mobility) for developing countries, or what is known in more technical terms as 'sequencing'.[42] Nevertheless, this should not be interpreted as a defence of capital controls. In a direct response to Bhagwati's critique of capital account liberalization, Shailendra J. Anjaria, director of the External Relations Department of the IMF, posited that capital account convertibility can be implemented

> in a prudent manner, supported by supervisory regulations that strengthen the financial system. Given the great benefits offered by freer international capital markets, however, the best response to volatile conditions is surely to strengthen those markets' foundations (through improved accounting and disclosure rules, for example) not close them down – especially since there is little evidence that the alternative, stopping the flow of capital, works well or for long.[43]

To this end the IMF and World Bank, through the new international financial architecture have been mandated to 'encourage' governments of emerging markets to impose 'sensible' policy responses in order to restrain the inflow of speculative capital and to encourage more productive, long-term capital formation (foreign direct investment, or FDI).[44] It should be noted that 'prudent' seems to be synonymous with market-directed policy (i.e. neoliberalism). We pick up on the institutions and norms provided by the international financial institutions in our discussion of corporate governance in the next chapter. For now I would like to go beyond the face value of the IMF's stance toward sequencing by situating it within the larger contradiction upon which the new architecture rests. This exercise helps us understand the political motivations underpinning the Fund's judgement calls regarding the Chilean and Malaysian capital controls.

It will be recalled from Chapter 1 that as the scope of transnational financial markets expands, the conditions for continued accumulation in the South weaken. Yet for financial markets to continue to grow there must be enough stability in the system to guarantee the continuation of free capital mobility across national borders. On the other hand, as the emerging market countries are forced to prise open their capital accounts as well as their current accounts, distribution tensions, increased volatility, and difficulty in signalling creditworthiness begin to mount. The need for the political elites and transnational bourgeoisie operating in these countries to address the resulting crisis of authority has produced the demand for increased policy autonomy in non-core countries, which could easily lead to departures from the neoliberal-based rules needed to guarantee the continued expansion of the Dollar Wall Street Regime and the power of global finance. Seen from this angle, the IMF's willingness to cede to particular capital controls is also an attempt to freeze the contradictions that emerge from the policy paradoxes in the South.

The Fund views capital controls as a response *second best* to that of using market liberalization as a corrective instrument. Top officials from the World Bank and the IMF have put forward the case that specific controls on some emerging markets are desirable as a temporary and second-best option – second only, that is, to direct liberalization (the *best* response).[45] Thus controls are a useful, temporary policy instrument to achieve breathing space for corrective action or, more to the point, neoliberal reforms (privatization, liberalization and flexibilization). It must be stressed that, contrary to the rhetoric of the post-Washington consensus, this position resembles old wine in new bottles rather than a Third Way compromise, for the simple reason that it does not depart from the Fund's conventional wisdom. According to this orthodoxy, to ensure stability during the reform process, policymakers should concentrate on liberalizing other parts of the economy before opening the capital account.[46] This stance suggests that the goal of free capital mobility is still the only route to attain stability and growth. Indeed, even after the Asian crash the Fund stalwartly stated that capital liberalization is 'an inevitable step in development and thus cannot be avoided, and ... can bring major benefits to a country's residents and government – enabling them to borrow and lend on more favourable terms and in more sophisticated markets.'[47]

Not all capital restrictions are equal in the eyes of the IMF, however. Despite the fact that fourteen emerging markets have implemented capital controls, Washington has applauded the Chilean unremunerated reserve requirement (URR) as the most successful control for averting the negative side effects of an abundance of short-term financial flows, most notably exchange rate appreciation and capital flight. We discuss the URL in more detail below. In stark contrast to this endorsement, the Fund remains opposed to Malaysian controls.[48] Why? To address this question it is necessary to go beyond the existing economic analyses by flushing out the political motives associated with the IMF's rulings. As Jomo K.S. points out, one way to accomplish this task is to widen the lens with which we view the controls: by recognizing that capital restrictions are not an end in themselves but rather a means to achieve a broader policy objective.[49] I would add that this wider goal is to serve the interests of the domestic political ruling classes that are trying to cope with the policy paradox in such a manner as to ensure the reproduction of their own power. This consideration is indispensable to grasping adequately the political dimension of how each control either threatens or supports the imperative of free global capital mobility. To this end, the following two sections examine the capital controls by providing a background sketch of the larger class-led policy strategies pursued by the Chilean and Malaysian states.

Chilean Capital Control, 1991–98

The unremunerated reserve requirement (URR) is often referred to by the international financial institutions as the prototype control. In brief, the Chilean capital control, which was in force from 1991 to 1998, required all non-equity foreign capital inflows to pay a one-year, non-interest-bearing deposit.[50] Levying a lower tax on investment encouraged longer-term investment periods. The URR was a reserve deposit initially set at 20 per cent that earned no interest and was applied to all portfolio inflows that entered the country. In July 1992, the rate of the URR was raised to 30 per cent and its holding period was set at one year, independently of the length of stay of the inflow. The capital restriction was seen as the best way to weed out the negative effects of arbitrage capital flows (buying a financial product cheaply in one market and selling it dearly in another) while harnessing their economic benefits, such as channelling more inflows in the direction of foreign direct investment and longer-term portfolio investments – as opposed to speculative or short-term private capital. Accolades aside, economists and policymakers remain divided on the ability of this control to affect both interest rate behaviour and moderate speculative capital inflows.[51] For its proponents, including the IMF, the apparent success of the URR lies not only in impressively high and consistent Chilean GDP growth rates – which hovered around 6.5 per cent per annum – but also in its ability to withstand contagion from the Mexican crisis and, relatively speaking (compared with Brazil and Russia), the Asian crisis. For its critics, the URR has largely failed to achieve its main objectives of luring longer-term investment into Chile and reducing macroeconomic instability.[52] Despite the lack of evidence the question that looms is, why has the URR been so popular with those interests tied to the IMF and wider Washington consensus?

The answer to this question is straightforward enough. The unremunerated reserve requirement was a means for the Chilean government to deal with the above-mentioned policy constraints in such a manner that did not threaten the imperative of free capital mobility. For one thing, the control did not counter the conventional wisdom of the IMF in terms of capital account liberalization and thus assisted in maintaining an environment that was friendly to the interests tied to capital market liberalization. Despite its restriction on short-term capital inflows, for instance, the government was zealously liberalizing capital outflows. Crucially, when a country opens its doors to outflows it becomes more attractive to fund managers, for the basic reason that they are guaranteed a quick exit whenever they desire. For another, the URR, and the larger overarching 'growth with equity' project, continued the Pinochet tradition of providing preferential access to international credit and domestic pension fund capital to large economic groups, which in turn facilitated further centralization and concentration of transnational capital in the small Andean country. The means to this end, which was embedded in the conventional wisdom of the IMF, remained in place through the neoclassical technocrats (the so-called Chicago Boys). As Marcus Taylor notes,

> The large Chilean conglomerates, such as Luksic and Angelini, have grown substantially through mergers and acquisitions, as have many foreign transnationals and particularly Spanish owned groups. This has culminated in a situation in which practically all sectors of the Chilean economy are controlled by large firms that in turn are subsidiary parts of the handful of huge economic groups based in the financial sector.[53]

Viewing the capital constraint as part of a larger policy helps to shed more light on the nature of its means to achieve the 'growth with equity' project that was pursued by a coalition of Christian Democrat and Socialist parties (the Concertación, or 'coming together'). It should be stressed that this regime, which came to power in 1989, not only faced the daunting task of forming the first democratic regime since the Pinochet dictatorship but also had to deal with the above-mentioned policy constraints marked by high levels of private, short-term capital inflows. The growth strategy pursued by the Concertación was premissed on reproducing existing power relations in the economy, which has been in place since the mid-1970s. This meant that the two 'growth poles' would remain in place. One was marked by a primary-resource export enclave (copper, forestry, fishing), with little value added to the production process and with few links to the rest of the economy. The other was marked by a boom in the unproductive sector of the economy (services and finance), which not only accounted for the majority of recorded growth but was also largely based on speculative capital – most of which was borrowed from abroad.[54] One way of facilitating these two growth poles whilst promoting political stability in the newly formed democratic structures was through the use of controls on capital inflows. It was believed that these controls would allow for higher interest rates to check money supply and inflation while luring capital inflows. Given the nature of the accumulation regime in Chile, however, it was imperative that the higher interest rates should not push up the exchange rate of the peso. Put simply, setting competitively high interest rates to attract short-term capital flows (demand) pushes up the external value of a currency. The latter is undesirable, of course, because it makes Chilean exports more costly. Thus the immediate policy problem was to manage the heavy inflow of largely short-term capital in such a manner as to prevent an exchange rate appreciation and to achieve more elbow-room for domestic monetary policymaking.[55]

In June 1991, the same month that the unremunerated reserve requirement was implemented, swathes of foreign exchange entered the country to exploit an interest rate differential given the relatively low rates in the recession-hit OECD countries. These flows led to the destabilizing consequences of a foreign exchange glut that made it difficult to follow a restrictive monetary policy – that is, high interest rates. The government responded by reversing its restraints on imports, and thereby burning off excess foreign exchange that benefited the wealthy, who could afford to purchase foreign luxury goods. While the URR, along with a wider 'growth with equity' strategy, succeeded in neutralizing the effects of new cash inflows – in particular moderating the inevitable exchange-rate appreciation – it has done little to improve the overall performance of the Chilean economy. Despite its impressive growth rates, for example, this expansion was not propelled by investment in the productive sector, which one would expect according to the logic underpinning conventional wisdom. Instead the growth was created by the inflow of short-term bond finance, secondary stock market trading and acquisition of privatized firms. Indeed, about 60 per cent of these flows was diverted into foreign direct investment within traditional sectors of resource-extraction – copper mining, pulp and paper. Like Mexico (see Chapter 2), and Chile's own history during the 1980s, the majority of these foreign direct investments involved the transfer of ownership through the re-purchase of existing assets. The remaining 40 per cent went into services, especially the financial sector.[56] As such, there was no new investment in terms of research and development (R&D), which financial flows were said to foster, so as to encourage higher wages and decrease the degree of dependency of the national economy on the fluctuation of world prices for raw resources. To be sure, this investment strategy expressed itself in Chile's balance of payments where the capital account (inward and outward flow of money) has increased to the detriment of its current account (imports and exports of goods and services) (see Table 4.2).

Two key types of short-term cash flow that entered the financial sector from 1990 to 1994 were mutual funds and secondary American Depository Receipts (ADRs). The latter, the more popular type of ADR in Chile, involves foreign purchases made in the local stock exchange for shares in Chilean firms. While mutual funds were organized in the major international capital markets, the issuance of ADRs was managed by a handful of large Chilean corporations. This in turn allowed for the further concentration of assets of the Chilean rentier class, whilst providing cheaper methods of financing than found at home due to the high interest rates. In contrast to the official objectives of the URR in deterring short-term inflows, the

Table 4.1 Chilean balance of payments ($ million)

	1980	1985	1990	1991	1992	1993	1994	1995	1996	1997	1998
Current account	−1971.0	−1414.0	−484.5	−98.6	−958.1	−2553.5	−1585.2	−1345.1	−3511.6	−3728.3	4143.7
Capital account	3241.0	−1395.0	2857.0	965.2	3134.2	2995.9	5293.5	2275.5	6665.9	7357.2	3180.4

Source: ECLAC 1999: 14.

two most common types of external liabilities are relatively liquid, such as ADRs. This means that both kinds of investment can be rapidly withdrawn from Chile through the formal foreign exchange market, if investors see fit to sell their assets in the domestic market. In 1994 secondary ADR represented an additional net inflow of 2 per cent of GDP, which could become a significant source of instability. As in the case of the nature of foreign direct investment in Chile, mutual funds and ADRs have not led to an increase in productive capacity, or economic growth, but instead in a change in the ownership of Chilean assets. The immediate consequence of this is, of course, a deeper commitment on behalf of the government to the current export-promotion strategy that favours transnational finance interests over others.[57]

Did the unremunerated reserve requirement inhibit the quantity of short-term capital flows vis-à-vis other emerging markets? The answer depends upon the measurement used. The Central Bank of Chile, for instance, classified short-term and long-term inflows on the basis of contracted maturity. In this way, short-term inflows are investments that remain in the country for less than one year. Using a different set of tools, Sebastian Edwards argues that residual maturity is a far more reliable measurement of a country's vulnerability since it takes into account the country's liabilities held by foreigners that are due within a year. When viewing the residual maturity of short-term inflows in Chile from 1991 to 1997, the percentage of short-term debt is not as low as when contracting maturities is applied. And, although by the end of 1996 Chile had a relatively low percentage of short-term residual debt, it was not significantly lower than that of Argentina – a country that did not impose capital controls. Interestingly, this percentage was higher than Mexico, which also did not have capital controls.[58]

Capital inflows dropped considerably after 1994 due to the combined effects of the Mexican currency crisis, the rise in US interest rates, and tighter financial regulation in Chile. Nevertheless, to lure capital flows the Chilean state still offers a plethora of incentives, such as the repatriation of capital one year after an investment, foreign investors' guarantees of the right to profit remittances, and a choice between either the tax regime applicable to national corporations or a fixed rate of taxation on their profits guaranteed for a certain period of time. More recently, the Chilean government announced its plans to abolish the 15 per cent capital gains tax levied on foreigners.[59]

The promotion by Chile of more liberalized trade of its financial and natural resources and labour-intensive extraction processes increased the power of finance and transnational interests during the 1990s; but this growth appears to have been sustained by large amounts of borrowing, largely through American Depositary accounts and easy access to international credit – at least for large corporations. The contradiction, however, remains that Chile's 'growth with equity' strategy reproduced the powerful position of transnational capitals at the expense of the working poor. For example, 'IMF sources show that in 1998 the richest ten per cent of Chilean society appropriated ten times the amount of the poorest twenty per cent (41 per cent against 4.1 per cent of total income).'[60] Critically, the larger strategy that the URR pursued weakened rather than strengthened the Achilles heel of the Chilean economy, namely its vulnerable dependence on external borrowing and investment. In fact, the high interest rates involved in the growth with equity strategy have assisted in shifting the debt burden from the public to the private sector.

Unsurprisingly, and despite the government's claims of a healthy economy, Chile finds itself in a structural position similar to that of the late 1970s immediately before its crash in 1982. Hence when these inflows began to taper off with the Asian crisis in 1997, the government was pressured to do away with the URR and begin courting overcautious potential investors and creditors through more lucrative terms. Ironically, precisely at a time when currency turmoil elsewhere would suggest that the URR might prove particularly useful, the Chilean authorities concluded that, whatever the benefits of the tax, they could no longer afford to turn away foreign capital. Seen in this light, the official justification of the URR to favour equity over debt financing and long-term over short-term financing fell apart. The country's debt-fuelled accumulation strategy required a steady stream of cash inflows – regardless of their nature. The concern to maintain these flows was well founded, as the financial crises in Asia and Russia propelled the huge stampede out of Latin American securities, mainly in the third quarter of 1998 ('guilt by association'). Chile experienced $2.1 billion of capital flight in 1998 alone.[61] In direct response to this, the unremunerated reserve requirement was suspended in September 1998.

The Malaysian Currency Control, 1998–99

The opening-up must occur in proper sequence; this is the moral of the Asian story. Some Asian states chose, mistakenly, to stress short-term borrowing by domestic banks over longer-term foreign investment. The sequence of these measures, not liberalization itself, compounded the suffering when the crisis erupted and confidence vanished.

Shailendra J. Anjaria, director of
External Relations Department, IMF[62]

Although Malaysia boasted one of the most open economies in terms of its current and capital accounts, it introduced one of the most stringent forms of capital restraint, both to stabilize its currency, the ringgit, and to control capital outflows. When the country witnessed, at the apex of the 1997 crisis, a 50 per cent devaluation of the ringgit and a 70 per cent fall in the value of the Kuala Lumpur Stock Exchange (KLSE), the government looked to the successful Chinese capital control as a possible solution.[63] In September 1998, the Malaysian authorities withdrew the ringgit (RM) from the international currency trading system and formally pegged it at RM3.8 to the US dollar. Moreover 'exporters were required to sell their foreign exchange to the central bank at a fixed rate; that currency was then sold for approved payments to foreigners, mainly for imports and debt service.'[64] The primary objective of the control was to maintain currency convertibility on the current account (trade in goods and services) whilst preventing the buying of foreign exchange for speculation and staving off capital flight. In this way the controls did not target foreign direct investment or the repatriation of interest, dividends and profits. Prime Minister Mohamed Mahathir, who rose to the leadership of the country's ruling United Malay National Organization (UMNO) in July 1981, added insult to injury by engaging in 'vitriolic rhetoric' not only in his tirades on the immorality of foreign currency trading and his suggestions that it should be made illegal, but also on his subsequent implementation of an 'economic recovery plan' that sought to go against the traditional IMF medicine of fiscal and monetary austerity. For Dr Mahathir, the primary cause of the crisis was to be located in the speculative activities of global finance and not in Malaysia's economic policy formation, and even less so in its crony capitalism – for example, nepotism and personal ties between state and firms. Needless to say, Washington and the IMF were less than amused with Mahathir's political reaction to the crisis. They were not alone: global finance also retaliated by engaging in investment strikes.

As suggested earlier, to make sense of the Fund's ruling against the Malaysian control we need to remember that the control was not an end in itself, but instead an aspect of a larger policy objective. Beyond the economic reasons given for the implementation of the control, the political motive underlying the broader policy aim is to be found in the aforementioned policy paradox: the dependence on global capital and investment flows requires political stability to ensure a constant stream of capital flows. On the other hand, the increasing presence of short-term, private and speculative flows leads to major policy constraints on governments. Up until the advent of the crisis, the Malaysian state had successfully straddled this divide through well-orchestrated policies that linked corporate interests to state power, a thriving export economy based on high levels of foreign direct investment in the areas of information technology, quasi-dollarization, and – critically – highly effective forms of social engineering aimed at ensuring political stability in a country that remains divided along inter-ethnic and intra-ethnic class lines.[65]

Seen in this light, the currency controls provided checks on capital outflows, the government was able to implement lower interest rates and achieve greater money supply than would otherwise be possible in the crisis environment. Malaysian-type capital restraints also assisted in temporarily overcoming the policy constraints associated with short-term capital inflows. As Jomo K.S. points out, controls on outflows stimulate the economy and postpone hard choices between devaluation and tighter money policy.[66] The question that raises itself here is, for how long? The Malaysian controls were a means to achieve the broader policy objectives of tending to the political legitimacy of the regime, political stability, and the reproduction of power structures through such policies of social engineering – all of which could be threatened by embracing IMF conditionality. Notwithstanding the lack of consensus regarding the controls in Malaysia, they fit the pattern of the regime's previous forms of populist rhetoric. By blaming foreigners for the country's economic ills – and, of course, playing down the fact that Mahathir and his cohorts benefited handsomely from the speculative activities – the government was actively promulgating a 'patriot–traitor' theme to regulate and reproduce the existing social order.[67]

One reason that the government had leeway to implement the controls in the first place was that Malaysia's exposure to foreign loans was relatively lower than the so-called IMF 3 (South Korea, Thailand and Indonesia).

> Critically, unlike the other three, Malaysian external liabilities did not exceed its foreign exchange reserves. Also, it seems that three quarters of the corporate foreign borrowings were accounted for by three partially privatized state-owned enterprises. Hence Malaysia was not obliged to seek IMF emergency credit or to accept IMF policy conditionalities.[68]

These conditionalities included: (1) government guarantees of private-sector foreign debt; (2) domestic demand contraction by sharp increases in real interest rates and government budget surpluses; and (3) structural reforms in finance, corporate governance, labour markets and the like.[69] Curiously, during the initial period of the Asian crisis in 1997 the then finance minister, Anwar Ibrahim, implemented what the Asian Development Bank has termed a 'virtual IMF policy'.[70] However, when the contagion seeped into the Malaysian economy in 1998 policy lines began to fracture over how best to respond to the ominous crisis. As the economy began to show signs of contraction, Prime Minister Mahathir not only quickly reversed Anwar's position by adopting an expansionary policy by the

middle of 1998, but sought to vilify his former protégé by representing him as an 'IMF stooge', and subsequently imprisoning the
finance minister on dubious charges of sexual impropriety. On a
deeper level, because Anwar's recovery strategy was considered to be
a 'virtual IMF policy', its rejection was a clear signal of Mahathir's
refusal to resort to contractual policies. At base this move signalled a
desperate attempt by Mahathir, and the dominant social forces associated with his regime, to secure his political survival by maintaining
policy autonomy over fiscal spending. By sacking Anwar Ibrahim
and designating him a traitor to the country, Dr Mahathir sought
to legitimize his subsequent 'recovery plan' – which included controls on capital outflows – as an economically sound alternative to
those measures proposed by the Fund. Yet with the desperate act of
designating himself Finance Minister, Mahathir revealed deep fissures
within the long-standing authoritarian regime.

Dr. Mahathir and his cohorts in the ruling party, the UMNO
feared the political consequences of IMF-type reforms, namely a
repeat of the downfall of the Indonesian prime minister, Suharto.
Thus the Fund's policy conditionalities were seen as a means to
deepen, as opposed to mitigating, the policy paradox facing the
Malaysian government. Having the option of denying rather than
tempting the devil, the government had more wiggle room to implement a policy that reproduced the status quo as opposed to the
preferred IMF strategy of organizing a witch-hunt to eradicate what
it believed to be the cause of the crisis: poor corporate governance, including highly concentrated ownership structure, excessive
government interventions, and underdeveloped capital markets. In
short, the Malaysian government was turning the Fund's blame game
on its head in the interests of consolidating its power base.[71] This
clearly did not sit well with the IMF. Rhetoric aside, dampening
capital flows threatened the dominant power relations in the global
economy in two related ways. First, in itself the control clearly
went against the spirit of free capital mobility. Second, the IMF was
threatened by the possible emulation of this manoeuvre designed to
increase policy autonomy. As I have argued, the currency control
was a means to support the broader policy strategy of the Mahathir
regime, namely the ability to achieve national policy autonomy to
reproduce existing power structures largely by keeping short-term

capital flows and the IMF out of Malaysia. Thus the more policy autonomy Mahathir and his followers could achieve, the more the regime was able to respond effectively to the crisis in such a manner as to retain control over its social engineering policies (i.e. maintain political stability) and protect economic interests of the dominant economic and political elites in Malaysia.

One of the principal reasons for the Malaysian economic miracle was the ability of the political elite to carry through painful neo-liberal restructuring effectively (by following prescriptions set by the Washington consensus) while at the same time preserving a strong semblance of stability within the multi-ethnic population. To subdue the intra-ethnic and inter-ethnic class tensions – primarily between Malays, Chinese and Indian Malaysians – a remarkable exercise in social engineering known as the New Economic Policy (NEP) was implemented between 1971 and 1990. As Christine Chin notes, this strategy served to reproduce the political power of the Malays while allowing them to take control of the economy, in line with two of the NEP's main goals: the distribution of corporate wealth from non-Malays to Malays; and the creation of a *Bumiputera* (sons/princes of the soil) Commercial and Industrial Community, which translates into the Malay business and professional middle classes.[72] Aside from the poverty-reduction objectives, the UMNO attempted to declass and *de-ethnify* tension by recasting struggle into the nationalistic terms of 'patriots and traitors'. In response to stagnation in the early 1980s, due largely to the country's dependence on primary exports, Dr Mahathir sallied forth with an updated version of the NEP in 1991, 'Wawasan 2020' ('Vision 2020'). To all intents and purposes Wawasan 2020 was a blueprint for creating a fully industrialized and developed country by 2020, but with the same social engineering strategies as the NEP. Through these policies, especially the unique strategy of ethnic tiering, the government attempt to establish social cohesion by creating a new national project: Malaysia Inc. The interests of the political and economic elites were presented as the interests of all patriots of Malaysia.

Although Malaysia is slowly recovering from its economic crisis, the debate over the effectiveness of the currency control continues to rage.[73] Those tied to the Washington consensus stalwartly defend their condemnation of the control. Not surprisingly, the underlying rationale of their rejection is based on the conventional wisdom mentioned earlier:

> The existing historical evidence suggests quite strongly that controls on outflows … have been largely ineffective. They are easily circumvented, encourage corruption and, in most historical episodes, have not helped the economic adjustment process. A major drawback of controls on outflows is that, in most cases, they are not used as a temporary device to face a crisis situation. Instead, they become a permanent feature of the country's incentive structure. It has been argued that a way of avoiding these problems, while still protecting the economy from international financial markets' instability, is to adopt controls on short-term capital inflows [like the Chilean URR].[74]

In addition to its public denouncements of the Malaysian control, the IMF has sought to discipline the Malaysian government further by excluding it from the G20, and therein from the institutional structures of the new international financial architecture, which for the first time incorporated 'systematically important' emerging markets into the international decision-making environment (see Chapter 3).[75] Regardless of the fact that the Kuala Lumpur Stock Exchange (KLSE) was ranked among the top ten bourses in the world in 1996, Malaysia was denied entry into the elite club of the G20 also on the grounds that some G7 members led by the US felt that Thailand, on the size of its economy and the absence of currency controls, was better suited.

As mentioned above, disciplinary action was not limited to the IMF. Global finance also condemned Malaysia through the powerful instrument of investment strikes. Because of the adverse effects on capital investment in the KLSE, as well as longer-term foreign direct investment, the Malaysian authorities abandoned the main control in mid-February 1999. Proving correct the platitude 'once bitten twice shy', the composite index of the KLSE continues to tumble, despite reinstatement in the Morgan Stanley Capital International indexes in 2000. Notwithstanding the recent removal of the last vestige of the currency control in May 2001, namely a 10 per cent exit tax on stock market profits, capital is not rushing back to Malaysia.[76]

Despite the fact that Malaysia was committed to current account liberalization the country's controls were considered an imprudent choice by global finance and the IMF, largely because they, along with its larger policy strategy, threatened the norm of free capital mobility as the only alternative. In other words, if Malaysian controls had proved successful, they would have had a powerful 'demonstration effect' to other emerging markets.[77] This becomes clearer when we conceptualise the disapproval of controls on outflows within the larger power structures involving the United States and global finance. First, restrictions on capital outflows hinder a quick exit by speculators, who, according to convention, may wish to escape for reasons of poor transparency standards or unsound macroeconomics. Policymakers in Washington also frown upon this type of control because it hinders the flow of Asia's high levels of savings towards Wall Street.[78] The American government feared a very real shift in the region towards a regulatory and inward-looking attitude, especially on the part of Hong Kong, Taiwan and Malaysia. Second, as mentioned above, there appears to be a close connection between liberalizing capital outflows and net capital inflow. According to a well-known mouthpiece of the consensus, John Williamson, 'The reason is that the elimination of outflow controls assures investors that it will not be difficult to get their money out again should they so wish, and in that way reduces the option value of holding funds outside the country.'[79] Third, in spite of the general opposition of the United States, largely through its vilification of the 'Asian model' (which has become synonymous with the term 'crony capitalism'; see Chapter 5), to restricting capital mobility of short-term flows, these controls pose an ideological threat to the Dollar Wall Street Regime and the structural power of the US (see chapters 1 and 3). For example, according to one source, 'US debts to the rest of the world total more than $2.7 trillion, equivalent to more than one quarter of gross domestic product. To finance this debt, the US requires an inflow of around $2 billion per day from the rest of the world.'[80] If they had been legitimized by the IMF, the Malaysian currency controls could have been emulated by others and would then seriously have hamperd the inflows the US needs to help feed its ever-expanding current account deficit.[81]

Paradoxically the Malaysian control was part of a larger national strategy aimed at overcoming the policy contradictions generated by free capital mobility and the underlying crisis of global capitalism, and in consequence of almost two decades of adherence to the macroeconomic tenets of the Washington consensus. Although it is patently clear that this broader policy strategy served the interests of Malaysia's political and economic elite, the control was used not to delink the Malaysian economy from the world market, but instead to fortify the ability of the national government to maintain economic and social stability so as to remain – and as competitively as possible – in what has become known as the global casino. Recent events in Malaysia suggest that erosion of public support for the Mahathir regime will continue with a slowing world economy.[82]

Continuing Instability for Emerging Markets?

Through its ability to send negative signals to the global financial markets, the IMF effectively punished Malaysia for implementing a form of capital control that ran counter to the interests of the Dollar Wall Street Regime. US-imposed leadership has also recently put an end to any imposition of capital controls in Chile. Like the NAFTA provision that ensured that Mexico maintain free capital accounts (see Chapter 2), the US–Chile Free Trade Agreement, signed in December 2002, contains a provision to restrict the Chilean government's 'use of capital controls for short-term speculative capital flows'.[83] There can be no doubt that, given the ongoing deepening of the global economic slowdown, and the unwillingness of international capital markets to invest in emerging market economies, the US has gained the upper hand in forcing restriction on the future use of capital controls. As has become increasingly evident with the demise of such countries as Turkey, Argentina, Uruguay and perhaps Brazil, financial flows to the South present, in the words of Joseph Stiglitz, 'a risk without reward: they lead to increased instability, not increased growth'. Stiglitz goes on to argue that

countries with heavy short-term indebtedness risk their political autonomy. If a leader that is not to Wall Street's liking emerges, markets may raise interest rates to exorbitant levels, threatening to bankrupt the country unless the people choose a leader more to the financial community's liking. The recent scare in Brazil before President Luiz Inacio Lula da Silva's election is a good example of this.[84]

The Chilean and Malaysian case studies reveal several important lessons. First, in both cases the controls were more than simple economic policy instruments aimed at dealing with contagion, as in the case of Malaysia, or the threat of short-term capital flows, as with Chile. Rather, they were means to a larger end: the consolidation of neoliberal rule by the political elite and dominant bourgeois interests. As noted in both cases, the extent of the crisis was not great enough to warrant an invitation to the IMF into either Chile or Malaysia during the implementation period of their respective capital controls. Thus the decision to opt for one type of control over the other resided in the particular historical configuration of class forces in each national social formation as well as in the position of each country within the global political economy. The extent of the crisis in Chile and in Malaysia is not only attributable to debt levels and foreign currency reserves; more fundamentally, it reflects the fact that neither country constitutes a 'systematically important emerging market' for the US (see Chapter 3). This observation implies that they did not receive as much 'hot money' as other 'important markets' such as Thailand, South Korea, Russia, Brazil and Argentina – all of which are members of the G20. Nonetheless, this does not detract from the fact that both controls remain archetypes of what the Fund considers a useful capital control (Chile) and a negative use of this policy mechanism (Malaysia), and therefore constitute a significant precedent for other 'systematically important' emerging markets.

Second, the Fund's judgement calls are deeply rooted in the self-interest of American structural power (the Dollar Wall Street Regime), which depends upon the successful reproduction of the imperative of free capital mobility by attempting to freeze the contradictions that underpin the new international financial architecture (see Chapter 1). Largely due to its appearance as a pluralistic multilateral lending institution and its exclusive emphasis on the economic dimensions of capital controls, the IMF is able not only to reproduce the 'common sense' assumption that free capital mobility is a natural phenomenon driven by the external forces of globalization but also to cloud the fact that the Fund's judgement call is profoundly political in nature. It follows from this that the IMF endorses, albeit cautiously and sparingly, the temporary use of

Chilean-type capital controls because they have a less negative effect on the scope of speculative activity for institutional investors – an activity from which many investment banks have drawn a great proportion of their earnings. This is one of the main reasons why the US government remains vehemently opposed to the implementation of a global tax, such as the Tobin tax, which would restrict short-term speculative behaviour. Moreover, as discussed in Chapter 3, because the Malaysian control was modelled on the Chinese capital control that was adopted by Hong Kong, Taiwan and China, the US fears that the Malaysian control could be adopted on a more permanent basis by other countries in the region.

Third, and relatedly, the IMF's judgement call reveals an important feature of the new architecture: the need to block protectionist tendencies in these key strategic countries as political elites and capitals in these countries attempt to deal with the above-mentioned policy paradox brought about by financial liberalization. Likewise, both case studies reveal that the policies chosen by these dominant social forces are driven more by their concern to deal with the policy paradox in such a way as to reproduce their own power by implementing strategies aimed at stabilizing their economies in reaction to the growing turmoil in the financial markets, than by an imperative to obey the rules of the Washington consensus. The fear that countries may start to close markets and turn away from neoliberal-based globalization has been expressed in a speech made by President Clinton: 'Unless they [the countries of the global South] feel empowered with the tools to master economic change, they will feel the strong temptation to turn inward, to close off their economies to the world. Now, more than ever, that would be a grave mistake.'[85]

Notes

1. Quoted in Naim 1999.
2. Eichengreen 1999a, Eichengreen et al. 1999.
3. Naim 1999.
4. Ibid.; Eichengreen et al. 1999.
5. Helleiner 1995: 323.
6. Gowan 1999.
7. Susan Strange calls these 'non-decisions', of which she identifies five that greatly shaped the present financial structure. For Strange, non-decisions

denote the failure of states 'to act when positive action would have been possible'. See Strange 1998b: 8.

8. Bello et al. 2000: 4
9. Cerny 2000: 201.
10. Gowan 1999: 98.
11. Greider 1997; Gowan 1999; Henwood 1999.
12. Raghavan 1998.
13. UNDP 1999: 31.
14. Strange 1998a: 92.
15. Pauly 1999.
16. Pauly 1999: 401.
17. According to the IMF data, 'the largest member of the IMF is the United States, with a quota of SDR [special drawing rights] 37,149.3 million, and the smallest member is Palau, with a quota of SDR 3.1 million. See www.imf.org/external/np/exr/facts/quotas.htm.
18. Strange 1998b: 165ff.
19. IMF, 'General Arrangements to Borrow (GAB) and New Arrangements to Borrow (NAB), A Factsheet', November 2002, see www.imf.org/external/np/exr/facts/gabnab.htm.
20. Bergsten 1998.
21. Rajan 2000.
22. Asian Development Bank 1999, quoted in Rajan 2000.
23. Wade and Veneroso 1998a, 1999b.
24. Wade and Veneroso 1998a: 18–19.
25. Guitián 1997: 22.
26. Quoted from www.investorhome.com/emh.htm.
27. Strange 1998b: 13.
28. Griffith-Jones 1996.
29. Ocampo 2001.
30. Dillon 1997: 70.
31. Ocampo 2000: 44.
32. Altvater 2002.
33. Gowan 1999: 11.
34. Felix 2002: 126–7; see also Shiller 2000; Patomäki 2001.
35. Haley 1999: 76.
36. Grabel 1996: 1763.
37. UNDP 1999.
38. This was made clear in the IMF's first comprehensive review of the Asian crisis; see Lane et al. 1999.
39. Grabel 1999.
40. Cf. 'World Bodies Called into Account', *Financial Times*, 24 September 1999; Sachs 1998; Wade and Veneroso 1998a.
41. Smith 1999.
42. Johnston 1998.
43. Anjaria 1998.
44. Cf. IMF, 'Report of the Acting Managing Director to the International Monetary and Financial Committee on Progress in Reforming the IMF

and Strengthening the Architecture of the International Financial System',
12 April 2000, www.imf.org/external/np/omd/2000/report.htm#11_F.

45. Cf. Stiglitz 1998.
46. Williamson 1997.
47. IMF 1997b.
48. See, for example, IMF 2000e, 2000f, especially parts 1–3; Sugisaki 1999.
49. Jomo 2001a.
50. For a more detailed study of the Chilean capital control from a historical
    materialist perspective, see Soederberg 2002.
51. Cf. Agosin and Ffrench-Davis 1996; Edwards 1999; Dooley 1996.
52. Naim 1999, pp. 14ff.
53. Taylor 2002: 63.
54. Petras et al. 1994.
55. Ffrench-Davis 1995.
56. Agosin 1998.
57. Fazio 2000.
58. Edwards 1999.
59. Latin American Weekly Report, 30 May 2000.
60. Taylor 2002: 12. For an excellent critique on the relation between neoliberal-
    led accumulation and policy formation on poverty levels in Chile, see Taylor
    2003.
61. IMF 2000f.
62. Anjaria 1998.
63. Cohen 2003.
64. Wade and Veneroso 1998b: x.
65. Dollarization refers to the legal adoption of the dollar as a replacement
    for the Malaysian ringgit. The 'quasi' suffix implies a 'partial' dollarization
    in the form of pegging the Malaysian currency to the US dollar.
66. Jomo 2001b.
67. Chin 2000.
68. Jomo 2001a: 41.
69. Wade and Veneroso 1998b: 18.
70. Asian Development Bank 1999: 13.
71. A good indication of this power structure is the concentration of corpo-
    rate ownership in publicly listed companies (PLCs). In 1998 'the largest
    shareholder owned 30.3 per cent, the top five shareholders owned 58.8 per
    cent, and the top twenty owned 80 per cent of total outstanding shares of
    an average PLC. Ownership data on the prominent large conglomerates
    indicate a similar concentration pattern.' Juzhong Zhuang et al. 2000: 22.
72. Chin 2000: 1042.
73. See Jomo 2001.
74. Edwards 1999: 82.
75. Alongside the G7/G8 and a representative from the European Union,
    Argentina, Australia, Brazil, China, India, Indonesia, Mexico, Saudi Arabia,
    South Africa, South Korea and Turkey. For more information, see John
    Kirton, www.g7.utoronto.ca/g7/G-20/G-20whatisit.html.
76. 'Ringgit Fears Keep Investors Away', Asiawise, 7 May 2001.

77. Wade and Veneroso 1998b.
78. This stance dovetails with the following observation made by the US Federal Reserve Chairman, Alan Greenspan: 'flood of imports into the US [is] unsustainable, for the current wealth in the US [is] not being created through producing goods and services, but the stock market'. 'Ministers Nervous about How Long US Expansion Can Last' *Financial Times*, 24 January 2000.
79. Wade and F. Veneroso 1998a: 22.
80. 'Oil and the Coming War against Iraq', *World Socialist Website*, 19 February 2003, www.wsws.org/articles/2003/feb2003/oil-f19.shtml; cf. 'US Trade Deficit Hits Record Level in 2002', *Financial Times*, 20 February 2003.
81. See Wade and Veneroso 1998a; Gowan 1999.
82. Since Mahathir sacked the popular finance minister Anwar Ibrahim, and subsequently took over himself, the UMNO has been losing public support. This has become evident with the growing power of the opposition Parti Islam se-Malaysia (Pas). 'Mahathir Issues Warning over Islamic Party', *Financial Times*, 22 June 2001.
83. 'Fair-trade Treaties Play Unfair Tricks', *Straits Times*, 17 February 2003.
84. Ibid.
85. Patomäki 2001: 114–15.

5

Deconstructing the New International Standard of Corporate Governance: An Emerging Disciplinary Strategy for the South?

The East Asian crisis of 1997–98 engendered a fierce debate over what should be done to quell the growing volatility in the international financial system, as we saw in Chapter 3. The US government and the US-dominated international financial institutions (IFIs) quickly monopolized the terms of the debate by steering attention away from policies that either threatened the principle of free capital mobility or reduced the power of the International Monetary Fund. Indeed, the only proposals that found their way to the negotiating table, and shaped the subsequent creation of the new international financial architecture, were those that sought to strengthen, as opposed to radically reform, the existing system. To date there are at least two discernible 'common sense' tendencies involved in these wider efforts to fortify the existing capitalist system via imposed US leadership and, more specifically, core–periphery coercion (see Chapter 3). First and foremost, financial liberalization is posited as a desirable policy because, like trade liberalization, it leads to economic growth and stability. Second, and related to this neoclassical assumption, debtor countries should be exposed more directly to the exigencies of transnational finance, so that the former may be forced to undertake market-based solutions to their current economic and political problems. Or, as a recent World Bank publication puts it, policy modifications are necessary so that governments, financial sectors and market participants in the global South 'adapt themselves to the new, competitive open market economy'.[1] According to the predictions of neoclassical economics, the results should be universally beneficial.

These two common-sense assumptions underlie the recent changing roles of the IFIs, such as the concerted effort to reinforce the
technical assistance provided for in the IMF's Article IV consultations,
whereby the Fund is able to scrutinize the degree to which the terms
of conditionality have been adhered to by the debtor nation. To this
end, both the World Bank and the IMF have recently systematized
twelve 'areas where standards are important for the institutional underpinning of macroeconomic and financial stability, and hence useful
for the operational work of the two institutions'. Specifically there
are twelve primary modules which constitute what the IFIs refer to
as the Reports on the Observance of Standards and Codes (ROSCs):
anti-moneylending and countering the financing of terrorism, data
dissemination, fiscal practices, monetary and financial policy transparency, banking supervision, insurance supervision, securities market
regulation, payments systems, corporate governance, accounting, audit-
ing, insolvency regimes and creditor rights.[2] Each unit represents an
'internationally agreed standard', which is then benchmarked against
country practices in a given area of state policy or market behaviour.
The chief aim of this exercise is to promote the 'proper management'
of financial liberalization in the developing world.

The ROSCs are novel in that they have not only expanded,
octopus-style, surveillance in the public sectors but also moved into
the private spheres of emerging market economies. It should be
noted that while participation in the ROSCs is, at least for now,
strictly 'voluntary', refusal to submit to such practices will inevitably
send negative signals to the international investment and financial
communities. The corporate governance module, which is the focus
of this chapter, falls under the 'official' responsibility of the World
Bank and its regional satellites such as the Asian Development
Bank (ADB), the Organization of Economic Co-operation and
Development (OECD) and, implicitly, the US-based credit-rating
agency, Standard & Poor's. Through these transnational institutions,
the international standard of corporate governance is inspected more
frequently and intensely than simply on an annual basis via the
Fund's Article IV consultations.

The OECD describes corporate governance as the 'structure
through which shareholders, directors and managers set the broad
objectives of the company, the means of attaining those objectives

and monitoring performance'.[3] The ultimate aim of adapting good corporate governance measures is to ensure that investors (suppliers of finance, shareholders or creditors) get a return on their money.[4] Up to now there has been very little critical work on the corporate governance module. Yet, given the disciplinary character imbued in corporate governance, both its content and form warrant further consideration. By analytically peeling away the layers of neutrality, this chapter attempts to expose how, and to what end, this standard was manufactured.

In this chapter I argue that, despite the claim that good corporate governance embodies 'universal principles', the definition advanced by the IFIs intentionally draws on the Anglo-American variant. This imposed standardization of corporate governance serves two over-lapping goals. First, it attempts to stabilize the international financial system by ensuring that emerging markets adapt to the exigencies of the neoliberal open market economy. Second, by placing greater emphasis on 'shareholder value' than on other variants of corporate governance, the interests of foreign capital are protected. Both these aims converge on a wider disciplinary strategy imbued in the cor-porate governance module of the ROSCs: an attempt not only to establish comprehensive webs of surveillance in order to police the behaviour of economies and states in the emerging markets better, but also to legitimize the subjective meaning of these codes by insisting that the ROSCs represent 'common values' across national spaces. This is despite the fact that they clearly serve the interests of Western institutional investors (e.g., public and private pension funds, insurance companies, bank trusts and mutual funds), which are closely tied to the relatively more powerful world financial centres, such as Wall Street and Main Street. Taken together this two-pronged strategy serves to construct a reality in which no alternative to the principle of free capital mobility is permitted to exist. Given the ongoing corruption within major US corporations, such as Enron, Xerox, K-Mart, Tyco, World Com, and so forth, it becomes even more urgent to explore the social construction of this international standard of corporate governance. I will discuss the issue of corporate scandal in the US in more detail in the last section of this chapter.

The discussion begins with the East Asian crisis of 1997–98. There are two reasons for this choice. First, given the fact that the debacle served as a catalyst in bringing about major changes in the international financial system, significant insight into the standardization of corporate governance can be gained by probing the IFIs' interpretation of the meltdown. Second, since crises not only bring about devastation and turmoil but also an opportunity for more powerful states and capitals to take advantage of the weakened negotiation power of crisis-plagued governments and markets, a broad discussion of the East Asian region helps to establish a concrete case from which the motives belying the imposed rules and standards may be understood.

The East Asia Debacle as Threat and Opportunity: The Origins of Standardizing Corporate Governance

East Asian state–capital relations are quite distinct from their Anglo-American counterparts.[5] Unlike the democratic political regimes based on individual rights and freedoms, and the strict separation of state and market, found in Anglo-American countries, their East Asian variants are characterized by authoritarian or dictatorial regimes with less regard for political and economic rights – including investors' rights.[6] The oft-invoked notion of the Asian 'developmental state' has its roots in a particular mode of late capitalist development underpinned by a national industrial strategy, which was socially constructed by powerful indigenous and foreign capitals.[7] These specific national configurations of class power formed tight networks of family-run companies, which eventually crystallized into a concentration and centralization of wealth and capital. Or, in more concrete terms, a close interaction between finance, industry and the state expressed itself institutionally by 'co-operative, long-term reciprocal relations between firms, banks and governments in a system which intermediates high savings into high corporate debt/equity ratios.[8] These characteristics not only set the East Asian form of capitalism apart from Anglo-American countries but were also largely believed – including by the international financial institutions – to be the inner strength of the 'Asian economic miracle'. The IFIs lavished praise on the Asian model's strong macroeconomic fundamentals (e.g. budget surpluses, high saving rates, low inflation,

export-oriented industries) and its commitment to an efficient allocation of investment whilst adhering to IMF advice to peg exchange
rates and liberalize capital accounts.[9] However, when the unsustainable debt burdens encouraged by these policies, not to mention the
swathes of hot money, destabilized the 'miracle economies', the IFIs
were the first to transform their paragons into pariahs.

Maintaining their usual hard-line neoliberal position, the IFIs
charged the East Asian region with general mismanagement of financial liberalization.[10] Unlike previous economic crises, the East Asian
debacle was closely identified with both state *and* market failure.
According to the IMF, the state failed to monitor economic activities properly and therefore failed to reduce exposure to foreign exchange risks in both the financial and corporate sectors. This factor,
moreover, was compounded by lax prudential rules and regulations,
as well as insufficient financial oversight by domestic institutions.[11]
East Asian governments were equally to blame for their misguided
policies that silently promoted the Achilles heel of East Asian capitalism: a high concentration of ownership, more popularly referred to
as cronyism.[12] Indeed, according to the Asian Development Bank, the
central weakness of the crisis-affected region is a high concentration
of ownership (see Table 5.1). The latter manifests itself in parent-
subsidiary formations (or 'pyramids') that are

> extraordinarily complex and opaque structures of private holding com-
> panies, layers upon layers of subsidiaries, as well as cross-holdings and
> informal links with yet more companies. Almost always, the pyramids
> included at least one bank with a licence to take deposits, and several
> publicly listed subsidiaries that could issue shares in the open market.[13]

According to the IFIs, crony capitalism was the root cause of
the crisis largely because of the high levels of moral hazard that it
tends to cultivate. The exclusionary communities that make up East
Asian markets breed ineffectiveness and corruption largely because
their structure diminishes the ability of outside actors and institutions to impose checks and balances. More important, cronyism
reduces the efficacy of essential mechanisms of shareholder protection, such as the board of directors system, shareholder participation
through voting during shareholder meetings, and transparency and
disclosure.[14]

Table 5.1 Control of publicly listed companies in 1996, weighted by capital marketization (% control)

Country	Sample companies (no.)	Family owned	Widely held	State owned	Widely held financial institutions	Widely held non-financial corporations
Indonesia	178	67.3	6.6	15.2	2.5	8.4
Korea	345	24.6	51.1	19.9	0.2	4.3
Malaysia	238	42.6	16.2	34.8	1.1	5.3
Philippines	120	46.4	28.5	3.2	8.4	13.7
Thailand	167	51.9	8.2	24.1	6.3	9.5

Source: Claessens, Djankov and Lang 1999, quoted in Asian Development Bank, 2000.

In reaction to the crisis, the Fund threw a $100 billion lifeline to rescue Indonesia, Thailand and South Korea in exchange for conditionality. What set this form of IMF conditionality apart from its previous policies was that it was targeted at correcting both market and state failure in the region. Aside from the Fund's traditional requirements to contract domestic demand through high interest rates, it required the closure of several banks and 'structural reforms in finance, corporate governance, labour markets, and so on, going far beyond what was necessary to stabilise the situation'.[15] For the IFIs, the eradication, or at least the diminished role, of the concentration of ownership in the corporate and banking sectors was the key to producing stability in the region. The primary way of achieving this was through the implementation of good corporate governance. Two motives underpin this concern. First, the growing levels of interdependency brought about by the liberalization of finance imply that regional stability was becoming quickly identified with global stability. Second, apart from the obvious opportunities associated with devalued currencies, the crisis offered an opportunity to attempt to impose reforms that would most benefit the interests of powerful Western institutional investors, such as guaranteed capital account liberalization and the protection of minority shareholder rights. As Walden Bello observes, this second motive was made quite clear in the speeches of White House officials during this period. In the words of the former Undersecretary of Commerce, Jeff Garten:

'Most of these countries are going to go through a deep and dark tunnel.... But on the other end there is going to be a significantly different Asia in which American firms have achieved much deeper market penetration, much greater access.'[16]

The next section of this chapter explores the genesis of the new standardization of corporate governance as a reaction to the Asian crisis. How this standard is manufactured and imposed by key international regulatory institutions is discussed in the following section. The chapter then turns to the content of the corporate governance standard, finally suggesting why this particular standard is being pursued vis-à-vis the wider power structures within the global political economy.

The New International Disciplinary Landscape of Standardizing Standards and Codes

The raison d'être

The standardization of corporate governance is intrinsically linked to the above preoccupations. The IMF and the World Bank argued that if protection of minority shareholders' rights was to be secured in foreign investment environments – wherein rampant insider trading is a daily phenomenon and companies can easily manipulate the relationships between their subsidiaries by cross-subsidization – East Asian governments and markets need to undertake corporate restructuring, to ensure more transparent and accountable companies. While we look at the justification for the imposition of a particular version of corporate governance below, it is useful to understand the *raison d'être* of the ROSCs. The East Asian crisis not only shook the global financial markets but also rattled the dominant neoliberal doctrine that free capital mobility was indeed a viable policy pillar to pursue. Or, in the words of the former Chief Economist of the World Bank, Joseph Stiglitz,

> The US Treasury had during the early 1990s heralded the global triumph of capitalism. Together with the IMF, it had told countries that followed the 'right policies' – the Washington Consensus policies – they would be assured of growth. The East Asia crisis cast doubt on this new world-view unless it could be shown that the problem was not with capitalism,

but with the Asian countries and their bad policies. The IMF and the US Treasury had to argue that the problem was not with the reforms – implementing liberalization of capital markets … but with the fact that the reforms had not been carried out far enough.[17]

Yet it is one thing to blame the crisis-hit countries and quite another to impose Western forms of corporate governance. While the IMF did have the leverage of massive bail-outs in South Korea, Thailand and Indonesia, the growing legitimacy crisis of the neoliberal-based policies of the Washington consensus implied that new forms of policy discipline were needed to ensure that these countries adhered to the same vision as the US Treasury and, more generally, US capital interests. Thus the form of imposing discipline on these states had to be revamped. This was accomplished in two broad ways.

The first way was through the creation of the G20 and Financial Stability Forum (FSF) in 1999 (see Chapter 3). It will be recalled that the G20 brings together, for the first time, finance ministers and central bank governors not only of the G7 and the European Union, but also their counterparts in 'systematically important' emerging market economies. The FSF, on the other hand, seeks to provide regular meetings of national authorities responsible for financial stability from G7 countries, including Hong Kong and Singapore, the IMF and the World Bank, the Bank for International Settlements, and OECD, alongside international regulatory and supervisory groups plus central bank experts in order to enhance discussions about financial supervision and surveillance. Taken together the main objective of the G20 and FSF is to achieve systemic stability by ensuring that emerging market economies adopt the rules of the global capital markets through adherence to free-market principles, including free capital mobility.

At the core of this stabilization strategy are the ROSCs. The member countries of the G20 and FSF voluntarily participate in the assessments of the twelve international units that constitute the ROSCs, such as transparency, macroeconomic policy, sound financial sector regulation and corporate governance. Thus, through various multi-level consultations, as appropriate, with relevant international bodies such as the IMF and the World Bank, and with the private sector (such as credit-rating agencies), it is believed that the integrity of the international financial system may be strengthened. The G20 countries are said to participate voluntarily in the policing and implementation of these international standards and codes of 'good governance'. The coercive element of capital and US dominance are thus diminished, or even hidden, in at least two ways. Although both points will become clearer as we analyse the corporate governance module in more detail, it is useful to flag them here. First, the intricate webs of governance seem to convey (falsely) a pluralistic arrangement involving both private and public organizations, and thereby contain built-in checks and balances. Yet, upon closer inspection, not only are the same players involved but also the private sector has been granted more power over policy formation in both states and markets in the South. Second, compliance with the ROSCs is not voluntary, as non-compliance would send negative signals to the international financial community, resulting in possible capital flight and investment strike.

Another way we can observe changes in the form neoliberal discipline imposed in the South is through the treatment of conditionality by the World Bank and the IMF. Ever since the 1950s IMF financing has relied on conditionality. In short, this term describes conditions in the form of policy implementations that debtor countries must undertake if they are to receive IMF financing. Lately, however, there has been much concern not only about the increase in the actual number of conditionalities, especially over the past decade, but also about their overly intrusive, and thus largely ineffective, quality. This latter point is particularly salient in light of the Fund's new mandate to manage financial liberalization properly in both private and public sectors in the developing world. Among the IMF's various attempts to reconstitute conditionality, especially as it pertains to core issue areas, is the reliance upon other international regulatory institutions. This move is vital in understanding how 'standardization' of corporate governance is achieved. Since 1999, the executive boards of the IMF and the World Bank have been engaging in more 'conditionality-sharing'. In what is referred to as 'streamlining' conditionality, for example, the IMF has recently replaced its Enhanced Structural Adjustment Facility (ESAF) with the Bank's Poverty Reduction and Growth Facility (PRGF). The PRGF is framed around, and in turn supports, the Bank's Poverty

Reduction Strategy Papers (PRSPs), which are a reinvented form of the much-criticized structural adjustment lending policies that the Bank practised throughout the 1980s and a large part of the 1990s. This move not only gives the Bank's policies some financial teeth, but also allows for a more comprehensive and coherent surveillance programme by permitting the IFIs 'to more effectively monitor, in greater detail, the countries' policy actions, the frequency of program reviews, and the role of prior actions.'[18] Despite the rhetoric of *broad public participation* and *greater country ownership*, PRGF conditionality shares the same coercive tendency as the SAPs in that recipient countries will not receive poverty reduction assistance if they do not show adherence to 'good governance' principles, which are all firmly rooted in the market-based ideology of neoliberalism. Within the larger parameters of the PRGF and the PRSP, both the Fund and the World Bank have been actively involved in developing guidelines and dividing the area of competence and responsibility vis-à-vis each of the eleven modules that make up the ROSCs.[19]

The upshot of this diffusion of power has led to the emergence of an intricate web of surveillance and discipline, which seeks to spin 'common-sense values' across and within national spaces. For example, while the ROSC module of transparency is under the purview of the IMF, the unit of securities market regulation is under the control of the International Organization of Securities Commissions (IOSCO); whereas, as mentioned earlier, corporate governance is under the purview of the World Bank (and, by extension, the ADB) and the OECD, and implicitly Standard & Poor's. It is useful to outline briefly how this extension of responsibilities to different intergovernmental and non-governmental organizations has the effect of sharpening the focus on the activities of both states and markets in emerging markets, and simultaneously depoliticizing the disciplinary strategy that promotes the interests of Western institutional investors.

The imposition of corporate governance

The surveillance and disciplinary characteristics of the institutions responsible for the corporate governance module are intended to replace conditionality by fortifying the IMF's Article IV consultations.

The World Bank, for its part, is able to police the implementation of what is considered 'good' corporate governance practices in debtor countries on a regular basis, essentially by making them an integral part of its anti-poverty and growth strategies, and withholding funds as the ultimate act of punishment. The function of the OECD, on the other hand, lacks this coercive characteristic. Nonetheless, in its capacity as a well-respected international think-tank for the wealthier nation-states, the OECD serves an important role not only in manufacturing the meaning of good corporate governance, but also in legitimizing this social construct through the appearance of consensus formation. In its attempts to formulate the principles of corporate governance, for example, the OECD went out of its way to invite not only the usual suspects – government officials, international policymakers, powerful international financial groups – but also trade unions and non-governmental organizations. In this way, the 'imagined community' of transnational civil society was considered to be adequately represented in the creation of the 'universal principles' governing corporate governance, a factor that the chapter discusses later.

Unlike the above two institutions involved in the wider disciplinary strategy of corporate governance, the third is a non-governmental regulatory body: namely, Standard & Poor's (S&P). The significance of Standard & Poor's arises when viewed in concert with the OECD and the World Bank: they have effectively granted the credit-rating agency de facto policing rights vis-à-vis corporate governance, or what James Rosenau refers to as 'control mechanisms'.[20] As with the IFIs, the authority of S&P derives from the specialized knowledge upon which its judgements are based, and the fact that 'capital markets acquiesce to and conduct themselves on the basis of [its] ratings'.[21] The rating agency's appearance as a nonpartisan institution, devoid of political affiliation and thus motive, also conceals its disciplinary nature in terms of ideologically reproducing the 'international' standard of corporate governance. In addition to its powers of moral suasion, S&P wields coercive power as well. Its ability to inflict potentially great economic harm to a country by downgrading its debt rating has serious ramifications for governments and markets alike; the most obvious factor being a negative signal to international creditors, institutional investors and traders, which is usually followed by capital flight and/or investment strikes. To take a recent example, in order to punish Japan for its slow progress on structural reform, S&P recently downgraded Japan's long-term debt rating, which has put Japan on a par with the only G7 country with a rating below the top-grade AAA – Italy.[22] Upon release of this news, institutional investors engaged in the so-called 'Wall Street Walk' out of Japan, while others stayed away (investment strike).

The specific linkages between these three regulatory institutions are discernible as follows. The Asian Development Bank advertises its use of S&P's version of corporate governance directly on its website. The meaning of corporate governance that S&P draws on is none other than the definition provided by the OECD, upon which the World Bank also appears to base its understanding of this standard. In its efforts to rate (quantify) corporate governance, S&P has transformed the OECD definition into a veritable disciplinary mechanism in its attempts to systematize it in the form of corporate governance scores (CGS). Interestingly, CGS comprises scores derived from corporate governance ratings at the country and company levels. Whilst *company governance* measures the effectiveness of the interaction among a company's management, board, shareholders and other stakeholders by focusing on what a company does and not on what is the minimum required by local laws and regulations, *country governance* measures the effectiveness of legal, regulatory and informational infrastructure. This latter focuses on how external forces at a macro-level can influence the quality of a company's corporate governance. Taken together, the CGS not only aims to police both political and economic spaces of an emerging market effectively, but also to expose both spheres more directly to the discipline of transnational finance.

The basic aim of the ROSCs and their respective intergovernmental and non-governmental organizations was to erect a regulatory scaffolding around both states and markets in the developing world so as to ensure compliance with ROSCs through constant and vigilant surveillance at the national, regional and global levels. However, to grasp 'who benefits' from this institutional reconfiguration, it is important to remain critical of the motives underpinning this supposed 'new' international financial architecture, by resisting mainstream explanations, which focus on either the US government's desire for a more equitable and democratic international regulatory structure governing finance, or on a move to signal a new multilateralism. Despite the appearance of institutional change, the power structures that underscore this project remain firmly entrenched in the parameters of what Stephen Gill refers to as the class-based G7 nexus.[23] This nexus embraces not only the political elite tied to the G7 but also their frequent interactions with powerful transnational capitals in such elites, and highly clandestine meetings and institutions such as the Trilateral Commission, the World Economic Forum, the Mont Pélérin Society, the OECD, and so forth.[24] These high-level social and business dealings also take place in key regulatory agencies such as credit rating agencies – the two largest being the US-based Moody's and S&P – as well as in the distant, yet highly powerful, UN cousins, the IMF and the World Bank. As Gill rightly emphasizes, the agenda-setting and policymaking processes of the G7 nexus revolve around the dominant interests of the US; this will be discussed in more detail later in the chapter. Suffice it to say here that the G7 nexus of international regulatory institutions, such as the one that is involved in constructing and policing good corporate governance in the global South, resemble closed policy (epistemic) communities of industrialized countries, which are marked by an elite group of like-minded individuals who promote their own interests without involving the wider public. This clandestine global management effectively depoliticizes the class-based attempt to strengthen – largely through legitimating and stabilizing – the existing system marked by tighter communicative lines and increased cooperation, as opposed to reforming it via democratization processes.

Nevertheless, the creation of common values, which underlies the formulation of the ROSCs, is not a procedural and technical exercise based on a pre-existing consensus. Instead it is a highly political attempt to construct an imagined community between states. The establishment of universal values is part and parcel of this disciplinary strategy, of which corporate governance is said to be an instance. The class nature of this strategy (who benefits) may be understood by taking a closer look at the *content* of how corporate governance has been socially constructed.

Constructing Common Values in the South

Corporate governance: one or many?

In contrast with the confident usage of the term by the international financial institutions, the vast literature devoted to the study of corporate governance, primarily in the fields of management science, economics and law, reveal that there is little agreement on the definition of the term let alone ample evidence to suggest a solid correlation between sound corporate governance and investment performance.[25] Some writers have forcefully argued that good corporate governance is a precondition for commercial competitiveness and thus should be of national importance;[26] others hold that there is only a weak link between company performance and sound corporate governance. As one observer puts it:

> no issue is thornier than the question of whether there's a link between the quality of a company's board and the quality of its market performance.… A lot of Corporate Governance suffers from procedural frills (how often a board meets … what questions they ask the CEO [Chief Executive Officer]). It's missing the boat. There isn't a correlation between those things and investment performance.[27]

Other studies reveal 'scattered, non-robust correlations between various performance measures and proportion of independent directors'.[28]

The contested utility of corporate governance should evoke suspicion as to why international regulatory institutions are eager to endorse its beneficial qualities, especially in the context of East Asian markets. The following quotations, extracted from a document on corporate governance by S&P, which appears directly on the ADB website, are cases in point:

> Over 80% of investors say they would be prepared to pay more for the shares of well-governed companies than those of poorly governed companies. (McKinsey & Co., 'Investor Opinion Study', June 2000)

> Foreign fund managers are being more discriminating over levels of governance and Asian corporations are becoming aware of the need to be good corporate citizens, for example in the treatment of minority shareholders. (Chairman of the Hong Kong Securities and Futures Commission, *Financial Times*, 25 April 2000)[29]

By presenting corporate governance as a fait accompli, these institutions ignore the ongoing debates that draw attention to the contested meaning of this term. As a recent World Bank publication claims, 'Corporate governance is the market mechanism most effective in protecting investors' rights; it is also necessary to secure a stable supply of long-term capital essential for sustained growth.'[30] Despite these claims, corporate governance is far from a ready-made, standardized term. One of the main reasons for the heterogeneity of the term is due to the fact that what is considered 'sound' corporate governance is shaped directly by social forces, which in turn structure their relationships between banks, corporations and the state to reflect national circumstances.[31] This distinction is observable even within continental Europe, where corporate governance takes on different meanings in different countries. Whereas the French equivalent, *gouvernement d'entreprise*, places emphasis on enterprise, the German, *Unternehmungsverfassung*, stresses a legal meaning rather than its managerial connotations.[32] This fundamental linguistic confusion surrounding corporate governance reveals two important and highly contradictory aspects that underpin the construction of an 'international standard'. First, and despite the manner in which corporate governance is packaged and sold by the Asian Development Bank, OECD and Standard & Poor's, the importance of the national framework remains a major obstacle in developing an international standard of corporate governance. Second, and relatedly, how is it that the regulatory institutions responsible for policing 'sound' corporate governance in the global South have arrived at a standardized definition?

Cognizant of the above concerns, the Business Sector Advisory Group on Corporate Governance to the OECD cedes that no one model of corporate governance works in all countries and in all companies. While this may be true in theory, the response of the IFIs to the East Asian crisis should make us wary of the sensitivity of these institutions to differing national frameworks. More importantly, the OECD contradicts this sensitivity regarding national specificities by insisting not only that 'universal' standards – such as fairness, transparency, accountability and responsibility – exist, but also that they can be applied across a broad range of legal, political and economic environments.[33] These four universals combine to form corporate governance as an international standard (ROSC), against which emerging markets are to be judged not only by the G7 nexus but also by Western institutional investors. Further, S&P's working definition of corporate governance, and subsequent CGS, refer to 'the extent to which a company adopts and conforms to codes and guidelines of good corporate governance practices'.[34] By virtue of the fact that S&P's codes and guidelines are derived from the OECD standards, countries and companies of emerging markets are measured against the benchmark of Anglo-American standards.[35] Another clue regarding the preference for the Anglo-American variant of corporate governance is the credit-rating agency's insistence that its CGS focus primarily on issues that affect the interests of shareholders – as opposed to stakeholders. As we will see in the next section, concern for stakeholders denotes a more bank-oriented model of corporate governance.

Manufacturing a standard

To untangle the particular interests behind this 'universal' norm it is helpful to examine closely one of the chief preoccupations of 'sound' corporate governance: to protect the rights of minority shareholders by mitigating what economists refer to as moral hazard. Conventionally this term describes the problems that arising when salaried managers run companies on behalf of dispersed shareholders; they may not act in the shareholders' best interests. However, there is a broader interpretation of moral hazard that extends beyond the relationship between shareholders and managers, or what is referred to as the *principal-agent* or *agency* problem. This concern is evident in the preamble of the OECD corporate governance document:

> Corporate governance is affected by the relationships among participants in the governance system. Controlling shareholders, who may be individuals, family holdings, bloc alliances, or other corporations acting through a holding company or cross shareholdings, can significantly influence corporate behaviour. *As owners of equity, institutional investors are increasingly demanding a voice in corporate governance in some markets.*[36]

In this wider meaning of moral hazard more interests are involved in the way in which a company is managed, as either good or bad governance affects the relations between controlling and minority shareholders (usually foreign capital), between shareholders and creditors, and between controlling shareholders and other stakeholders (e.g. suppliers and workers). While the point can only be flagged at this stage, it is important to note that the nature of the East Asian corporate governance system, which is premissed on concentrated ownership, contradicts the universal element of fairness in that this structure usually violates the rights of minority shareholders and other investors. Specifically, according to an Asian Development Bank study,

> This could take the form of paying themselves special dividends, committing the company into disadvantageous business relationships with other companies they control, and taking on excessively risky projects inasmuch as they share in the upside while the other investors, who might be creditors, bear the cost of failures.[37]

Unlike their Anglo-American counterparts, banks in East Asia are significant stakeholders of non-financial corporations (i.e. banks are both owner and creditor). Also, the notion of public disclosure in the case of family-run businesses is antithetical to the business climate of many East Asian countries. It should be noted, however, that this sentiment extends well beyond the East Asian region. According to a study conducted by the World Bank,

> In developing economies, firms tend to have greater need of external capital to sustain growth, but these economies typically are unable to provide adequate protection for investors through a developed and well-functioning financial market. In underdeveloped financial and capital markets, there is a greater probability of moral hazard and adverse selection, and investors are frequently exposed to risk.[38]

Within this context, then, the issue of 'universal' elements underpinning 'sound' corporate governance becomes problematic, to say the least. For our purposes, a more appropriate question would be, which form of national corporate governance do these 'universal' principles reflect. To unpack this problem it is helpful to scrutinize how moral hazard is, or is not, dealt with in two main ideal-types of corporate governance systems: (1) the Anglo-American variant found, for example, in the US and the UK; and, (2) the bank-oriented model, which reflects the system in Japan (and other East Asian countries) and continental European countries.[39]

In contrast to the bank-oriented model, the *Anglo-American model* of best practices and codes, for instance, places considerably more emphasis on free-market operation, where the enterprise is primarily an instrument for achieving the maximization of shareholder value.[40] Within the context of this system, there is more voice given to shareholders, especially in terms of what is considered their most important right: voting. The respect for shareholder voting rights is believed to facilitate a commitment of corporate resources to value-maximizing ends.[41] This principle reflects the modest levels of ownership concentration in the US corporate system, where large companies are listed in stock markets and have their ownership dispersed among institutional and individual investors. Apart from limiting the role played by banks in the management of companies, the moral hazard problem is overcome by a competitive environment encouraged by liberalization (less state intrusion). As a result, restraints are placed on managerial discretion by, at least in theory, providing balance between internal controls (such as the board of directors) and external controls (such as hostile takeovers).[42] Managerial discretion is also mitigated in the Anglo-American model; banks play a limited role in the management of companies. According to this perspective, the survival of the fittest – not the biggest – will delimit high levels of ownership and thus mitigate moral hazard.

In the Anglo-American system of corporate governance the market acts as the ultimate 'disciplinarian' of moral hazard, such as the short-termism and opportunism of managers. Underlying this claim is the neoclassical preference for market forces over state intervention, under the belief that the market provides the most flexible and efficient coordinating and adaptive mechanism in the face of complex interdependence and turbulent environments.[43] The more exposure corporations and banks have to market forces, the more pressure is placed on inefficient family-run firms. It is argued that this is an inevitable squeeze on profits brought about by increased competition, which acts inventively for the benefit of consumers, through making the best use of scarce resources.[44]

On the other hand, the *bank-oriented model* rests on the central proposition that the purpose of the firm should be defined more widely than the maximization of shareholder welfare alone. In this ideal-type, most companies are private, the ownership of listed companies is highly concentrated, family ownership is very important, hostile takeovers are rare, and pyramidal control schemes are common, such as in the East Asian case. Moreover, this type of corporate governance allocates a high degree of importance to bank ownership of equity. This is evident not only in East Asia but also in many continental European countries, such as Belgium, Germany, Sweden, Portugal, and so on.[45] Another distinguishing feature of this model of corporate governance is its assumption that there should be some explicit recognition of the well-being of other groups having a long-term association with the firm – and therefore an interest, or 'stake', in its long-term success, by those such as employees, financiers, suppliers, and even customers. Moral hazard is therefore rendered redundant in the bank-oriented model because of a deep mistrust of the degree to which markets may not 'suitably capture the full social benefits or levy the full social costs of market activity'.[46]

In this second ideal-type of corporate governance, moral hazard is ostensibly overcome through the attempts at achieving two objectives: efficient management and control. These objectives are reached when a corporation builds a reputation for the ethical treatment of its suppliers, clients and employees; this then creates trust relations, which in turn support profitable investments and mutually beneficial exchanges.[47] Boards of directors, for example, are usually large and have a limited number of outside directors. Although shareholders have more rights, in theory, than in the Anglo-American model, in practice the chief executive officer is in control. That characteristic has serious implications not only for the manner in which markets are organized but also for the type of relations between states and markets. As in the case of East Asia, state intervention in the economy is not viewed by market participants as detrimental to the efficient allocation of scarce resources, especially in terms of reducing competition ('crowding out'); but is seen instead as a necessary force in overcoming unavoidable obstacles of short-termism and greed-driven herd behaviour. More important, there is no conclusive evidence in the literature to suggest that the Anglo-American variant leads to more stability, such as lower capital costs and greater competition, than the bank-oriented model found in Germany and Japan. In a Brookings Institution study, Mitsuhiro Fukao demonstrates that the underlying structure of Japanese and German companies is more conducive to stronger shareholder participation, and more stable management and corporate relations with creditors, suppliers and employees than is usually the case in the United States and the United Kingdom.[48]

There is more to the dominance of the Anglo–American model of corporate governance than the preference of one ideal-type over another. The option to model a putative 'international standard' on Anglo–American codes and best practices is rooted in the wider power relations in the global political economy. Specifically, this model of corporate governance reflects the interests of Western institutional investors, most of whom profit from the market-centric system of the United States, where they are able to operate in a less restricted fashion, as opposed to the bank-centric systems found in Western Europe and Japan. The next section looks at this system in more detail. It seeks to expose the links between stabilization of the international financial system by attempting to impose 'internationally agreed standards' in the developing world and the protection of Western institutional investors by creating an environment that suits the interests of these powerful transnational actors.

The Political Economy of Dominance: Institutional Investors

The landscape of a market-centric system

The implicit use of the Anglo–American definition of corporate governance in the creation of an 'international standard' is closely tied to powerful institutional investors, who weave in and out of emerging markets to turn as large a profit in the least amount of time as possible. As noted by Sir Adrian Cadbury, head of the UK Committee responsible for drafting a code of best practices concerning corporate governance, increasing shareholder activism in general and the pressure from institutional investors in particular play an important role in 'forcing those demanding capital to comply with international standards regarding disclosure and governance'.[49] But who are the majority of these shareholders? According to the former general manager of the Bank for International Settlements (BIS), Alexandre Lamfalussy,

> net inflows of capital into the developing world amounted to $100 billion in 1990 and $175 billion in 1993[;] they reached an average of about $240 billion per year during 1996 and 1997. A shift of 1 per cent in the total assets of '*Western*' institutional investors towards securities purchases in emerging markets would amount to more than $200 billion; an equal shift in the gross external assets of the banks reporting to the BIS would amount to another $90 billion; and a 1 per cent shift in these banks' total assets would represent a multiple of this figure.[50]

Although Lamfalussy considers 'Western' to include Canada, the United States, Europe and Japan, the most prominent institutional investor base in the international financial markets is the US. 'By mid-1995, U.S. institutional investors held assets of $10.2 trillion, or nearly 22 percent of all U.S. financial assets ... by the end of 1995 their percentage ownership in the largest 1,000 US corporations had increased to 57.2 percent, up from 46.6 percent in 1987.'[51] Viewed from this angle, we can see how the goal of protecting the interests of these powerful shareholders becomes intimately connected with the overarching concern of the G7 nexus to stabilize the international financial system. This requires some explication.

US institutional investors and shareholder activism

Commensurate with their growing economic strength, US institutional investors have decided to flex their muscles by demanding a voice in the overall management of the company, especially in terms of performance issues – that is, how corporations create value for themselves and their shareholders. Although shareholder activism may be traced back to the 1930s with individual shareholder concern over corporate accountability, the sheer size of the new financial players has made not only companies but also governments aware of the dangers involved if the investors' ultimate threat, investment strike or capital flight, is carried out.[52] Shareholder activism has not remained within the confines of the US, however. Indeed, as mentioned earlier, powerful US institutional investors have been at the forefront in lobbying the G7 nexus to assist in creating the conditions in the emerging markets that would lead to some sort of 'corporate democracy' – that is, a democratic system in which 'citizens' participate through the exercise of votes.[53] Only within corporate democracy would 'shareholder activism' truly become effective in protecting the interests of institutional investors operating in authoritarian regimes, especially those found in many financially attractive East Asian and top-tier Latin American countries such as Brazil, Argentina (at that time) and Mexico. This concern is closely tied to the Clinton administration's strategic priority to ensure that the ten 'Big Emerging Markets'[54] (or BEMs) continually adhere to the same neoliberal policies propelling at least the appearance of growth in the US. According to the US Commerce Department,

> by the end of the decade US trade with the BEMs may exceed trade with Europe or Japan, and in another 10 years could surpass trade with Europe and Japan combined. The CIA estimates that between now and 2010 the handful of BEM countries will account for 44 per cent of the non-US growth in world imports.[55]

While it is important to identify one of the key interests, that of US institutional investors, involved in the construction of the 'international' corporate governance standard, we must not lose sight of the underlying nature of global capital accumulation, which has ultimately facilitated the economic and political clout of these financial players. The growing reliance on a mode of accumulation whereby money dominates over productive capital leads to the necessity of effectively expanding (as opposed to valorizing) capital by continually increasing one's exposure to risk, and thus to higher returns. This risk-driven form of profit-seeking behaviour acts as the mainspring for the construction of financial instruments, such as mutual funds. These funds, which are nothing more than a collection of bonds and stocks that allow investors to avoid risking all their money on a single company, have been designed to facilitate investment in geographical spaces where information on foreign companies and markets is not readily accessible to the individual investor. This is the case most notably in developing countries where interest rates are high, representing increased risk. A global capitalist system driven by the imperative of free capital mobility is only able to feed the growing hunger for higher returns by creating opportunities involving higher risk. This has led to the recent phenomenon of the 'hedge fund craze'. Once the preserve of wealthy individuals, currently everyone from institutional investors to the 'mass affluent' (those with as little as $10,000 to invest) is buying into these highly speculative organizations. According to *The Economist*, 'In the first half of [2001], almost twice as much money flowed into [these funds] as in the whole of 2000. Worldwide, there are now reckoned to be over 6,000 such funds, controlling assets worth over $500 billion.'[56]

The discipline of the US financial system

As a result of state-led efforts of deregulation, the US financial system had become virtually 'market-centric' by the end of the 1990s, which essentially refers to the absence of explicit state intervention into the financial system (in contrast with the bank–centric model, which does not view state intervention as raising moral hazard). The hallmark of this market-centric system has been the centralization and concentration of financial power in the core Anglo-American countries – that is, the United States and the United Kingdom.[57] To allow continually more and more Americans to participate and benefit from this form of capital expansion (e.g. private and public pension funds, bank trusts, insurance companies, and mutual funds), the US government constantly undertakes measures to deregulate financial activity and thereby widen the scope of risk for these financial institutions. For instance, due to the continual narrowing of the profit margin in wholesale banking in the US, especially that derived from lending to high-quality sovereign borrowers, it has been necessary to raise commission income by searching for higher returns on riskier international banking, primarily through security holdings (e.g. stocks, bonds, notes, certificates of deposit). This has been facilitated by the exponential growth of markets for derivative instruments and the growing presence of new players: namely, the more mobile and less vulnerable institutional investors, which operate collectively (herd behaviour) and on a relatively short-term horizon. Moreover, this move has enabled bank assets not only to become more profitable but also to shift from balance sheet to off-balance-sheet commitments (or vice versa), and, in so doing, render the lender–borrower relationship less transparent and inevitably more unstable. Internationally, the flow of net bond and note financing caught up with net international bank lending by the mid-1990s, and then overtook it. To maintain its competitive position in a world market dominated by securitization, the US government repealed the Glass–Steagall Act in 1999. As a result US investment banks have been allowed to increase their leverage in the pursuit of more high-risk, high-yield bonds and uncertain, but potentially large, capital gains on equity and bond investments. Significantly, the repeal of Glass–Steagall was both a beacon and a response to the ever-diminishing returns to banks and the need to compete in the era of securitization with as little state regulation as possible, so long as there exist adequate institutional standards in the market – that is, 'well-managed' liberalization. It was a beacon in that, despite the growing instability of the international financial architecture, the US government clearly believes that further capital account liberalization is the only viable manner of growth for the global political economy. At the same time, this shift should be understood as a response to the inherent contradictions of capital accumulation in the US.

Yet, as we have seen, the disciplinary force of shareholder activism is strengthened institutionally by the G7 nexus, specifically the OECD, Standard & Poor's and the World Bank/Asian Development Bank. To ensure their ever-expanding sprawl, institutional investors also depend on the G7 nexus to break down, or at least make more porous, East Asian pyramids so as to establish a level playing field within the national social formation while embedding the markets within Anglo-American behavioural norms. One step towards this goal is the act of universalizing standards such as corporate govern-ance, which in effect acts to recreate the existing power structures of the neoliberal market-centric system. The reconfiguration of the G7 nexus in the form of ROSCs reflects these deeper changes in the nature of global capital accumulation as well as the ever-changing needs of the powerful social forces tied to it. There is, however, a contradiction involved in promoting an Anglo-American version of corporate governance, which, although important, may only be flagged at this point. While corporate governance is at the heart of the operations of multinational corporations, the promotion of an Anglo-American model serves the interests of the shareholders and financial institutions that are not multinationals. Thus the tensions between financial capital and productive capital interests come to the fore here.

Neoliberal Discipline beyond Corporate Governance

As many scholars argue, prevailing social forces, tightly intertwined with the neoliberal market-centric system, do not simply maintain their privileged position in the global political economy by default. Given the highly contradictory nature of finance-led global capital accumulation and the ever-present class-based conflicts attached to the capitalist system, dominant political ruling classes and the transnational bourgeoisie are required to reclaim their power continually through both coercive and ideological means.[58]

The issue of whether or not the ROSCs are effective in bringing about this larger class-based strategy, although a worthy subject of further research, is beyond the scope of the chapter. Suffice it to say that, if we look beyond the rhetoric, the crisis-affected countries of East Asia are not substantively undertaking the recommended reform prescribed in the standard of corporate governance. For one thing, such reform entails painful, and potentially dangerous, political and economic restructuring, which most politicians and capitals are loath to undertake. To illustrate this, consider a recent survey that revealed that 50 per cent of South Korean and Taiwanese companies were under family control. In Thailand and Malaysia, the proportion was between 60 and 70 per cent of companies, and in Indonesia and the Philippines, the least developed in this group, it was even higher. In these countries, 'only ten families controlled over half of their countries' total market capitalization.'[59] According to a recent ROSC on the fiscal transparency of South Korea, state forms of intervention are far from assuming a market-centric system. According to the IMF's own data

> [the South Korean] government owns 65 percent of the assets of the banking sector (made up of a majority stake in three major banks and minority stakes in two more) as well as four non-bank financial institutions.... The government also extends loans and guarantees for commercial operations through the budget, but it also provides such support outside

the budget, which amount to hidden subsidies to loan and guarantee recipients.[60]

However, this does not discount the effects of the nascent disciplinary strategy of standardizing corporate governance – not to mention the other ten modules governing state policy and market behaviour – in other, economically less powerful countries in the global South. Nor does it reduce the magnitude of the attempt by the G7 nexus to construct socially and reproduce the commonsense assumption that there exists a natural trajectory of economic development aimed at establishing a 'coherence' between OECD and non-OECD countries so that they may more efficiently reap the rewards of a neoliberal world order based on free capital mobility. For example, in an attempt to reinforce this common sense, the OECD foreshadows the world in 2020 by arguing that

active participation in the global economy depends upon the strengthening or creation of effective economic, human, social and institutional capacities. Most non-OECD countries need institutional reforms necessary to promote 'supply-side' capacities, notably private sector development and enterprise competitiveness.[61]

It should be stressed, however, that the standardization of corporate governance, and more generally the ROSCs, are but one moment in the larger effort to erode national differences in the name of international stability. The World Trade Organization and the Multilateral Agreement on Investments, the European Union, and the North American Free Trade Agreement, and, as we will see in the next chapter, the Monterrey consensus, are all part of a larger disciplinary strategy pursuing the same objective: to open new playing fields to facilitate the penetration of powerful transnational institutional investors into new markets. Whilst it is still too early to decipher the effects of the efforts to build a new international financial architecture through, for example, the standardization of corporate governance, it is not too soon to attempt to dispel the common sense assumption that these strategies are based on universal values. As this chapter has argued, corporate governance, in its present form and content, represents specific material interests tied to the interests of the Dollar Wall Street Regime and powerful transnational capitals.

Despite the claims of neoclassical economists and neoliberal politicians that the root of financial instability lies in imprudent government policies and crony capitalism in the Third World, the volatility of the global financial system is in fact due to the underlying crisis of capitalism and the constant attempts by transnational capitals to overcome the barriers to capital valorization by engaging in short-term thinking for immediate financial gain. Ostensibly money managers of capitals base their judgement regarding the quantity, time and place to invest on 'rational' and 'scientific' (objective, value-free) risk modelling, which, in algebraic complexity, draws on a variety of variables, including the 'sound economic fundamentals' of a company or country. Yet the common sense about the reliability of 'sound fundamentals' as providing a guidepost has come under attack, since the Asian crisis (see Chapter 3).[62] More recently, the recent string of financial scandals in the US has revealed that the market values of the top multinational corporations have been but an illusion. Robin Blackburn rightly notes that

> Enron's demise was significant not just because of its size – other concerns failing at the same time, such as K-Mart or LTV, had more employees and pensioners – but because it had represented the cutting-edge of neoliberal corporate strategy, living proof that financialization and deregulation were the wave of the future.[63]

Apart from the fraudulent behaviour of the top management and accounting firms of these 'failed corporations', the speculative behaviour of investors was a major contributing factor to the overvalued shares. As prominent Yale economist Robert J. Schiller observes, 'the Dow Jones Industrial Average stood at around 3,600 in early 1994. By 1999, it had passed 11,000, more than tripling in five years, a total increase in stock market prices over 200 percent. At the start of 2000, the Dow passed 11,700.' Although most countries in Europe doubled stock market valuations over the period between 1994 and 1999, and stock markets in East Asia and Latin America made impressive gains, the US saw by far the largest increase. Shiller argues that basic economic indicators in the US did not coincide with this huge increase in market valuation. Moreover, he notes that 'US personal income and gross domestic product rose less than 30 per cent, and almost half of this increase was due to inflation. Corporate profits rose less than 60 per cent, and that from a temporary recession-depressed base.' The conclusion may be drawn that stock prices have been driven up by speculation as opposed to 'genuine, fundamental information about value'.[64]

When the situation is viewed from the above perspective, an important point may be gleaned from the recent wave of corporate scandals in the US, represented by the collapse of giants such as Enron, Global Crossing, Tyco, WorldCom, Xerox, Arthur Andersen, and so forth. The scandals are best understood as attempts at overcoming the barriers of capital valorization in the ongoing crisis of capitalism, as opposed to being perceived as expressions of mere flaws in existing forms of 'corporate governance'. Speculative bubbles do not result from either inaccurate algebraic modelling or the herd behaviour of institutional investors. Instead, they are part and parcel of the crisis of overaccumulation: finance will remain the motor of capitalist growth, as long as the productive realm remains relatively unprofitable. This form of capital accumulation is in itself highly volatile, largely because profits are based on a range of assumptions of how particular markets will perform (or underperform) in the future. While the dominance of finance is structurally rooted in the crisis of global capitalism, its power is neither self-regulating nor automatic – an unproblematic 'once and for all' type of power – but needs to be socially reproduced and thus legitimated through state intervention, and required the traditional coercive elements of state power (such as the military and police) as well as the coercive aspects of financial power (investment strikes and capital flight), to enforce market rules.[65] To be sure, the capitalist state plays an essential role in re-creating the dominance of finance and responding to and mediating manifestations of crisis by way of damage control. Wolff puts it this way: 'The goal, as always, is to keep the capitalist economy from suffering the kind of deterioration that might interact dangerously with political and cultural developments. The economic hegemony of the capitalist system and the political hegemony of the United States must be globally assured.'[66]

Notes

1. Jang 2001: 73; IMF 1997a.
2. According to the IMF, 'Standards in the areas of data, fiscal transparency, and monetary and financial policy transparency have been developed by the Fund while others have been developed by other standard setting bodies including the World Bank and the Basel Committee on Banking Supervision,' IMF 2002; cf. IMF 2001a, 2001b.
3. OECD 1998.
4. Cf. Vives 2000; Pound 1995; Schleifer and Vishny 1997.
5. The term 'East Asia' is used widely here to embrace Southeast Asian countries, such as the Philippines, Malaysia, Indonesia and Thailand. Whilst sensitive to the very real differences within each national social formation, the broader generalizations drawn here are believed to reflect adequately the state–capital relations in these countries. Moreover, these countries share more differences with the Anglo-American version of state–business relations than there are between them. For a critical insight into the models of capitalism debate, see Coates 2000.
6. Jang 2001.
7. Cf. Zysman 1983; Johnston 1999.
8. Wade and Veneroso 1998a.
9. Kapur 1998.
10. Damodaran 2000.
11. Lane et al. 1999.
12. Zhuang 2000; Claessens et al. 2000; Walker and Fox 2000.
13. 'In Praise of Rules', *The Economist*, 7 April 2001: 21; Cerny 2001.
14. Cf. Lazonick and O'Sullivan 2000.
15. Wade and Veneroso 1998b: 18.
16. Bello 1998.
17. Stiglitz 2002: 213.
18. IMF 2001b: 104.
19. See IMF, 'IMF Poverty Reduction Growth Facility', www.imf.org/external/np/exr/facts/prgf.htm.
20. Rosenau 1995; cf. Sinclair 1994.
21. Rosenau 1995: 32.
22. 'Japan Suffers Fresh Blow with S&P Downgrade', *Financial Times*, 28 November 2001.
23. Gill 1994.
24. For an excellent theorization of these transnational bourgeois linkages see van der Pijl 1993, 1998.
25. Van den Berghe and De Ridder 1999; Keasey et al. 1997; Ricketts 1998.
26. See, for example, Monks and Minow 1996; Bain and Band 1996; Barry 1998, 1999.
27. Pozen quoted in Van den Berghe and De Ridder, 1999: 16.
28. Bhagat and Black 1998; Lannoo 1999.
29. The S&P summary of corporate governance and its corporate governance scores are posted directly on the Asian Development Bank website.

30. Jang 2001: 81.
31. Fukao 1995; Van den Berghe and De Ridder 1999; Doremus et al. 1998; cf. La Porta et al. 1999.
32. Lannoo 1999.
33. OECD 1999.
34. The key components of Standard & Poor's Corporate Governance Scores are as follows:

    1. **Ownership**
       - Transparency of ownership
       - Concentration and influence of ownership
    2. **Financial Stakeholder Relations**
       - Regularity of, ease of, access to, and information on shareholder meetings
       - Voting and shareholder meeting procedures
       - Ownership rights (registration and transferability, equality or ownership rights)
    3. **Financial Transparency and Information Disclosure**
       - Type of public disclosure standards adopted
       - Timing of, and access to, public disclosure
       - Independence and standard of auditor
    4. **Board and Management Structure and Process**
       - Board structure and composition
       - Role and effectiveness of board
       - Role and independence of outsider directors
       - Board and executive compensation, evaluation and succession policies

    Source: www.standardandpoors.com/ResourceCenter/RatingsCriteria/ CorpGovScores/index.html.
35. See, for example, www.standardandpoors.com/ResourceCenter/Ratings Criteria/CorpGovScores/index.html.
36. OECD 1999: 3, emphasis added.
37. Zhuang et al., 2000: 6; Johnson et al. 2000.
38. Jang 2001: 79.
39. In employing these ideal-types, the chapter is not denying the existence of differences within the Anglo-American or bank-oriented models. Indeed there are distinctions between, for example, the United Kingdom and the United States. However, this does not discount the basic premiss of this section, which in turn supports the larger argument of the essay: namely, the existence of important similarities, such as the weight allocated to moral hazard, in each ideal-type.
40. Van den Berghe and De Ridder 1999: 40; Ackoff 1994; CalPERS 1998.
41. Van den Berghe and De Ridder 1999.
42. Vives 2000: 3.
43. Jessop 1999, 2000.

44. Cf. Lamfalussy 2000.
45. Cf. Vives 2000; Doremus et al. 1998.
46. Jessop 2000.
47. Vives 2000.
48. Fukao 1995.
49. Cadbury 1996.
50. Lamfalussy 2000: 73, emphasis added.
51. Brancato 1997: 19–20.
52. Brancato 1997.
53. Jessop 1983: 285.
54. China (including Taiwan and Hong Kong), India, Indonesia, Brazil, Mexico, Turkey, South Korea, South Africa, Poland and Argentina.
55. Stremlau 1994/95: 18.
56. 'The Latest Bubble?', *The Economist*, 1 September 2001: 45. It should be noted that these hedge funds differ from the macro-hedge funds discussed in Chapter 3, for example the LTCM.
57. See Henwood 1998.
58. See, for example, Cox 1993b; Gill 1995.
59. 'In Praise of Rules', *The Economist*, 7 April 2001: 6.
60. IMF, 'Reports on Observance of Standards and Codes (ROSCs): Republic of Korea, Fiscal Transparency, 23 January 2001, www.imf.org/external/np/rosc/rosc/asp.
61. OECD 1997: 20.
62. For a good critique of the use of sound economic fundamentals as a standard with which to measure the health of an economy, see Patomäki 2001.
63. Blackburn 2002: 26.
64. Shiller 2000: 4.
65. Gill and Law 1993.
66. Wolff 2002: 127.

6

Linkages between the New International Financial Architecture and the Emerging Development Architecture: The Case of the Monterrey Consensus

In our attempt to deconstruct the common-sense understanding of the new international financial architecture, through the identification and examination of its underlying contradictions, we have been able not only to go beyond its institutional structure but also to deepen our grasp of this new initiative as a class-led strategy aimed at reproducing the status quo in the global political economy. The question that emerges here is, why does imposed US leadership strive to appear to be inclusive and cooperative vis-à-vis the South? To address this question we need to look more closely at how powerful international policymakers have attempted to link the objectives of the NIFA with the emerging international development architecture. This chapter seeks to explore the linkages between the international financial and development architectures by examining the recently forged Monterrey consensus. The broad analytical framework introduced in Chapter 1 will be drawn on implicitly here in order to understand the nature of the linkages by situating its meaning within the inherent contradictions and class-based power relations that define the global capitalist system. Specifically it is important to identify the underlying contradictions that the Monterrey consensus seeks to freeze, particularly the tensions between the Dollar Wall Street Regime, the ongoing crisis of overproduction, and free capital mobility and the South.

On 8 September 2000, heads of state committed themselves to reducing poverty in the world by 2015. To meet this objective of the Millennium Declaration, the UN Secretary-General, Kofi Annan, called for a Financing for Development (FfD) conference to take place in Monterrey, Mexico, in March 2002.[1] Following the spirit of global economic governance, FfD sought to forge new alliances between states, business and global civil society in order to achieve more equitable economic and financial governance in the world economy. For Annan, new partnerships cannot be reached without the inclusion and participation of all relevant 'stakeholders', most notably the World Bank, the IMF and the WTO. While this move was indeed one of the most innovative features of the FfD, it also served as a wellspring that fed much suspicion regarding the underlying motives.

One observer has gone so far as to state that the 'UN is weak and compromised and is now signing off on a political document which delivers nothing on debt, nothing on redistribution and reparations, nothing on the regulation of markets and corporations and nothing for the global South.'[2] According to the Bretton Woods project, approximately 700 civil society organizations (CSOs), which attended the 'Foro Global' that was held prior to the FfD conference, denounced the official report as 'it failed to offer new mechanisms to mobilise new financial resources to achieve the Millennium Development goals'.[3] Indeed the general consensus among CSOs is that the Monterrey document is nothing more than an attempt to repackage the long-dominant US-backed Washington consensus, which is marked by a set of neoliberal policies that have encouraged the dependence of developing nations on foreign investment, export-led growth, privatization, and government reduction in social expenditure.[4] The paradox that emerges here is as follows: the continued application of trade and financial liberalization by governments of developing nations, which constitutes the backbone of policy recommendations in the Monterrey report, is not only highly problematic in the current era of increasing protectionism in the North and growing financial volatility but also, and relatedly, widely seen as contributing to, rather than alleviating, poverty, human degradation and political turmoil in the South.

In what follows, it will become clearer that the primary reason for re-creating the neoliberal doctrine within the Monterrey consensus is based in the shifting architecture of aid to the South. Despite all the media attention given to the new commitments by richer states to spend more on development assistance, especially in the context of the G8 Summit in Kananaskis, Alberta, in 2002, foreign aid has become privatized over the past two decades due to general capitalist restructuring strategies. The latter were assisted through the market-led growth strategies pursued by the IMF and World Bank. As such, official government aid has lagged far behind private capital investment in developing countries. The worrying trend is that there appears to be a reduced flow of private capital from richer to poorer countries, especially after the recent spate of financial debacles in the South and the current global recession.[5]

Before proceeding with our discussion it is, once again, important to flag what is meant here regarding the 'South'. Particularly significant in terms of foreign capital investment flows is the heterogeneity of the South. As we saw in Chapter 1, for the former US Undersecretary of Commerce for International Trade, Jeffrey Garten, there are ten 'big emerging markets',[6] which 'alone contain nearly one-half of the world's population, have the most rapidly growing economies in the world, and have governments currently committed to trade-led growth and cooperation with the United States'.[7] There is another South, however. Following Samir Amin, this term embraces two categories: excluded and marginalized states – both of which include the so-called 'highly indebted poor countries'.[8] As I have argued in the previous chapters, most of the 'big emerging markets' have recently been incorporated into the rules and regulations of the G20, which falls under the ambit of the new international financial architecture, involving the IMF, World Bank, the G7, the Bank for International Settlements, and the European Union. It is interesting to note that the remaining countries of the South have not been included in this surveillance and disciplinary scheme aimed at ensuring that both public and private sectors adhere to 'proper' (read: neoliberal) management under the current reign of free capital movements (see Chapter 5 on corporate governance).

Like the NIFA, the content of the Monterrey consensus reinforces and legitimizes the coercive power of transnational capitals, most notably their ability to exercise flight or investment strikes if domestic conditions are not to their liking, such as capital controls, too many regulatory policies, undisciplined and costly (or unionized) labour markets, political instability, high environmental standards, and so forth.[9] Thus, from the perspective of capitals, the G7, and US-led international financial institutions (IFIs), the only solution to the current problem of declining aid to the ('other') South is to ensure that developing countries continue to adopt sound neoliberal policy, which implies that they open their markets up even further to the exigencies of transnational capitals.

From the above perspective, I argue that the Monterrey consensus not only serves further to legitimate an emerging official development discourse, most notably the second generation reforms of the IFIs, which, in similar vein to global governance, attempt to recast neoliberalism in terms of common values and goals through emphasis on inclusion, partnership and poverty reduction, but also seeks to legitimate, via semblances of inclusionary politics, imposed US leadership. Specifically, the Monterrey consensus is, in the first instance, concerned with reproducing and thus legitimating the growing power of transnational capitals. Thus it is not so much about reducing poverty as about managing the ever-increasing polarization of capitalist social relations in the South. In this sense, the Monterrey document not only depoliticizes the coercive power of transnational capitals by portraying their role as equal partners with civil society and states of the South but also represents their growing role in the development agenda as some sort of natural occurrence.

In what follows I not only demonstrate a continuity between the second generation reforms and the Monterrey consensus but also flush out certain issues that the latter avoids, such as the attempt to legitimate the increasing power of transnational capital in nation-states, and the increasing forms of imposed US leadership (see Chapter 3) evident in the debates about performance-based grants and sovereign bankruptcy procedures. The latter are examined in the third section of the chapter. Before shifting our analysis to the key solutions proposed by the Monterrey report, it is helpful to begin the discussion by grasping the meaning and context from which its precursor, the Washington consensus, emerged. In doing so we go over some ground already traversed in the previous chapters of the book, but this is an important exercise in terms of revisiting the underlying contradiction upon which the new international financial architecture rests in order to tie the argument of the book together:

the NIFA is a class-led project designed to re-create the norm of free capital mobility, particularly in the South.

The Washington Consensus and the Crisis of Capitalism

The fall the Bretton Woods system in 1971 ushered in a new policy and ideological orientation in the United States known as neoliberalism, which is premissed on the steadfast belief that political and social problems should be solved primarily through market-based mechanisms as opposed to state intervention. Neoliberalism quickly became the dominant policy of the international financial institutions, such as the IMF and World Bank, congealing into what many authors have referred to as the Washington consensus. Although the term conjures up images of conspiracy among US policymakers and capitals vis-à-vis the global South via the medium of the IFIs, this intellectual doctrine should be understood more as a general resolve by American political elites and the bourgeoisie that market-led reform in the developing countries would be beneficial in addressing the US's declining economic strength during this period. On the other hand, the implementation of market-led strategies aimed at export promotion industrialization clearly served the interests of indigenous bourgeoisies, too. Take, for instance, the growing polarization of Latin American societies marked by growing numbers of working poor, at one extreme, and a new class of super-rich Latin American billionaires who benefited from the buyout of public enterprises, at the other.[10] Notwithstanding this observation, the American bourgeoisie, particularly large manufacturing and financial fractions, as well as consumers throughout the industrialized world, were the greatest beneficiaries of the imposition of market-led reforms throughout the South.

In response to the waning degree of US hegemony, the American government was able to conceal its unilateral policies through the seemingly multilateral nature of the international financial institutions. Key policy instruments of the consensus were at the heart of the structural adjustment programmes administered by the IFIs, which, despite the immense diversity among developing countries, were largely homogenous in nature. As we will see below, the SAPs also assisted in creating a greater, not lesser, dependency of Third World governments on global capital markets as opposed to bilateral aid, not to mention higher poverty rates than before the debt crises of the early 1980s. Having established the capitalist nature of the Washington consensus, three caveats need to be raised at this point, as they help illuminate the context from which the Monterrey consensus surfaced.

First, and in contrast to the UN's understanding of the IFIs as 'equal partners', these multilateral institutions are not neutral and independent public authorities acting above states, but rather public authorities for transmitting the policy of the states.[11] Voting power within the IMF, for instance, is heavily skewed in favour of its largest shareholder, the United States. With its 17 per cent voting share, the American government can easily veto any changes to the IMF Charter that it perceives as going against national interests. The G7 countries, excluding the United States, have a combined voting power of 42.5 per cent compared to the meagre 39 per cent of all developing countries. Moreover, since the US donates more than 50 per cent of the World Bank standby capital, it wields hegemonic influence within this institution, usually at the expense of those countries that cannot afford to contribute such amounts. Additionally, since the entirety of World Bank loans is taken from the private financial markets at preferential rates, the Bank is dependent on the US, the G7 countries, and the international financial markets for the bulk of its working capital. Seen from this angle, it should not come as a surprise that during a second preparatory conference for Financing for Development in February 2001,

> the US representative to the UN insisted that the mandates of the WTO, IMF and World Bank 'should be respected'. The US, he said, was 'concerned that the development financing process might be used as a vehicle for the United Nations to interfere in their governance and decision-making mechanisms.' Any such attempt, he warned, would be opposed by the US.[12]

Such blatant expressions of US imposed leadership will become more evident in our discussion of performance-based grants and the management of sovereign debt, which will be dealt with later in the chapter.

Second, the Washington consensus, as its Monterrey counterpart, is not solely political in nature, but rather has its roots in the changing nature of the world economy. Put differently, although powerful leaders and policymakers in Washington created neoliberal policies that eventually formed the Washington consensus this process did not occur in a vacuum, but instead in reaction to the economic and political manifestations of what we have identified as the crisis of overproduction (see Chapter 1). It will also be recalled that an important outcome of this crisis has been the growing dependence of corporations, governments and consumers – in both the advanced and the developing worlds – on debt financing. The United States emerges as one of the largest debtor nations, albeit with loans held primarily in US dollars. Nonetheless, to finance its immense current-account deficit (or trade deficit) it requires approximately $2 billion a day. According to the IMF, this poses 'one of the biggest risks to the world economy'.[13] It should be noted that the $5 billion increase in foreign aid spending that Bush pledged at the Financing for Development meeting in Monterrey in 2002, which is to take effect in 2006, will more than likely come out of yet another debt package – that is, if the American public sanction more development aid as their own levels of indebtedness reach unsustainable proportions.[14]

Third, and related, the growing protectionism, unilateralism and fiscal overrun pursued by the Bush administration need to be understood as a historical moment of this crisis of overproduction, and not simply a reaction to the horrific events of 9/11. In other words, the performance-based grants that were proposed before the destruction of the World Trade Center, and the government's stance on sovereign bankruptcy, are intrinsically tied to the efforts to maintain US competitiveness and a dominant position in the world economy, especially in the face of the deepening of the crisis. For instance, according to MIT economist Paul Krugman the Bush administration is proposing an additional $600 billion in tax cuts and spending $15 billion on 70-tonne artillery pieces, and considering developing three different advanced fighters that even administration officials have suggested is too many.[15] Indeed, the financing for the largest package on military spending in more than two decades has been sold along patriot–traitor lines at home and the simplistic maxim of 'you are either for or against America' (the so-called 'Bush Doctrine') abroad. In the short run, the construction of nationalism and moral virtue, which has become synonymous with Bush's 'war on terrorism', has taken priority over other policy concerns. The fear of public backlash has made many policymakers wary of criticizing the administration's budget for the fiscal year 2002, which came wrapped in the colours of the American flag. To legitimate further the increased spending on the war effort, the Treasury Secretary has openly stated that America's huge external deficit is, contrary to the position of the IMF, 'a meaningless concept' (the so-called 'O'Neill Doctrine). For O'Neill, 'the deficit merely reflects the fact that foreigners, attracted by superior returns, want to invest in America.'[16] The message to the American public is clear enough: 'spend, especially by purchasing US products, regardless of your debt levels.' Indeed, if one is to believe the government and media, it is the patriotic duty of the American citizen to spend in order to ease the economy out of its slump. Consumer spending, combined with Bush's military Keynesianism, it is widely believed, will steer the US economy towards a so-called 'soft-landing' (e.g. maintenance of relatively low interest, inflation and unemployment rates). Ironically, the 'meaningless concept' of the US external deficit turns out to be rather significant for developing countries, as it is a 'fundamental' that private capital markets are used to gauge the creditworthiness of a debtor country.

This discussion acts as a primer in understanding not only why the nature of aid assistance has changed so drastically over the past decade, but also why advanced industrialized countries, especially the most powerful of all, the US, remain reluctant to increase their current levels of spending on development aid. While the chapter returns to this point, it first looks at how market-led reforms have produced both a threat and an opportunity for the developed world, since the Monterrey consensus is a direct reaction to these concerns.

Neoliberalism under Fire:
New Threats and Opportunities

Given the ongoing crisis, why would capitals and policymakers from advanced industrialized countries be interested in expanding their markets southward? The answer is that developing countries pose an opportunity for the industrialized countries to overcome the barriers posed by the crisis. As Gerald K. Helleiner notes,

In purchasing power parity terms, developing countries already account for fully 44 per cent of world output. According to the World Bank, by the year 2010 they will account for 56 per cent of global consumption and 57 per cent of global capital formation. How many know that during the 1991 recession in the industrial world three-quarters of the increase in world exports, which buffered their problems, went to developing country markets? How many G7 businessmen know that developing-country offers of increased market access in the Uruguay Round were together worth more to the United States than those of either the European Union or Japan, or that they were worth more than those of the United States to both Japan and the European Union?... The developing countries are economically as well as demographically important, and they are very rapidly increasing their importance in the global economy.[17]

Helleiner's observations highlight the opportunities for capitalist expansion, and thus the ability to prolong high profit levels. To help capitals take advantage of the opportunities that an expansion to the South can offer, the international financial institutions have promoted liberalization of trade and finance sectors so as to create more freedom for foreign capital to enter and exit developing countries more quickly and uniformly across national spaces. More specifically, to overcome the barriers created by the crisis, the US government needs to undertake at least three strategies to assist their capitals to expand their markets: (1) attract and retain large amounts of international financial flows so as to finance its current account deficit and corporate debt; (2) secure cheaper labour markets through the construction of huge reserve armies and discouragement of union formation; and (3) expand consumer markets for its goods. Nevertheless, important barriers stand in the way of realizing these opportunities. One menacing impediment is the eroding levels of legitimacy for the neoliberal project due to higher levels of poverty and economic vulnerability in the South.

Almost two decades since the expansion of IMF conditionality within the debt crisis was issued, the gap between rich and poor countries has never been wider.[18] The world's twenty-five richest individuals possess income and assets now worth $474 billion, which exceeds the entire GNP of sub-Saharan Africa.[19] For many transnational capitalists and key international policymakers, rampant poverty in the South, if left unchecked and unmanaged, could breed discontent, which in turn could threaten not merely neoliberal domination, but more importantly the global capitalist system, from which they, as the minority of the world's population, continue to benefit. The preoccupation with the anti-capitalist backlash has become even more pressing in the post-9/11 world. As we will see below, the Bush administration has used these horrific events to push through unilaterally reforms affecting the lives of millions of poor people, especially those living in what is categorized as 'highly indebted poor countries' (HIPCs) (more on this below), where, the US government believes, poverty will lead to more acts of terrorism against its country. This anxiety tempered the mood of the 2002 World Economic Forum, where sessions entitled 'New Sources of Vulnerability: Thinking the Unthinkable', 'The Future of Terrorism: What are the Next Threats?' and 'Crisis Management: Look Out Ahead' were the order of the day, as opposed to a few years ago in Davos when people like Bill Gates were running seminars like 'Wiring the World.'[20] Kofi Annan's speech at the World Economic Forum, held in New York City's plush Waldorf–Astoria Hotel, a few months after September 11th, echoed this growing fear. According to Annan the problem is 'that power and wealth in this world are very, very unequally shared, and that far too many people are condemned to lives of extreme poverty and degradation.... The perception, among many, is that this is the fault of globalization, and that globalization is driven by a global elite.'[21]

The growing discontent of neoliberal-led growth has been accompanied by the strengthening of political linkages and trans-national networks among those groups and individuals who feel a general sense of alienation from the processes of globalization. For instance, transnational social movements, under the banner of anti-globalization, pose an important ideological threat to the ongoing exploitation of human and ecological resources in the Third World by transnational corporations. The most spectacular of these has been the 50,000 civil society organization World Social Forum (WSF) held three times in Porto Alegre since 2001. As Hilary Wainwright notes,

The representative of the World Bank was turned away from the [WSF] conference. Twice as many French ministers, seeking moral credit for the forthcoming elections made their way to Brazil, than to the World Economic Forum in New York. The latter gathering of the economic elite is increasingly adopting the rhetoric of a social agenda; leaders of Coca-Cola, McDonald's and Siemens amongst others feel moved, or shaken, to issue a statement on 'corporate citizenship'. The *Financial Times* intones about the need to seek profits in a way that 'respects the reasonable interests of others'. It adds in a give-away line, 'but we cannot make this a legal requirement'.[22]

For a growing number of people living in the South, neoliberal policies emulated in the structural adjustment policies have not made good on their promises either to address the yawning gap between income disparities, or building economically stronger, more resilient economies. Argentina is an obvious case in point, where, in a country with a population of 35 million, 19 million were classified poor as of June 2002, 'with earnings of less than $190 a month; 8.4 million were considered destitute, with monthly incomes below $83'.[23] This represents a poverty rate of 54 per cent of the population, whereas in 1993, according to the World Bank, the poverty rate was a mere 17.6 per cent.[24] Unfortunately, Argentina is far from an anomaly, in terms of either poverty rates or sovereign bankruptcy. Poverty rates and informalization of the workforce, including child labour, are growing rampantly throughout the South, especially in South Asia and the Pacific.[25] Even the country hosting Financing for Development, Mexico, boasts an increase in poverty rates, currently hovering around 40 per cent, since the NAFTA came into effect in 1994.[26] In the wider context of the crisis of overproduction in global capitalism, which is compounded by increased policy constraints imposed historically by structural adjustment programmes, it is becoming increasingly difficult for governments of developing countries to sell the virtues of the Washington consensus without taking a fall in popularity and legitimacy.

Although governments of developing nations are continuing to implement neoliberal policies, which are deemed necessary to attract and retain much-needed foreign capital inflows, they are desperately seeking ways of 'humanizing' the form of these policies. The veritable growth industry of anti-poverty programmes in the

South over the past decade is a case in point. Some pundits have gone so far as to call for a new development agenda and increased policy autonomy that will assist them in overcoming what the executive secretary of the UN Economic Commission for Latin America and the Caribbean, José Antonio Ocampo, describes as a 'crisis of the state'.[27] A return to a more inward-looking form of capital accumulation – for example, closed capital accounts, or what Samir Amin and others have referred to as the 'delinking' process – is, once again, moving into the policy debates in developing nations.[28] This poses a substantive threat to those interests that benefit from the attempts by the IFIs and other transnational actors (credit agencies, the Financial Stability Forum, the World Economic Forum, the Trilateral Commission, etc.) to homogenize policy formation in the South, which hinges on keeping capital, labour and consumer markets liberalized and well disciplined. Briefly, by granting the local bourgeoisie more control over the accumulation process, the delinking strategy delimits the opportunities for the strategy of market expansion of advanced countries continually to impede the realization of self-centred development in the South, especially as the G7 countries are more aggressively expanding to the developing world in order to overcome the barriers to capital valorization in this current crisis phase.

The threats to the legitimacy of neoliberalism, and thus to the global capitalist system, and opportunities to overcome the profitability barriers inherent within the crisis of overproduction comprise the key explanations for the growing concern of the developed countries for poverty alleviation and continued neoliberal reform in the South. The second-generation reforms and the Monterrey consensus are cases in point, but so too are the Free Trade Area of the Americas (FTAA) and the recent preoccupation of the G8 organisers to make the 'New Economic Partnership for African Development' (Nepad) a top priority for the Kananaskis summit. In all these blueprints for neoliberal-led forms of capital accumulation, the negative effects of globalization, such as increased poverty rates, growing dependency on international capital markets, and increased economic vulnerability, are not mentioned in the neoliberal solutions offered in the Monterrey report. What is promoted, however, is the need for both public and private sectors of developing countries to embrace market-based governance institutions and practices. According to a recent World Bank publication, policy modifications are necessary so that governments, financial and trade sectors, as well as participants in the developing world, can 'adapt themselves to the new, competitive open market economy'.[29]

The next section begins with an overview of the changing nature of aid to the developing world and official discourse in development, before turning to a critical assessment of two key solutions that are present both in the second-generation reforms, which represent the reformulated Washington consensus, and the Monterrey document: trade and financial liberalization.

Old Wine in a New Bottle: Recasting Neoliberal Domination

Second-generation reforms: reformulation of neoliberalism in the international financial institutions

Early criticism of the effectiveness of the structural adjustment programmes emerged within the World Bank in the late 1980s. According to one observer, 'after a decade of following the World Bank advice, living standards in Africa have fallen by 2 per cent annually, unemployment has quadrupled to 100 million and real wages have plunged by a third.'[30] In response to this crisis in legitimacy, especially regarding its increasingly apparent defunct role in the post-Bretton Woods era, the World Bank underwent an overhaul, not only in terms of its transformation from a top-down, predominately economic focus towards an allegedly more human-oriented stance (or, 'empowered development') but also in terms of balancing its stress on increasing productivity with fighting poverty. Since mid-1995, the World Bank has shifted its focus from financing infrastructural projects in the South to poverty-alleviation programmes. The IMF also plays an important role in the fight against poverty. A concrete manifestation of this new focus has been the creation of a joint programme entitled the Poverty Reduction Strategy Papers (PRSPs). According to the Bank's president, James Wolfensohn, while the IMF 'has the responsibility for macroeconomic stabilization for our client countries and for surveillance[, w]e have the responsibility for the structural and social aspects of development ... the two functions are like breathing in and breathing out.'[31] The PRSPs are inspired by the Bank's Comprehensive Development Framework (CDF), which is based upon the 'human development framework' of Nobel laureate Amartya Sen. According to Sen, development should not be based on narrow economic measurements, such as personal incomes or GNP, but instead on the real freedoms that people enjoy. In fact, these freedoms serve as both the *primary end* and *principal means* of development.[32] Reflecting this, the PRSPs emphasize 'partnership with the poor' and 'country ownership' of programmes. As Marcus Taylor notes,

> Despite the rhetorical insistence on country ownership as a means for greater participation in formulating national development agendas, the recipient country merely gets to facilitate a product developed according to World Bank priorities and aimed to tie numerous aspects of social policy formation to the larger macroeconomic framework established by the Bank and IMF.[33]

From the above perspective, then, the PRSPs are not about doing away with conditionality, but should be seen instead as direct responses to the above-mentioned 'threats to neoliberalism', which are, in turn, targeted at reconfiguring and deepening neoliberal domination over the growing number of poor in the South. Indeed in these recent transformations – generally referred to as the second-generation reforms – the World Bank has not replaced its stress on the importance of the adoption of market-led growth, but legitimizes it by softening the impact of neoliberal rule, but also reproduces the coercive power of transnational capital in these countries.[34] On the other hand, these poverty-alleviation programmes pursued by the Bank are accompanied by increased powers of surveillance and control over both public and private spheres in the South. For instance, the Reports on the Observances of Standards and Codes (ROSCs), which include data dissemination, fiscal policy transparency, corporate governance, and so forth (see Chapter 5). What is more, the Comprehensive Development Framework is thrown into a different light when we observe that its sister institution never fully changed its overt position on its preference for free-market policies, especially its promotion of capital market liberalization, which in turn grant more power to transnational capital interests. Former chief economist of the World Bank Joseph Stiglitz puts it more bluntly when he states that the IMF serves 'the interests of global finance'.[35] This explicit agenda is then 'breathed into' the implicit policies of the World Bank, as powerful states, the IFIs and the WTO attempt to construct socially a universal norm that is based on the assumption that both free capital and trade markets are not only inevitable but necessary for economic progress and general well-being. The Bank's *World Development Report 2002: Building Institutions for Markets* is a case in point:

> [This Report] goes beyond the 2000/2001 Report by analysing what institutions *do* to promote growth and facilitate access and by suggesting *how* to build effective institutions. And it emphasizes how institutions can help people make better use of the assets they own and how to accumulate more.[36]

The reformulation of the World Bank's focus on 'human development' and anti-poverty mirrors the basic assumption of the Monterrey consensus: substantial poverty reduction is more about disciplining the poor to accept the dictates of neoliberal domination than creating a more just world. This is largely because the latter goal would entail a radical restructuring of the present power relations as opposed to their reproduction.[37] Put differently, both strategies mirror each other in their attempts to 'embed' the values and norms of neoliberalism in the rapidly deteriorating social, political and economic life in the South.[38] One clear example of this is the proposal for performance-based grants.

Performance-based grants as a neoliberal disciplinary mechanism[39]

How are social relations 'managed' (disciplined) in the highly indebted poor countries so that they too may become 'opportunities' for capital expansion, and thus overcome present barriers to the crisis of overproduction? One way has been to shift popular understanding of external threats, or 'common enemies' of capitalist democracies, from communism to nationalism. More recently, especially in the United States, the linkages between nationalism and terrorism in the South have been amplified. While the constructed threat of rogue states has been an overriding concern for the US in the post-Cold War era (see, for example, Samuel Huntington's *The Clash of Civilisations*[40]), the Bush administration took this preoccupation to new heights after September 11th. For the US government, the higher the poverty rates the higher the potential for that environment to breed terrorism. In the words of President George W. Bush,

> Poverty doesn't cause terrorism. Being poor doesn't make you a murderer.... Yet persistent poverty and oppression can lead to hopelessness and despair. And when governments fail to meet the most basic needs of their people, these failed states can become havens for terror. It is time ... to close the divide between wealth and poverty, opportunity and misery. It is time for governments to make the right choices for their own people.[41]

Seen from the above perspective, in order to deter future terrorist aggression against America the government has to gain more control over what occurs within these countries so as to reproduce the existing status quo, and ensure that these countries adopt market-led policies so that they may overcome poverty. This was the larger context in which the second-generation reforms were born, as it became increasingly clear that the Washington consensus and the self-imposed role of the IMF as 'lender of last resort' would not do in ensuring the reproduction of neoliberal domination in the South. This was largely because the Meltzer Commission not only drew much public attention to the shortcomings of the IFIs but also heightened the legitimacy crisis of neoliberal restructuring of the global South, especially in the HIPCs. The Commission charged the IMF, for instance, with giving too little attention to improving financial structures in developing countries and too much to expensive rescue operations. Likewise, by its own evaluation of its performance in Africa, the World Bank found a 73 per cent failure rate: only one in four programmes, on average, achieved satisfactory, sustainable results in terms of reducing poverty and promoting the creation and development of markets and institutional structures that facilitate development.[42]

While the US Department of the Treasury agreed with some recommendations proposed by the IFI Advisory Committee, particularly that the IMF and World Bank were in need of reform, it was firmly

opposed to the Committee's suggestion that the IFIs should strive
to become more multilateral in terms of their decision-making and
policy implementation processes. To appeal to Congress, the US
Treasury dressed up its criticism by attacking the lack of 'patriotic'
interest in the Committee's report:

> The critical test in evaluating the desirability of alternative reform pro-
> posals should be an assessment of whether they would strengthen or
> weaken the capacity of the institutions to address economic challenges
> that are critical to U.S. interests. In our view, the core recommendations
> of the majority, taken together, would substantially harm the economic
> and broader national strategic interests of the United States, by reducing
> dramatically the capacity of the IMF and MDBs [multilateral development
> banks] to respond to financial crises, and by depriving them of effective
> instruments to promote international financial stability and market-oriented
> economic reform and development.[43]

For the Bush administration, a far more palatable option in
dealing with pressing issues in the Third World such as increasing
poverty rates and economic crises is unilateral-inspired solutions that
work in the interests of the US. In terms of poverty alleviation,
one way of achieving more control over the World Bank, as well as
the HIPCs, was through the International Development Association
(IDA). IDA credits refer to World Bank loans that are loaned at near
zero interest rates to the poorest seventy-two countries – that is,
those which register less than $1,500 per capita annual income. Prior
to the G8 Summit in Genoa, President George W. Bush proposed
that up to 50 per cent of its $6 billion annual outlay for grants be
made available to the world's poorest countries, the HIPCs. This is a
lot coming from one of the least generous donors. Apparently there
is little dissent within the key policymaking circles in the US regarding the grants proposal. Indeed, despite differences on other policy
recommendations put forward by the IFI Advisory Commission, its
chair, Allan H. Meltzer, and the US Undersecretary of the Treasury,
John Taylor, seem to agree that performance grants are a more effective form of control and surveillance over states and markets of the
South than traditional loans. For one thing, grants can be project-
linked and executed under competitive bids (which includes foreign
market participants) with payments shared by both the World Bank

and the beneficiary. For another, the grant scheme would allow for an independent audit and payments based on clearly quantifiable basic needs aimed at improving the quality of life and, relatedly, economic growth: primary education, health, sanitation and water, as well as the numbers of babies vaccinated, improvement of literacy rates, and so on. Or, in the words of the architects of performance grants: 'No results; no funds expended. No funds diverted to offshore bank accounts, vanity projects or private jets.'[44]

It should be mentioned that there is far from a global consensus regarding the grants proposal. In fact, the initiative has revealed deep divisions between the World Bank, the European Union and the US, which is perhaps one reason why it was not tabled at the Monterrey meeting. The World Bank and the EU fear that unless the US government is committed to increasing its contributions dramatically the proposal would ultimately bankrupt the Bank as well as reduce its policy leverage. Other critics have argued that the grants proposal would make the World Bank more powerful, since poor countries' governments would be willing to agree to even more conditions regardless of the consequences to obtain what is largely, although falsely, perceived as free money. The grant proposal poses a threat of 'mission creep', which describes 'a concern that IDA might unfairly compete with the smaller UN agencies if it has a sizeable grant program.'[45] What is more, the performance-based grants would be based upon highly subjective criteria, most of which would be designed in the interests of the United States. In addition, the goals of these grants will undoubtedly be shaped by the requirements of America's 'war on terrorism'. The amount of spending earmarked for this war is substantial. In October 2002, for instance, President Bush signed into law a huge increase in defence spending: $335 billion, which represents the biggest increase since Ronald Reagan's Cold War.[46]

While the International Development Association proposal reveals US imposed leadership in its starkest form, it is not the first attempt to gain more control over the poorer countries. In September 1999, for instance, the aims of IMF concessional lending were widened 'to include an explicit focus on poverty reduction in the context of a growth oriented strategy'. The role of the IMF was essentially to assist the World Bank in its surveillance and control over the management of aid flows in the South. This mirrors the World Bank's human development framework, discussed earlier, which is 'to be prepared with the participation of civil society – including the poor – and other development partners'. In line with these aims, and the wider PRSPs, the Fund has replaced its Enhanced Structural Adjustment Facility (ESAF) with the Poverty Reduction and Growth Facility (PRGF). According to the IMF, the latter differs from the former in the following manner. First, through the PRGF, the IMF aims to integrate the objectives of poverty reduction and growth more fully into its operations in the poorest member countries, or, more specifically, the HIPCs. Indeed, the PRGF was designed to give the IMF a more central and legitimate role in the 'HIPC initiative', which was proposed by the IFIs in 1996.

Broadly, the HIPC initiative aims to reduce the amount of debt owed by eligible countries in order to prevent them defaulting on their outstanding loans. Behind the veil of concern over easing the debt burden of the world's poorest countries, the HIPC initiative is actually designed and controlled by creditors to extract the maximum possible in debt repayments. The initiative is managed by the World Bank Group, and relies on the IMF's PRGF. To reach its goal, the PRGF places more emphasis on 'good governance' than its predecessor, which, as mentioned earlier, refers to the 'proper management' of liberalization policy along with public goods, achieving greater transparency, active public scrutiny, and so forth[47] – all of which is prescribed in the ROSCs. This move not only gives the Bank's policies some financial teeth but also permits a more comprehensive and coherent surveillance programme by allowing the IFIs to monitor more effectively, in greater detail, the countries' policy actions, the frequency of programme reviews, and the role of prior actions.[48]

Like the PRGF, the grants proposal seeks to expose the South further to the exigencies of transnational capital, especially those perceived by the US to be 'failed states' (a term that coincides with terrorism), most of which are classified as highly indebted poor countries (Afghanistan, Somalia, Nicaragua, Benin, and so forth). In addition this strategy also aims at creating greater dependence on wealthy countries, and US domestic politics in particular. The new focus on the ownership of reforms is as much a response to the widespread criticism that the IMF is not only too intrusive but also too ineffective in heading off crises. For Treasury Secretary O'Neill, crisis prevention, as opposed to the crisis management and big loan packages that marked the Clinton administration, is to be the main focus of the IMF. This concern emerges most dramatically with Washington's present stance regarding the Argentine default.

The Monterrey solution

Although the Financing for Development conference was ostensibly concerned with a substantial reduction in the levels of poverty, the world's richest countries failed to commit to levels of official development assistance. The numbers gain more meaning when we take a longitudinal view of the structural changes of development aid. At the Earth Summit in Rio de Janeiro in 1992, the governments of wealthy (OECD) countries adopted what is referred to as 'Agenda 21', which includes an aid target of 0.7 per cent of GDP. To date, only five countries (the Netherlands, Denmark, Norway, Sweden and Luxembourg) meet the 0.7 per cent target; while the United States, the world's wealthiest country, allocates a mere 0.1 per cent of its GDP to development assistance, and Britain, despite all the talk of Chancellor Gordon Brown, contributes a meagre 0.23 per cent, less than the EU average of 0.33 per cent. The bottom line is that if the world's wealthiest countries were to spend 0.7 per cent of GDP on aid, development assistance would be $114 billion more than developing countries are currently receiving.[49]

Underlying these figures has been the trend of official development finance, and in particular its largest component, bilateral aid, to lag behind private flows since the early 1990s (see Table 6.1). Indeed, over the past decade aid as a share of central government spending has fallen from 0.82 per cent to 0.58 per cent.[50] It is important to note that transformation of the structure of lending is also deeply rooted in the crisis of overproduction, especially the restructuring strategies undertaken by major industrialized countries to overcome limitations to capital valorization over the past decade. This tendency, for instance, reflects the outcome of almost two decades of market-led development, stemming primarily from the policies tied to the Washington consensus and the largely state-led initiative to grant finance more power through, for example, the process of financial disintermediation and, more recently, the repeal by the US government of the Glass–Steagall Act in 1999. This move allows US investment banks to increase their leverage in the pursuit of more high-risk, high-yield bonds and uncertain, but potentially large, capital gains on equity and bond investments. On the other hand, to break the barriers to capital valorization there was a need for states to implement trade rules that would allow their transnational capitals to reach labour and consumer markets, not to mention the lax taxation and environmental standards of the developing world. The WTO has played a key role in facilitating the further reduction of trade barriers in the developing world, which also explains the rise of foreign direct investment (FDI) to the South over the past decade. Moreover, the General Agreement on Trade and Services, which was originally agreed at the WTO in 1994, will remove any restrictions and internal government regulations in the area of service delivery that are considered to be barriers to trade, such as libraries, schools, hospitals, banks, rubbish collection and even water.

The question that emerges here is, if an increase in official assistance is not forthcoming, where is the financing for development to originate? The Monterrey document makes clear that financing is to be extracted from international capital markets. In order to overcome high levels of poverty, developing countries must be in a position to lure in private international capital flows by attempting 'to achieve a transparent, stable and predictable investment climate, with proper enforcement and respect for property rights, embedded in sound macroeconomic policies and institutions that allow businesses, both domestic and international, to operate efficiently and profitably and with maximum development impact.'[51] The upshot of this neoliberal orthodoxy has not only been increased poverty, dependence and vulnerability in the developing world but also the concentration and centralization of wealth in the G7 countries. Thus themes of threats and opportunities weave in and out of the two key policy initiatives in both the Washington consensus, including the second-generation reforms, and the Monterrey report: namely, trade and financial liberalization.

Who has benefited from over twenty years of trade and financial liberalization? And, broadly speaking, how are these two forms

Table 6.1   Net long-term resource flows to developing countries, 1991–2000 ($ billion)

	1991	1992	1993	1994	1995	1996	1997	1998	1999	2000[a]
Total	123.0	155.8	220.4	223.7	261.2	311.2	342.6	334.9	264.5	295.8
Official flows[b]	60.9	56.5	53.6	48.0	55.1	31.9	42.8	54.6	45.3	38.6
Private flows	62.1	99.3	166.8	175.7	206.1	279.3	299.8	280.3	219.2	257.2
Capital markets	26.3	52.2	100.2	85.6	99.1	147.8	127.2	103.5	33.8	79.2
Debt flows	18.8	38.1	49.2	50.5	63.0	98.7	97.0	87.9	0.6	31.3
Bank lending	5.0	16.2	3.4	8.7	30.5	33.7	45.2	50.0	−24.6	0.7
Bond financing	10.9	11.1	36.6	38.2	30.8	62.5	49.0	40.9	25.4	30.3
Other	2.8	10.8	9.2	3.6	1.7	2.4	2.7	−3.0	−1.6	0.3
Equity flows	7.6	14.1	51.0	35.2	36.1	49.2	30.2	15.6	34.5	47.9
Foreign direct investment	35.7	47.1	66.6	90.0	107.0	131.5	172.6	176.8	185.4	178.0

[a] Preliminary   [b] Based on OECD DAC's *Geographic Distribution of Flows*.

Source: World Bank Group 2001: 36.

of liberalization related? It is to these questions that the discussion now turns.

A Critical Assessment of Trade and Financial Liberalization as Tools in Development

On the merits of trade liberalization

A universal, rule-based, open, non-discriminatory and equitable multi-lateral trading system, as well as meaningful trade liberalization, can substantially stimulate development worldwide, benefiting countries at all stages of development. In that regard, we reaffirm our commitment to trade liberalization and to ensure that trade plays its full part in promoting economic growth, employment and development for all. We thus welcome the decisions of the World Trade Organization to place the needs and interests of developing countries at the heart of its work programme, and commit ourselves to their implementation.

The Monterrey Consensus, 'Final Outcome of the International Conference on Financing for Development'[52]

The former ambassador to the United Nations from Peru, Oswaldo de Rivero, argues that of the 158 developing countries only four newly industrialized countries (NICs) remain economically viable after the recent East Asian crash of 1997/98: namely, 'two city-states (Singapore and Hong Kong) and two small countries (South Korea and Taiwan). Yet these countries constitute only 2 per cent of the population of what the experts have been calling, for the last forty years, the "developing world".'[53] De Rivero goes on to point out that these four NICs possess at least two related features that are absent in other developing countries, especially the HIPCs. First, there is a significant technological progress in production methods and thus an ability to achieve higher-level exports – that is, by moving away from low-value-added primary production. Second, there has been a significant demographic shift from the poor to the middle class.[54] One-quarter of the world's population earn under $1 per day, with 100 million children living or working on the streets.[55] Indeed, an increasing amount of these poor people, especially women and children, work in the in the so-called informal economy. As Elmar Altvater suggests, the informal economy has grown as a result of rising unemployment and underemployment, with, for example, the percentage of informal labour in total employment ranging from 30 per cent in Chile to 84 per cent in Uganda.[56]

Despite promises made at the Doha trade negotiations, and growing criticism from the international financial institutions, the US has long taken a protectionist stance towards agriculture and textiles (not to mention steel), which account for 70 per cent of the Third World's exports. The US government (both houses) recently passed a farm bill that would increase government spending on agriculture by 80 per cent. This translates into an increase of $82 billion over the next ten years, or about $1 billion a day, to protect American farmers (three-quarters of the money will go to the biggest and richest 10 per cent) – in short, a form of protectionism that will severely hurt the major activity of Third World countries.[57]

The European Union is equally protectionist. The regional trade bloc spends 25 per cent more subsidizing farmers through its Common Agricultural Policy (CAP) than on development assistance, most of this money ($35 billion) earmarked for subsidies to large commercial farms. According to a study by Marc L. Busch and Eric Reinhardt on the GATT/WTO trade dispute settlement, the WTO has been no more effective in resolving conflict between the US and the European Union than the General Agreement on Tariffs and Trade it replaced. The study goes on to reveal that, and in contrast to the optimism of the Monterrey report, 'the higher the political and economic stakes involved in the WTO case, the less likely the losing side has been to comply with a ruling against it'.[58] Put another way, the more economically powerful a country, the more able it is to protect its citizens from the effects of the crisis of capitalism through its ability to counter or dominate key multilateral institutions – the WTO in this case. The upshot of these actions – not properly addressed in the Monterrey document – is the deepening of poverty in the South, as opposed to its alleviation. Moreover, increasing agricultural protectionism poses a threat to the legitimacy of the Doha negotiations that aim to overcome existing non-tariff barriers in agriculture and textile products in the South.

If fair trade exchanges between powerful trading partners are not taking hold, then how are poorer countries to overcome increasing rates of poverty, especially in the wake of the deepening economic slowdown in the G7 countries? By neglecting the asymmetrical features of production and exchange in the global capitalist world order, as well as the ongoing crisis of overproduction, which is spurring on the bouts of protectionist policies, the Monterrey consensus document fails to address one of the main reasons for the growing levels of poverty in the Third World. It augments the problem by insisting that it will disappear when the developing nations adopt more trade liberalization, especially those laid out in the current Doha negotiations, and 'good governance' (read: neoliberal policy formation).

On the merits of financial liberalization: increased instability and vulnerability

Like trade liberalization, financial liberalization poses both threats and opportunities to transnational capitals and the US. Or, as one observer has phrased it: 'when financial transactions across the globe add up to 360 times the value of transactions in goods and services, the global economy is walking on eggshells'.[59] Within the wider context of financialization, the neoliberal-led Washington consensus has had at least two important consequences for the developing world. First, through its policies, the consensus has assisted in increasing the dependency of emerging market economies on short-term flows as their primary source of credit. Second, this move has led to the concentration of power in an increasingly smaller number of institutional investors (pension and mutual funds), which, in effect, has led to a situation where decisions relating to capital allocation have become more and more centralized.[60] Taken together, these two trends have led to the growing dependence of both states and markets of the developing world on the coercive power of a transnational rentier class, most but not all of whom are from the North.[61]

There are several worrisome trends in private international financial flows that the Monterrey consensus failed to highlight as it toed the official IMF line, echoing the need to maintain open capital accounts. First, as Ocampo observes, the majority of private flows have been concentrated in middle-income countries, the so-called emerging markets such as South Korea, China, Mexico and Taiwan, with the majority of cross-border capital flows continuing to circulate within industrialized economies. Foreign exchange markets control a large proportion of these transactions, most of which are dominated by US investment banks.[62] Second, as the past several crises have demonstrated, a high concentration of the most volatile flows tend to gravitate to middle-income countries, while low-income countries have thus been marginalized from private flows and have continued to depend on official aid. Third, despite the implementation of neoliberal policies, most notably trade and financial liberalization, the ongoing productivity crisis has not led to the investment of these funds in the sphere of production and thereby employment; instead, as mentioned above in the Mexican case, growing speculative activities have become an end in themselves in that they are reinvested in the more profitable financial sphere.[63] According to the World Bank, at least a part of the decade's increase in capital inflows to developing countries 'may reflect transactions tied to capital outflows, perhaps to avoid taxes' (round-tripping).[64] Finally, the share of developing countries in these flows declined sharply after major financial crises in Mexico (1994/95) and East Asia. The World Bank report on *Global Development Finance 2002* predicted no significant recovery in capital flows in the emerging markets until perhaps 2003. This in turn prevents a somewhat optimistic calculation based upon not simply an economic recovery in the developed world, but one coupled with low interest rates. In *Global Development Finance 2003* the World Bank downgraded this prediction considerably, to 'It is unlikely, however, that private flows to developing countries will return to the levels of the 1990s.'[65]

Internal dissent in the US regarding the free capital mobility imperative was evident when Congress baulked when the Clinton administration attempted to bail out Mexico in the 1994/95 peso debacle (see Chapter 2). In response to legislation authorizing $18 billion of additional US funding for the IMF, Congress established the International Financial Institution Advisory Commission (more popularly known as the 'Meltzer Commission') in November 1998 to advise on future US policy towards several multilateral institutions: the IMF, the World Bank Group, the regional development banks, such as Inter-American Development Bank, the Bank for International Settlements, and the WTO.[66] Interestingly enough, although this decision would affect over half the world's population, the debate only involved US nationals.

Relatedly, the Asian crash revealed deep fissures both within the US and among the G7 countries regarding the desirability of continued freedom of cross-border financial flows. High-profile US policymakers and economic pundits, such as former Federal Reserve chairman Paul Volcker, and Joseph Stiglitz, began to question not only the wealth-creating properties of free capital mobility but also the lack of structural coherence for continued capital accumulation.[67] The events of the Asian bust made painfully clear that the underlying tenets of the Washington consensus were more than faulty. Some writers have argued that it is simply not the case that liberalized financial markets will 'consistently price capital assets correctly in line with future supply and demand trends, and that the correct asset pricing of liberated capital markets will, in turn, provide a continually reliable guide to saving and investment decisions ... and to the efficient allocation of their economic resources' – this is commonly referred to as the efficient market hypothesis.[68]

The significance of these debates lies in the fact that they represent an ideological renewal of capital controls as a necessary mechanism to reduce market volatility by seeking to curb short-term speculation. One popular way of achieving this is by imposing a steep tax on short-term inflows, an example being the Tobin tax.[69] This solution drives a stake through the heart of the Washington consensus, for a new Bretton Woods arrangement necessitates an interstate system based on serious political and economic compromises, which could serve to weaken the position of the US by limiting the immense flows of finance that act to buoy up its ever-increasing twin deficits. As Benjamin J. Cohen observes, of the possible reasons why governments may hesitate in implementing capital controls, the political opposition of the United States appears to be the most decisive.[70] Despite the fact that the burden of proof has shifted from those advocating capital controls to those in favour of capital mobility, this debate has received little attention in the Monterrey document.

A year after the Asian debacle, OECD governments unsuccessfully sought to implement the Multilateral Agreement on Investments (MAI), which would effectively give transnational finance capitals even more power within national social formations. Not to be defeated, however, the US and other wealthy nations have attempted to reimpose the power of transnational financial capital in the General Agreement on Trade in Services, which is the services arm of the WTO. Among the services covered in the GATS are financial services. The latter entail the insurance, banking and securities industries, including trading in different financial instruments and currencies, asset management, and other sectors, such as the provision of financial information or financial advisory services. Finance is not insubstantial. According to the official GATS website,

> The sector is estimated to involve US$1.2 trillion per day in foreign exchange transactions. International financing extended by banks around the world reporting to the Bank for International Settlements (March 1997) is estimated at $7 trillion, including $5.1 trillion net international lending. Total world banking assets are put at more than $40 trillion, insurance premiums over $2 trillion.[71]

With the approval of a law granting fast-track authority for President George W. Bush to negotiate trade deals, more of these

attempts to impose free capital mobility within legal trade docu-
ments for the global South can be expected.[72] Essentially the 'fast
track trade negotiation authority' (or simply 'fast track') provides
the president with the power to negotiate trade agreements without
the participation of the US Congress.[73] When a trade agreement
is negotiated using fast track, Congress must approve the entire
agreement within a very short period of time, without the power
to amend or remove specific articles or chapters.[74]

While it is difficult to see how open capital accounts and the
flow of hot money serve to alleviate poverty in developing nations, especially the highly indebted poor countries, which receive
minimal cross-border financial flows, it is clear that the imperative
of free capital mobility works in the interests of the United States.
The flows from the South help to feed its growing current account
deficit, caused by the crisis of capitalism, whilst allowing large institutional investors, most of which are based in the US, to profit
from arbitrage – that is, exploiting interest and/or currency rate
differentials across national spaces.

The case of Thailand

De Rivero's observation may also be illustrated by looking at three
of the IMF star performers ('emerging markets') we have discussed
thus far: Mexico (Chapter 2), Chile and Malaysia (Chapter 4). While
there are important historical differences among these countries,
all three share common characteristics, in terms of two seemingly
separate growth poles that mark their accumulation strategies: (1)
a high reliance on low-skilled, low-wage labour to supply their
export-platform industries; and (2) financialization. We see similar
trends when we look more closely at another 'star economy', which
enjoyed 'the world's highest growth rate from 1985 to 1995 – av-
eraging almost 9 per cent annually', only to be the first among the
greatest three casualties of the Asian debacle in 1997.[75]

Like its Malaysian and Mexican counterparts, Thailand's industrial boom was largely based on cheap labour. Similar to Mexico,
Thailand became a low-wage key export platform for assembly-in-
tensive products manufactured for Japanese, Taiwanese and American
firms for re-export to third countries. This coincided with the 1985

Plaza Accord, which effectively increased the external value of the yen, thereby making Japanese exports more expensive. In the search for cheaper labour markets in which less sophisticated components could be assembled, Thailand, with its relatively stable political regime, close proximity to Japan, and well-disciplined workforce, became a favourite for Japanese capitalists. Thus the attractiveness of the relationship rested on the baht's competitive value. As long as the yen remained appreciated, assets in other Asian countries appeared ludicrously cheap to Japanese investors. The Thai government was a manifestation of the changing relations between labour and capital, which included moves towards export manufacturing, the privatization of public enterprises, and the state's promotion of more explicit power to transnational capitals in policymaking and decisions regarding the allocation of public assets. The legitimacy of the Thai state was intimately tied to the steady infusion of transnational capital, so as to provide jobs and material concessions to the more powerful sectors of labour, particularly the burgeoning urban, non-bureaucratic, white-collar workers, who were quite vocal in their discontent with the bureaucratic state and who played a key role in organizing multifaceted struggles of discontent.[76]

Augmenting this social strife, and the emerging 'crisis of authority' for the ruling classes (see Chapter 1), was a fundamental contradiction underlying Thailand's ongoing accumulation regime as an integral low-wage zone within the larger East Asian development complex centred on Japan.[77] On the one hand, the country was experiencing an increase in cost pressures as it entered into competition with other countries in the region, including newer 'tigers' in the region (such as China and Vietnam), for market shares. On the other hand, it had to cover the costs of new rounds of investment and technological innovation, cope with the rise in the dollar to which the national currency is pegged, and address workers' demands for higher wages and social welfare benefits.[78]

Thai social relations of production, including the state, capitals and labour, were to undergo even more strain with the burst of Japan's asset bubble in the early 1990s. For Thailand, the collapse of Japanese asset prices meant a substantial decrease in Japanese investment and the precipitation of intensified class-based struggles as the Thai state became more and more reliant on capital from the global financial markets. From early 1990s onwards substantial inflows of portfolio investment funds, as opposed to foreign direct investment, were to dominate the Thai economy.[79] To attract and retain capital inflows the Thai government undertook a series of competitive deregulations in order to make the country accessible to foreign capital or to provide guarantees on foreign direct borrowing by corporations. Japan came to play a central role in the regional organization of credit, or what has been referred to as 'carry trade', in short-term investments, particularly in property development.

An inherently weak economy, where the higher presence of speculative capital outweighed productive investment, was swiftly and easily annihilated by a series of blows, as in the Mexican case (see Chapter 2). These powerful hits included the Chinese devaluation in 1994, when the People's Bank of China devalued the Chinese renminbi to promote labour-intensive exports; the 1995 agreement between the Japanese Finance Ministry and the US Treasury to depreciate the yen against the dollar, thereby undermining the viability of cheap Thai exports; and the mere mention by the Japanese Ministry of Finance officials that an interest rate hike might be necessary to strengthen the yen, which had fallen a full 40 yen against the dollar to 127 yen in the preceding two years.[80] The possible removal of one of the pillars of the 'carry trade' created the impetus for a run on the baht and the collapse of Thai assets prices. Commercial and investment bankers immediately began to call in their Thai loans. Ostensibly the fact that the current account was in deficit to the tune of 8.2 per cent of GDP in 1996 struck fear into the hearts of many investors, who were reminded by investment analysts that this was roughly the same figure as that of Mexico when that economy suffered its financial meltdown in December 1994. However, Table 6.2 reveals that while the trade deficit in 1996 peaked in comparison with previous years, current account deficits were the norm for the country; while Table 6.3 reveals that much of the financing for the trade deficit was amassed from private financial markets mostly on a short-term basis – that is, until the baht was substantially devalued in 1997, which meant labour and goods at bargain rates. In the summer of 1997, almost fifteen years after its last bail-out by the IMF, Thailand would, once again, be subject to IMF conditionality, and to its newly increased forms of surveillance and neoliberal discipline under the new international financial architecture.[81]

In the attempts to assist the Asian countries (notably the IMF3: Thailand, Indonesia and South Korea) in regaining investor confidence, and thus to contain contagion, the Fund only deepened the sense of panic by drastically slashing government expenditures to achieve a budget surplus, bank closures and high interest rates. According to the first systematic review within the IMF of the policy response to the crisis, its origins lay in serious vulnerabilities in banking and corporate sectors, or, more generally, in crony Asian capitalism.[82] The Fund argued that this form of capital development rested on a highly concentrated ownership structure (e.g. 'bamboo networks' and 'pyramids'), excessive government intervention, opaque exchange and regulatory regimes that encouraged short-term foreign currency exposure, as well as problematic stock imbalances – all of which existed in conjunction with the volatility of short-term capital flows and external shocks – most notably terms-of-trade deterioration and slowing growth of export markets. Using its newly found powers, the IMF called for structural reforms that had few precedents in depth and breadth, most notably in its obsession with directly entering the banking and financial sectors of these sovereign states.[83]

Yet if 'middle-income' countries such as Malaysia, Thailand, Mexico, and Chile are slowly 'submerging', what hope is there for the highly indebted poor countries? The Monterrey consensus holds that the best answer to this uneven development, which the report fails to acknowledge has been largely brought about by neoliberal responses to the underlying crisis of global capitalism, is to break the dependence of developing countries on cheap labour and natural resources by further exposing them to increased trade liberalization, whilst attempting to reduce trade barriers in both the industrialized and the developed countries – that is, more neoliberalism.[84] Yet the main obstacle to increasing trade liberalization in the global South lies primarily with the richer nation-states. In its recent publication, *Global Development Finance 2002: Financing the Poorest Countries*, the World Bank suggests that development and poverty reduction are hindered by 'tariffs in high-income countries on imports from developing countries, [which,] though low, are four times those col-

Table 6.2 Thailand's external trade, 1985–2000 (million baht)

	1985	1987	1989	1991	1993	1994	1995	1996	1997	1998	1999	2000
Exports	193,366	233,383	516,315	725,630	935,862	1,137,600	1,406,311	1,412,111	1,806,699	2,247,454	2,213,965	2,777,733
Imports	251,169	334,209	662,679	958,831	1,166,595	1,369,037	1,706,3587	1,832,836	1,924,281	1,774,076	1,907,100	2,494,160
Balance	−57,803	−34,356	−14,6364	−233,201	−230,733	−231,437	−357,276	−420,725	−117,582	473,378	306,865	283,573

Source: Asian Development Bank 2001.

Table 6.3 Thailand's external indebtedness, 1985–99 (US$ million)

	1985	1987	1989	1991	1993	1994	1995	1996	1997	1998	1999
Total outstanding	17,546	20,385	23,537	37,772	52,717	65,596	100,093	107,778	109,731	104,943	96,335
Long-term debt, public and publicly guaranteed	9,854	13,912	12,513	13,309	14,776	16,266	16,881	16,929	22,324	28,113	31,011
Long-term debt, private non-guaranteed	3,370	2,837	4,640	11,971	15,307	20,152	39,117	48,235	47,142	43,931	38,475
Short-term debt	3,200	2,664	6,112	12,492	22,634	29,179	44,095	42,613	37,836	29,600	23,418

Source: Asian Development Bank 2001.

lected from developed countries (0.8 per cent as opposed to 3.4 per cent).[86] The most restrictive barriers are targeted at labour-intensive manufacturers and agricultural commodities, which in turn push more and more people into the informal sector. According to the UNDP, industrialized countries devoted more than $353 billion, or approximately seven times the total aid of the ODA (Overseas Development Assistance), to protect agriculture in 1998. At the same time, the policy choices available to governments in poorer countries are narrowed by conditionalities imposed by international financial institutions and bilateral donors.[86]

The discussion will now briefly explore a key policy issue that, while having a direct bearing on both financing for development and the eradication of poverty, was not adequately discussed during the Financing for Development meeting – despite having ramifications for over half the world's population – though it was hotly debated in the United States: namely, sovereign bankruptcy procedures. The significance of the following section is that it sheds light on the power structures underlying the Monterrey report, as well as revealing the attempts by the US to mitigate the above-mentioned threats to the existing capitalist order.

The Excluded Debate: The Case of the Sovereign Debt Restructuring Mechanism

At first glance the US and the IMF may appear to have acted inconsistently with regard to the countries, circumstances and conditions in which to effect bail-outs. The year before the Argentine meltdown, the Treasury Department was quick to sign over a $16 billion bail-out package when Turkey defaulted in 2000, just over fourteen months into its currency peg to the US dollar; whilst in August 2001, a year prior to Argentina's default, the US government supported a large stand-by loan package. More recently, and after the Argentine meltdown, in August 2002 the IMF came to the rescue of a larger neighbour, offering Brazil $30 billion to calm the country's roiled markets. According to Brazil's central bank, its debt-to-GDP (gross domestic product) ratio was 61.9 per cent by the end of July 2002.[87] Prior to the Brazilian debt crisis of 1982, its debt service ratio was 63.3 per cent (1979).[88] Yet the IMF did not rush to rescue Argentina, the largest-ever sovereign default in dollar terms ($155 billion), in December 2001. White House and Treasury officials say that by letting Argentina suffer the consequences of its own mismanagement, the US government wishes to send out a clear signal that it 'would be a reluctant financial fire-fighter and that the markets should not bet on a bailout'.[89] Why the discrepancy? Part of the answer lies in self-interest on the part of the US. As Susan Strange observed over two decades ago,

> Without its ever being stated in so many words, the Fund's operational decisions made its resources available neither to those in greatest need nor to those with the best record of good behaviour in keeping to the rules, but paradoxically to those members whose financial difficulties were most likely to jeopardise the stability of the international monetary system.[90]

Given the high levels of indebtedness of developing countries, as well as the fact that the key players in this debt load are institutional investors in the private sector, guaranteeing stability of the international monetary system today no longer implies bail-outs, but rather arrangements for market participants to have more direct control over policy formation in the global South. For the US, this has also implied more direct American control over the IMF. During the spring 2002 meetings of the IMF and the World Bank in Washington DC, the G7 finance ministers and the IMF's monetary and finance committee endorsed a twin-track approach to improving procedures for dealing with sovereign bankruptcies. It is important to register that what the G7 ministers received, however, was a watered-down version of what was originally proposed by the IMF's deputy managing director, Anne Krueger, in November 2001.

Broadly, Krueger's original proposal suggested a 'sovereign debt restructuring mechanism' (SDRM–1) that would entail a new international legal framework based on the features of domestic bankruptcy proceedings in the private sector. The SDRM was essentially aimed at creating a binding set of laws through which crisis-stricken countries could halt panics and keep investors from pulling their money out of the nation – buying time for political leaders to work out debts in an orderly fashion – much like Chapter 11 of US bankruptcy law. Under the proposal, the Fund was to become responsible for overseeing the SDRM–1. The latter describes a process in which countries in crisis would call a stop to debt payments as they negotiated with private-sector lenders, under the jurisdiction of a new international judicial panel. During these negotiations, the debtor country would effectively be protected from litigation by the IMF. The conditions of repayment after a country declared bankruptcy would be negotiated among the creditors by supermajority, whereby 60–75 per cent of creditors agree to terms of restructuring, which would then be binding for the rest of the creditors and, of course, the debtor country. The proposed role of the IMF would be to oversee voting and adjudicate disputes in this process. As Krueger notes, 'the Fund's role would be essential to the success of such a system'.[91] For the SDRM–1 to be realized, however, the IMF's Articles of Agreement (i.e. its constitution) would have to undergo reform. As noted earlier, for any such change to occur, the US, which wields veto power, has to agree.

The US government did not agree with the conditions set out in the SDRM–1, however. After being heavily criticized by the Treasury Undersecretary, Krueger revised her proposal (SDRM–2) so as to enhance the role and power of creditors. Essentially the SDRM–2 was more in line with Taylor's insistence on a decentralized, market-based approach that made broader use of 'collective action clauses' (CACs) in bonds issued by a sovereign government's provisions. These CACs allow a supermajority of bondholders to approve a restructuring; thus it becomes easier to restructure debt by allowing a majority of creditors to impose a deal. A supermajority of creditors is deemed important as it overcomes the problem of 'collection action', which occurs when individual creditors 'consider that their interests are best served by preventing what is termed a "grab race." The latter occurs when creditors try to get the best deal possible from the debtor government so as to enforce their claim as quickly as possible. This grab race is believed to hinder other creditors and thus may lead them in capturing the limited assets available.'[92] Krueger's modified SDRM–2 effectively reduced the amount of control the IMF had over how the standstill (a temporary suspension of payments) would work, or even how debts would be restructured. What is more, the SDRM–2 is far from transparent, or inclusive. The only seemingly independent forum attached to the SDRM–2 process is the Dispute

Resolution Forum (DRF). The powers of the DRF are limited in two ways. First, although the IMF has stated that the DRF should be independent of the Fund, it has also indicated that it would retain a veto over DRF decisions. Second, the SDRM–2 does not include citizen participation in the resolution processes of financial crises.

On the one hand, the SDRM–2 prefers a laissez-faire approach, allowing market participants more power in the default procedure. This presents a device clearly designed to increase the coercive power of transnational capital over debtor countries. Private financial institutions, led by their association, the Institute of International Finance, have played a tactical game of supporting collection action clauses in the apparent hope of killing the plan for a judicial mechanism that would in effect reduce their power.[93] On the other hand, as is clear from the Treasury's response to the Meltzer Commission, mentioned earlier, it does not want the IMF to assume a life of its own or to see the creation of a new and truly global financial institution that could oversee such processes, as this could entail moving towards multilateral as opposed to unilateral forms of norm creating and decision-making processes.[94] The latter could threaten US strategies aimed at dealing with the manifestations of the crisis of overproduction.

Official debates on the SDRM have excluded developing countries. In fact, up until the Annual Meeting of the IMF and the World Bank – which included the G7 Finance Ministers – in early Autumn 2002, official discussions surrounding sovereign debt default have taken place between the Fund and the US Treasury. Given the importance of this issue to industrialized countries, acting on behalf of the interests of transnational capitals that have supplied the credit to emerging markets, the SDRM was not on the table at the Monterrey gathering. Indeed a fair, independent and transparent process for negotiating debt restructuring would prove fatal to the disciplinary effects involved in bankruptcy. Neither the debtor country nor its citizens should have a voice in the negotiations. An act of exclusion, as many Argentines know too well, is necessary to bring together 'like-minded' groups and individuals to the table. The SDRM is also reserved for important emerging market economies, and thus not applied across the board to all classes of debtors, such as the highly indebted poor countries.[96] More importantly, the debates surrounding the SDRM seem to normalise the fact that sovereign debt default, which is a reality for Argentina, and may equally become one for Uruguay, and perhaps Brazil, with countless more to follow, is an acceptable prospect. Indeed, the fact that international policymakers are seriously debating the issue suggests that this is to be a regular occurrence in the world economy. Relatedly, another feature of the debate that is neglected is that sovereign debt default runs contrary to the neoliberal logic that unfettered market freedom leads to economic viability for the South.

Performance-based grants and methods to deal with sovereign bankruptcy both relate directly to the issue of poverty and its alleviation. So why were these topics not debated at the Monterrey gathering? Why were they so blatantly sidestepped in the report? The absence of these two policies, alongside the neglect of the political and economic ramifications of the debates surrounding the Meltzer Commission, makes it quite clear that American domination over other advanced industrialized states and the developing world, as well as the perceived threats and opportunities of US political and economic elites to this rule, will continue to shape the definition and parameters of development well beyond the Monterrey consensus.

Financing for Whose Development? The Linkages Revealed

When viewed from these alternative angles, it is clear that the Monterrey consensus attempts to re-create the current conditions of exploitative and uneven global capital accumulation primarily by manufacturing the common-sense assumption that the adoption of neoliberal reforms is an inevitable and logical strategy for developing countries in order to attract sorely needed foreign investment. Thus, in stark contrast to the mainstream understanding of global economic governance, there is a steering mechanism in the official development discourse: the US-dominated international financial institutions and transnational capitals. Moreover, it is indeed analytically and politically dangerous to conceal the class-based nature of this steering mechanism behind the rosy, pluralist level playing field painted by advocates of global economic governance.

While the adoption of hyper-neoliberal policies may lure invest-ment to the continent, the questions that emerge are not only 'at what price?' but also 'who pays?' The New Partnership for African Development, Nepad, for instance, 'targets a highly ambitious annual foreign investment of $64 billion – more than seven times higher than the total amount of investment in Africa in 1999'.[96] One only has to look at Argentina, Uruguay, Brazil, and even Mexico to learn where Africa is headed, should it embrace this blueprint for economic renewal, based on the premiss, indeed condition, of free capital mobility and trade liberalization.

This is not to say that the aims of the Millennium Summit are unimportant. We do need to work on reducing the proportion of people (currently 20 per cent) who are unable to access, or to afford, food and safe drinking water, as well as ensure that all children receive the minimum of a primary education by 2015. Yet, over two decades of neoliberal-led policies informed by the Washington consensus and its reinvented form, the second-generation reforms, have clearly shown that open capital and current accounts, and the massive erosion of national policy determination tied to such strate-gies, are not conducive, indeed run contrary, to these aims. While the limitations posed by the inherent nature of uneven development of the capitalist world market should be kept in mind, serious con-sideration should be given to alternative models of growth. These include: fundamentally transforming aid procedures and practices by untying aid; promoting fair trade practices within and between nation-states; endorsing co-operative farming and manufacturing sectors; legitimizing competing development strategies that seek to move towards a delinking from the IFIs and WTO so as to make national governments accountable first and foremost to the poor and trade unions as opposed to foreign investors, and so forth. Additionally, these alternatives that provide the disenfranchised with economic security, education and health should not be universally prescribed, but rather developed through dialogue with those indi-viduals and groups who are to benefit from their implementation. Finally, the struggles involved in forging and financing developing policies designed to empower the poor can only be realized if a parallel strategy is put in place: not only rolling back the power of transnational capitals but also keeping this power in check by adequate forms of government intervention, particularly vis-à-vis financial liberalization. Only such a dual-pronged approach will ensure that progressive struggles avoid following the underlying agenda shared by the SGRs, the Washington consensus, the Monterrey consensus, and the new international financial architecture: namely, class-led attempts to reconstruct unceasingly the coercive and ideological power of transnational capital and the United States in neutral, rational, inevitable, universal and egalitarian terms.

Notes

An earlier version of this chapter appears in *Alternatives*, forthcoming, 2004.

1. For more details on the Millennium Declaration, see the United Nations website at www.un.org/millennium/declaration/ares552e.htm.
2. Focus on the Global South, 'The Road to Monterrey Passes through Washington' *Focus on Trade* 75, March 2002, at www.arena.org.nz/monterrey.htm.
3. Bretton Woods Project, 'Development Finance Summit a Fiasco, Say Campaigners', *Bretton Woods Update* 27, at www.brettonwoodsproject.org/topic/reform/r2726ffd.html.
4. See, for example, the World Council of Churches (Washington Consensus) statement on the 'Monterrey Consensus Document', at www.Washington consensusc-coe.org/Washington consensusc/what/jpc/critique.html; John Foster, 'Doing the Monterrey Shuffle' *North–South Institute*, Ottawa, 2002; Canadian Council for International Cooperation, Reality of Aid: *An Independent Review of Poverty Reduction and Development Assistance*, available at www.devinit.org/realityofaid/kpolchap.htm; Iris Marion Young, 'Financing Development: A Summary and Critique of a UN report' *IDEA Newsletter*, June 2001, available at:www.carleton.ca/idea/newsletter/reports_062001_8.html.
5. 'A Survey of International Finance' *The Economist*, 18 May 2002: 27.
6. Interestingly, the term 'emerging markets' was created by the World Bank's International Financial Corporation in the 1980s to lure investors into countries that otherwise would have been snubbed as 'developing'; there has been further bifurcation in the South.
7. Stremlau 1994/95.
8. Amin 1999.
9. Gill and Law 1993.
10. Veltmeyer et al. 2000.
11. On this see Gowan 1999: 32ff.
12. *Focus on the Global South* 2002, at www.focusweb.org.
13. 'The O'Neill Doctrine' *The Economist*, 27 April 2002: 12.
14. 'O'Neill Set to Prevent Federal Default', *Guardian Unlimited*, 19 March 2002; www.guardian.co.uk/uslatest/story/0,1282,-1595956,00.html.

15. Paul Krugman, 'Bush's Aggressive Accounting', *New York Times*, 5 February 2002.
16. 'The O'Neill Doctrine'.
17. Helleiner 1996: 18–19.
18. According to the World Bank, 'The average income in the richest 20 countries is 37 times the average in the poorest 20 – a gap that has doubled in the past 40 years.' World Bank 2000: 3.
19. See excerpt from *The Reality of Aid 2002*, at www.devinit.org/realityofaid/.
20. 'Economic Forum Shifts Its Focus to New Dangers', *New York Times*, 3 February 2002.
21. 'Annan Cautions Business as World Forum Ends' *New York Times*, 5 February 2002.
22. Hilary Wainwright, 'Globalise the Left', *Red Pepper* 93, March 2002, at www.redpepper.org.uk.
23. Clare Augé, 'Argentina, Life after Bankruptcy', *Le Monde Diplomatique*, September 2002.
24. World Bank 2000: Table 4.
25. See, for example, World Bank 2000; ILO 2002; UNDP 2002.
26. Cf. Cypher 2001.
27. Ocampo 2002.
28. Amin 1990.
29. Jang Ha-sung 2001: 73.
30. Pender 2001.
31. Wolfensohn 1999: 3.
32. Sen 1999: especially ch. 2.
33. Taylor 2003.
34. Gill and Law 1993.
35. Stiglitz 2002: 207.
36. World Bank 2002.
37. For a more detailed critique of the World Bank's agenda as a capitalist strategy, see Cammack 2002.
38. Janine Brodie's work on the 'social' vis-à-vis neoliberal globalism takes us further into the paradox brought about by disciplinary neoliberalism. As Brodie argues, 'Neoliberal globalism simultaneously minimizes spaces and strategies for social intervention and maximizes the need for it.' Brodie 2002.
39. On disciplinary neoliberalism, see Gill 1999.
40. Huntington 1996.
41. E. Anthony Wayne, Assistant Secretary for Economic and Business Affairs, quoting the President of the United States, George W. Bush, 'U.S. Foreign Policy: The Growing Role of Economics', remarks to Baltimore Council on Foreign Affairs Baltimore, Maryland, 3 April 2002; available at www.state.gov/e/eb/rls/rm/2002/9155.htm.
42. The International Financial Institutions Advisory Commission official report is available at www.house.gov/jec/imf/ifiac.htm. There are numerous websites dedicated to the Meltzer Commission Report. See, for example, www.adb.

org/Documents/Slideshows/Meltzer_Report/default.asp?p=eroprsnt; www.nadir.org/nadir/initiativ/agp/free/bello/meltzer.htm.

43. US Department of the Treasury, 'Response to the IFI Advisory Commission'; available at www.treas.gov/press/releases/reports/response.pdf.

44. Lerrick and Melzter 2002: 1.

45. Vander Caceres Salazar, 'Taken for Granted? US Proposals to Reform the World Bank's IDA Examined'. Bretton Woods Project, available at www.brettonwoodsproject.org/topic/reform/r27granted.htm.

46. 'On a Hair Trigger', *The Economist*, 24 October 2002.

47. IMF, 'The IMF's Poverty Reduction and Growth Facility (PRGF)', available at www.imf.org/external/np/exr/facts/prgf.htm.

48. IMF 2001: 104.

49. Mark Tran, 'The Monterrey Poverty Summit', *Guardian*, 18 March 2002.

50. The Reality of Aid 2002, available at www.devinit.org/ktrends.pdf.

51. United Nations, 'Final Outcome of the International Conference on Financing for Development,' Summit Segment of the International Conference on Financing for Development on 22 March 2002 in Monterrey, Mexico; available at www.un.org/esa/ffd/0302finalMonterreyConsensus.pdf.

52. Ibid.

53. De Rivero 2001: 4.

54. Ibid.

55. UNDP 2000.

56. Altvater 2002: 86ff.

57. 'What the President Giveth…', *The Economist*, 30 March 2002: 13.

58. 'Drive to Head Off Transatlantic Trade Rifts', *Financial Times*, 13/14 April 2002: 4.

59. Ugarteche 2000.

60. Harmes 1998: 101.

61. Peter Gowan defines the rentiers as 'those who derive their income from extracting royalties from future production'. See Gowan 1999: 1.

62. Ocampo 2000. On the trends in private capital flows, see the World Bank Global Development Finance 2001: Building Coalitions for Effective Development Finance', available at www.worldbank.org/prospects/gdf2001/tocvol1.htm.

63. For a more detailed discussion of this phenomenon in the Chilean case, see Soederberg 2002.

64. World Bank 2001: 33.

65. World Bank 2002; World Bank 2003: 1.

66. See the Meltzer Commission Report, available at www.house.gov/jec/imf/ifiac.

67. See, for example, Cohen 2003.

68. Felix 2002.

69. Dillon 1997: 95.

70. Cohen 2003.

71. 'Opening the World Markets for Services', downloaded on 10 August 2002 at http://gats-info.eu.int/gats-info/guide.pl?MENU=ccc-5.

72. For example, the upcoming signing of the Free Trade Area of the Americas

in 2005, which is to become the largest trade bloc in the world spanning from Alaska to Argentina. More information available at www.ftaa-alca. org.

73. For a critique of this policy, see, for example, www.ibew.org/stories/ 01daily/0112/011217_ft.htm; www.globalexchange.org/fasttrack/why.html,

74. Faux 2001.

75. CIA Factbook; see http://geography.about.com/library/cia/blcthailand. htm.

76. Phongpaichit and Baker 1995.

77. Gills 1993: 205.

78. Jessop 2000.

79. Jansen 1997.

80. Bello 1998.

81. 'In light of the Asian crisis, the IMF recognises that the focus of surveillance must extend further and more deeply beyond short-term macro-economic issues. This would mean a closer and more detailed examination of the functioning of the financial sector, capital account issues, and external vulnerability.' In IMF, 'IMF Surveillance,' available at www.imf.org/exter-nal/np/exr/facts/surv/htm.

82. Lane et al. 1999; cf. Wade and Veneroso 1998a.

83. The Fund, for instance, mobilized large stand-by credits and loans in return for changes in government policies, such as: (a) government guarantees of private sector foreign debt; (b) domestic demand contraction by sharp increases in real interest rates and government budget surpluses; and (c) structural reforms in finance, corporate governance, labour markets, etc., going far beyond what was necessary to stabilize the situation. See, for example, 'A Survey of Asian Business: In Praise of Rules', *The Economist*, 7 April 2001; Zhuang et al., 2000; Wade and Veneroso 1998a; Bello 1998.

84. United Nations 2002.

85. World Bank 2002a: xii.

86. Randel et al. 2002.

87. Mark Weisbrot and Dean Baker, 'Paying the Bills in Brazil: Does the IMF's Math Add Up?', Center for Economic and Policy Research, Washington DC, 25 September 2002; available at www.cepr.net/Brazil-debt-final.pdf.

88. Kapstein 1994: 72.

89. 'Argentina Faces Harder U.S. Line', *International Herald Tribune*, 7 January 2002.

90. Susan Strange, quoted in Pauly 1997: 115.

91. Miller 2002: 4.

92. Jack Boorman, 'Sovereign Debt Restructuring: Where Stands the Debate?', speech given at conference co-sponsored by the CATO Institute and *The Economist*, New York, 17 October 2002; available at www.imf.org/external/ np/speeches/2002/101702.htm.

93. 'G7 "Breakthrough" on Debt Default', *Financial Times*, 28/29 September 2002.

94. See, for example, 'US Scorns IMF Plan for Bankrupt Governments', *Financial Times*, 6/7 April 2002; 'IMF Scales Down "Bankruptcy" Plan', *Washington*

Post, 2 April 2002; 'Economics Focus: Sovereign Bankruptcies', *The Economist*, 6 April 2002: 67.

95. Romilly Greenhill, 'IMF Meetings Give Go-ahead for Bankruptcy Plan – But on Whose Terms?', Jubilee 2000 UK, 1 October 2002; available at: www.jubilee2000uk.org/analysis/articles/imfo11002.htm.

96. 'Canada Rejects Critics of Africa Aid Plan', *Globe and Mail*, 26 May 2002.

References

Ackoff, R.L. (1994), *The Democratic Corporation: A Radical Prescription for Recreating Corporate America and Rediscovering Success* (New York: Oxford University Press).

Aglietta, M. (1979), *A Theory of Capitalist Regulation: The US Experience* (London: Verso).

Agosin, Manuel R. (1998), 'Capital Inflows and Investment Performance: Chile in the 1990s', in Ricardo French-Davis and Helmut Reisen (eds), *Capital Flows and Investment Performance: Lessons from Latin America* (Paris: OECD), pp. 111–46.

Agosin, Manuel R., and Ricardo Ffrench-Davis (1996), 'Managing Capital Flows in Latin America', in Mahbub ul Haq et al. (eds), *The Tobin Tax: Coping with Financial Volatility* (New York: Oxford University Press), pp. 89–120.

Akyüz, Yilmaz (2002), *Reforming the Global Financial Architecture: Issues and Proposals* (London: Zed Books).

Altvater, Elmar et al. (eds) (1991), *A Guide to the Debt Crisis: From Argentina to Zaire* (London: Zed Books).

Altvater, Elmar (2002), 'The Growth Obsession', in Leo Panitch and Colin Leys (eds), *Socialist Register 2002* (London: Merlin Press), pp. 73–92.

Álvarez, Alejandro B., and P. Gabriel Mendoza (1993), 'Mexico 1988–1991: A Successful Economic Adjustment Program?', *Latin American Perspectives* 78(20): 32–45.

Amin, Samir (1990), *De-linking: Towards a Polycentric World* (London: Zed Books).

Amin, Samir (1999), 'For a Progressive and Democratic New World Order', in Francis Adams et al., *Globalization and the Dilemmas of the South* (London: Macmillan), pp. 17–32.

Anjaria, Shailendra J. (1998), 'The Capital Truth: What Works for Commodities Should Work for Cash: A Commentary', *Foreign Affairs* (November/December); also at www.imf.org/external/np/vc/1998/111098.htm.

Arestis, P., and M. Sawyer (1999), 'What Role for the Tobin Tax in World Economic Governance?', in J. Grieve Smith and J. Michie (eds), *Global Instability* (London: Routledge), pp. 151–70.

Armijo, Leslie Elliot (ed.) (1999), 'Mixed Blessing: Expectations about Foreign Capital and Democracy in Emerging Markets', in Leslie Elliot Armijo, *Financial Globalization and Democracy in Emerging Markets* (New York: Palgrave/St Martin's Press), pp. 17–50.

Armijo, Leslie Elliot (ed.) (2002), *Debating the Global Financial Architecture* (Albany, NY: SUNY Press).

Arrighi, Giovanni (1994), *The Long Twentieth Century: Money, Power, and the Origins of Our Times* (London: Verso).

Asian Development Bank (1999), *Rising to the Challenge in Asia: A Study of Financial Markets*, Vol. 8: *Malaysia* (Manila: Asian Development Bank).

Augelli, E., and C. Murphy (1988), *America's Quest for Supremacy and the Third World: A Gramscian Analysis* (London: Pinter).

Bain, N., and D. Band (1996), *Winning Ways through Corporate Governance* (London/New York: Macmillan).

Banco de México (1991), *Informe Anual 1990* (México: Banco de México).

Bank for International Settlements (1996), *66th Annual Report* (Basle: BIS).

Bank Information Centre (2002), 'The International Financial Institution Advisory Committee (Meltzer Commission), July 30; available at www.bicusa.org/usgovtoversight/meltzer.htm.

Barry, Norman (1998), *Business Ethics* (London: Macmillan).

Barry, Norman (1999), *Anglo-American capitalism and the Ethics of Business* (Wellington: New Zealand Business Roundtable).

Barry, Norman (2002), 'The Stakeholder Concept of Corporate Control is Illogical and Impractical', *Independent Review* 6(4): 541–53.

Bello, Walden (1998), 'East Asia: On the Eve of the Great Transformation?', *Review of International Political Economy* 5(3): 424–44.

Bello, W., N.K. Malhotra, N. Bullard and M. Mezzera (2000), 'Notes on the Ascendancy and Regulation of Speculative Capital', in W. Bello, N. Bullard and K. Malhotra (eds), *Global Finance: New Thinking on Regulating Speculative Capital Markets* (London: Zed Books), pp. 1–26.

Bergsten, Fred C. (1998), 'Reviving the "Asian Monetary Fund"', International Economic Policy Briefs (Washington, DC: Institute for International Economics); available at www.iie.com/policybriefs/news98-8.htm.

Bhagat, Sanjai and Bernard Black (1998), 'The Relationship Between Board Composition and Firm Performance', in Klaus J. Hopt et al. (eds), *Comparative Corporate Governance: The State of the Art and Emerging Research* (Oxford: Oxford University Press), pp. 74–95.

Bhagwati, Jagdish (1998), 'The Capital Myth: The Differences between Trade in Widgets and Dollars', *Foreign Affairs* 7(3): 7–12.

Bienefeld, Manfred (1993), 'Structural Adjustment: Debt Collection Device or Development Policy? Paper prepared for Sophia University Lectures on 'Structural Adjustment: Past, Present and Future', given at Sophia University, Tokyo on 24–25 November, mimeo.

Blackburn, Robin (2002), 'The Enron Debacle and the Pension Crisis', *New Left Review* 14: 26–51; available at www.newleftreview.net/PDFarticles/NLR24802.pdf.

Bonefeld, Werner and John Holloway (1995), 'Introduction: The Politics of

Money', in W. Bonefeld and J. Holloway (eds), *Global Capital, National State and the Politics of Money* (London: Macmillan), pp. 1–6.

Bonefeld, Werner (1999), *The Recomposition of the British State during the 1980s* (Aldershot: Dartmouth Press).

Brancato, Carolyn Kay (1997), *Institutional Investors and Corporate Governance: Best Practices for Increasing Corporate Value* (Chicago: Irwin).

Brenner, Robert (1998), 'Uneven Development and the Long Downturn', *New Left Review* 229 (May–June): 1–265.

Bretton Woods Commission (1994), *Bretton Woods: Looking to the Future* (Washington, DC: Bretton Woods Commission).

Bretton Woods Project and Oxfam (2001), 'Go with the Flows? Capital Account Liberalisation and Poverty'; available at www.brettonwoodsproject.org/topic/financial/f22gowithflows1.html.

Brodie, Janine (2002), 'Globalization, Governance and Gender: Rethinking the Agenda for the 21st Century', remarks prepared for Inaugural Panel 'World and Regional Contexts'. Central American and Caribbean Regional Conference, 'Poverty Reduction, Good Governance, and Gender Equality', Managua, Nicaragua, 28–30 August, mimeo.

Buch, Claudia M. (1999), 'Chilean-Type Capital Controls: A Building Block of the New International Financial Architecture?', Kiel Discussion Essays (Kiel: Institut für Weltwirtschaft).

Burnham, Peter (1991), 'Neo-Gramscian Hegemony and the International Order', *Capital & Class* 45 (Autumn): 73–91.

Cadbury, Adrian (1996), *Corporate Governance* (Brussels: Instituut voor Bestuurders).

CalPERS (1998), *Corporate Governance Principles and Guidelines* (Sacramento, CA: California Public Employee Retirement System).

Cammack, Paul (2002a), 'Neoliberalism, the World Bank, and the New Politics of Development', in U. Kothari and M. Minogue, eds, *Development Theory and Practice: Critical Perspectives* (London: Palgrave), pp. 157–78.

Cammack, Paul (2002b), 'Making Poverty Work', in L. Panitch and C. Leys (eds), *Socialist Register 2002* (London: Merlin Press), pp. 193–210.

Cardoso, Eliana and Ann Helwege (1995), *Latin America's Economy: Diversity, Trends, and Conflicts* (Cambridge, MA: MIT Press).

Carnoy, Martin (1984), *The State and Political Theory* (Princeton, NJ: Princeton University Press).

Cartapanis, A., and M. Herland (2002), 'The Reconstruction of the International Financial Architecture: Keynes' Revenge?', *Review of International Political Economy* 9(2): 271–97.

Castañeda, Jorge (2001), 'Mexico: Permuting Power', *New Left Review* 7 (January–February): 17–41.

Cerny, Philip G. (ed.) (1993), *Finance and World Politics: Markets, Regimes and States in the Post-hegemonic Era* (Aldershot: Edward Elgar).

Cerny, Philip G. (2000), 'Money and Power: The American Financial System from Free Banking to Global Competition', in Grahame Thompson (ed.), *The United States in the Twentieth Century: Markets*, 2nd edn (London: Hodder & Stoughton), pp. 175–213.

Cerny, Philip G. (2001), 'Internalizing Neoliberalism: The New Meiji Revolution?', paper presented to the Hong Kong meeting of the International Studies Association, 26–28 July, mimeo.

Chin, Christine B. (2000), 'The State of the "State"', in Globalization: Social Order and Economic Restructuring in Malaysia', *Third World Quarterly* 21(6): 1035–57.

Clarke, Simon (1988), *Keynesianism, Monetarism and the Crisis of the State* (Aldershot: Edward Elgar).

Clarke, Simon (1994), *Marx's Theory of Crisis* (New York: St Martin's Press).

Claessens, S., S. Djankov and L. Lang (2000), 'The Separation of Ownership and Control in East Asia Corporations', *Journal of Financial Economics* 58(1/2): 81–112.

Cockcroft, James D. (1990), 'Mexico's Political Earthquake', *Monthly Review* 42(7): 39–50.

Coates, David (2000), *Models of Capitalism: Growth and Stagnation in the Modern Era* (Cambridge: Polity Press).

Cohen, Benjamin J. (2003), 'Capital Controls: The Neglected Option', in Geoffrey R.D. Underhill and Xiaoke Zhang (eds), *International Financial Governance under Stress: Global Structures versus National Imperatives* (Cambridge: Cambridge University Press); available at www.polsci.ucsb.edu/faculty/cohen/inpress/capcontrolneglect.html.

Commission on Global Governance (1995), *Our Global Neighbourhood: The Report of the Commission on Global Governance* (Oxford: Oxford University Press).

Committee on Agriculture, Nutrition, and Forestry (1998), Testimony Barbara P. Holum, Commissioner Commodity Futures Trading Commission, 16 December; available at www.cftc.gov/opa/speeches/opaholum-22.htm.

Cox, Robert W. (1987), *Production, Power, and World Order: Social Forces in the Making of History* (New York: Columbia University Press).

Cox, Robert W. (1993a), 'Gramsci, Hegemony and International Relations: An Essay in Method', in Stephen Gill (ed.), *Gramsci, Historical Materialism and International Relations* (Cambridge: Cambridge University Press), pp. 49–66.

Cooney, Paul (2001) 'The Mexican Crisis and the Maquiladora Boom: A Paradox of Development of the Logic of Neoliberalism', *Latin American Perspectives* 28(3): 55–83.

Cox, Robert W. (1993b), 'Structural Issues of Global Governance', in Stephen Gill (ed.), *Gramsci, Historical Materialism and International Relations* (Cambridge: Cambridge University Press), pp. 259–89.

Cox, Robert W. (1994), 'Global Restructuring: Making Sense of the Changing International Political Economy', in Richard Stubbs and Geoffrey R.D. Underhill (eds), *Political Economy and the Changing Global Order* (Toronto: McClelland & Stewart), pp. 45–61.

Cox, Robert W., with T.J. Sinclair (1996), 'Global Perestroika (1992)', in *Approaches to World Order* (Cambridge: Cambridge University Press), pp. 296–313.

Cutler, Claire A., Virginia Haufler and Tony Porter (eds) (1999), *Private Authority and International Affairs* (Albany, NY: SUNY Press).

Cypher, James M. (2001), 'Developing Disarticulation within the Mexican Economy', *Latin American Perspectives* 28(3): 11–37.

Damodaran, Sumangala (2000), 'Capital Account Convertibility:Theoretical Issues and Policy Options', in Walden Bello et al. (eds), *Global Finance: New Thinking on Regulating Speculative Capital Markets* (London: Zed Books), pp. 162–3.

Davis, Diane E. (1993), 'The Dialectic of Autonomy: State Actors, Class Actors, and the Roots of Economic Crisis in Mexico, 1964–1982', *Latin American Perspectives* 20(3): 46–74.

De la Rocha, Mercedes González (2001), 'From the Resources of Poverty to the Poverty of Resources? The Erosion of a Survival Model', *Latin American Perspectives* 24(4): 72–100.

De Rivero, O. (2001), *The Myth of Development: The Non-Viable Economies of the 21st Century* (London: Zed Books).

Dillon, John (1997), *Turning the Tide: Confronting the Money Traders* (Ottawa: Canadian Centre for Polity Alternatives).

Dooley, Michael P. (1996), 'A Survey of Literature on Controls over International Capital Transactions' (Washington, DC: IMF).

Doremus, Paul N. et al. (1998), *The Myth of the Global Corporation* (Princeton, NJ: Princeton University Press).

Eatwell, John and Lance Taylor (2000), *Global Finance at Risk: The Case for International Regulation* (Cambridge: Polity Press).

ECLAC (1999), *Statistical Yearbook for Latin America and the Caribbean 1999 Edition* (Santiago, Chile: Economic Commission for Latin America and the Caribbean).

Edwards, Sebastian (1999), 'How Effective are Capital Controls?', *Journal of Economic Perspectives* 13(4): 65–84.

Eichengreen, Barry (1999), *Toward a New International Financial Architecture: A Practical Post-Asia Agenda* (Washington, DC: Institute for International Economics).

Eichengreen, Barry, et al. (1999), 'Liberalizing Capital Movements: Some Analytical Issues', *Economic Issues* 17 (Washington, DC: IMF); available at www.imf. org/external/pubs/ft/issues/issues17/index.htm.

Epping, Randy Charles (2001), *A Beginner's Guide to the World Economy: Eighty-One Basic Economic Concepts that Will Change the Way You See the World* (New York: Vintage Books).

Faux, Jeff (2001), 'Fast Track to Trade Deficits: Mushrooming Foreign Debt Begs for Strategic Pause before Approving New Agreements', Economic Policy Institute, Issue Brief No. 170 (Washington, DC: Economic Policy Institute).

Fazio, Hugo (2000), *La transnacionalización de la economía chilena: Mapa de la Extrema Riqueya al año 2000* (Santiago: Editorial LOM).

Federal Reserve Board (1996), 'The Challenge of Central Banking in a Democratic Society', remarks by Chairman Alan Greenspan at the Annual Dinner and Francis Boyer Lecture of the American Enterprise Institute for Public Policy Research, Washington DC, 5 December; available at www.federalreserve. gov/boarddocs/speeches/1996/19961205.htm.

Felix, David (2002), 'The Economic Case against Free Capital Mobility', in Leslie Elliot Armijo (ed.), *Debating the Global Financial Architecture* (New York: SUNY Press), pp. 126–58.

Ffrench-Davis, Ricardo, et al. (1995), 'Capital Movements, Export Strategy and Macroeconomic Stability in Chile', in Ricardo Ffrench-Davis and Stephany

Griffith-Jones (eds), *Coping with Capital Surges: The Return of Finance to Latin America* (Boulder, CO: Lynne Rienner), pp. 99–144.

Ffrench-Davis, Ricardo (2000), *Reforming the Reforms in Latin America: Macroeconomics, Trade, Finance* (London: Macmillan).

Fischer, Stanley (1999), 'On the Need for an International Lender of Last Resort', revised version of a paper prepared for delivery at the joint luncheon of the American Economic Association and the American Finance Association, New York, 3 January (Washington, DC: IMF); available at http://imf.org/external/np/speeches/1999/010399.htm.

Fukao, Mitsuhiro (1995), *Financial Integration, Corporate Governance, and the Performance of Multinational Companies* (Washington, DC: Brookings Institution).

Germain, Randall D. (1997), *The International Organization of Credit: States and Global Finance in the World-economy* (Cambridge: Cambridge University Press).

Gill, Stephen (1993), 'Neo-liberalism and the Shift towards a US-centred Transnational Hegemony', in Henk Overbeek (ed.), *Restructuring Hegemony in the Global Political Economy: The Rise of Transnational Neo-liberalism in the 1980s* (London: Routledge), pp. 246–82.

Gill, Stephen (1992), 'The Emerging World Order and European Change: The Political Economy of the European Union', in Leo Panitch and Ralph Miliband (eds), *Socialist Register 1992* (London: Merlin Press), pp. 157–96.

Gill, Stephen (1994), 'The Global Political Economy and Structural Change: Globalising Elites in the Emerging World Order', in Yoshikazu Sakamoto (ed.), *Global Transformation* (Tokyo: United Nations University Press), pp. 169–99.

Gill, Stephen (1995), 'The Global Panopticon? The Neoliberal State, Economic Life, and Democratic Surveillance', *Alternatives* 2: 1–49.

Gill, Stephen (1999), 'The Constitution of Global Capitalism', paper presented to the British International Studies Association, University of Manchester, 20–22 December, mimeo.

Gill, Stephen (2003), *Power and Resistance in the New World Order* (London: Palgrave).

Gill, Stephen and David Law (1993), 'Global Hegemony and the Structural Power of Capital', in Stephen Gill (ed.), *Gramsci, Historical Materialism and International Relations* (Cambridge: Cambridge University Press), pp. 93–124.

Gills, Barry K. (1993), 'The Hegemonic Transition in East Asia: A Historical Perspective', in Stephen Gill (ed.), *Gramsci and International Relations* (Cambridge: Cambridge University Press), pp. 186–212.

Giddens, Anthony (ed.) (2001), *The Global Third Way Debate* (Polity: Cambridge University Press).

Gowan, Peter (1999), *The Global Gamble: Washington's Faustian Bid for World Dominance* (London: Verso).

Grabel, Ilene (1996), 'Marketing the Third World: The Contradictions of Portfolio Investment in the Global Economy', *World Development* 24(11): 1761–76.

Grabel, Ilene (1999), 'Mexico Redux? Making Sense of the Financial Crisis of 1997–98', *Journal of Economic Issues* 33(2): 375–81.

Gramsci, Antonio (1992), *Selections from the Prison Notebooks*, trans. Q. Hoare and G.N. Smith (New York: International Publishers).

Greider, William (1997), *One World, Ready or Not: The Manic Logic of Global*

Capitalism (New York: Simon & Schuster).

Griffith-Jones, Stephany (1996), 'International Capital Flows to Latin America', in Victor Bulmer-Thomas (ed.), *The New Economic Model in Latin America and its Impact on Income Distribution and Poverty* (London: Macmillan), pp. 127–43.

Guitián, Manuel (1997), 'Reality and the Logic of Capital Flow Liberalization', in Christine P. Ries and Richard J. Sweeney (eds), *Capital Controls in Emerging Economies* (Boulder, CO: Westview Press), pp. 189–224.

Gurría, José Angel, and Sergio Fadl (1995), 'Mexico's Strategy for Reducing Financial Transfers Abroad', in Robert Grosse (ed.), *Government Responses to the Latin American Debt Problem* (Miami: North–South Center Press), pp. 121–49.

Haley, Mary Ann (1999), 'Emerging Market Makers: The Power of Institutional Investors', in L.E. Armijo (ed.), *Financial Globalization and Democracy in Emerging Markets* (London: Macmillan), pp. 74–90.

Haley, Mary Ann (2001), *Freedom and Finance: Democratization and Institutional Investors in Developing Countries* (New York: Palgrave)

Harmes, Adam (1998), 'Institutional Investors and the Reproduction of Neoliberalism', *Review of International Political Economy* 5(1): 92–121.

Harmes, Adam (2001), *Unseen Power: How Mutual Funds Threaten the Political and Economic Wealth of Nations* (Toronto: Stoddart Publishing).

Hart, Michael (1990), *A North American Free Trade Agreement: The Strategic Implications for Canada* (Halifax: Institute for Research on Public Policy).

Hart-Landsberg, Martin (2002), 'Challenging Neoliberal Myths: A Critical Look at the Mexican Experience', *Monthly Review* 54(7); available at www.monthlyreview.org/1202hartlandsberg.htm.

Helleiner, Eric (1994), *States and the Reemergence of Global Finance: From Bretton Woods to the 1990s* (Ithaca, NY: Cornell University Press).

Helleiner, Eric (1995), 'Explaining the Globalization of Financial Markets: Bringing the States Back In', *Review of International Political Economy* 2(2): 315–41.

Helleiner, Gerald K. (1996), 'Development and Global Governance', in Roy Culpepper and Caroline Pestieau (eds), *Development and Global Governance* (Ottawa: International Development Research Centre/North–South Institute).

Henwood, Doug (1994), 'Anti-Market Forces', *Left Business Observer* 64.

Henwood, Doug (1999), *Wall Street: How It Works and for Whom* (London: Verso).

Holloway, John (1995), 'Global Capital and the National State', in Werner Bonefeld and Holloway (eds), *Global Capital, National State and the Politics of Money* (New York: St Martin's Press), pp. 116–40.

Huntington, Samuel P. (1996), *The Clash of Civilizations and the Remaking of World Order* (New York: Simon & Schuster).

Ikeda, Satoshi (2002), '20th Century Anti-systemic Historical Processes and US Hegemony: Free Trade Imperialism, National Economic Development, and Free Enterprise Imperialism', in Ramon Grosfoguel et al. (eds), *The Modern World-System in the 20th Century* (Westport, CT: Greenwood Press), pp. 103–23.

ILO (2002), *A Future without Child Labour* (Geneva: International Labour Organization).

IMF (1983), *IMF Survey*, 16 January (Washington, DC: IMF).

IMF (1986), *IMF Survey*, 2 June (Washington, DC: IMF).

IMF (1989), *IMF Survey,* 30 October (Washington, DC: IMF).

IMF (1992), *Mexico: The Strategy to Achieve Sustained Economic Growth* (Washington, DC: IMF).

IMF (1995), 'IMF Managing Director Welcomes G-7 Support for IMF', News Brief No. 95/15, 16 June (Washington, DC: IMF); available at www.imf. org/external/np/sec/nb/1995/nb9515.htm.

IMF (1997a), 'IMF Builds on Initiatives to Meet Challenges of Globalization', *IMF Survey*, 9 June (Washington, DC: IMF).

IMF (1997b), 'Capital Account Liberalisation and the Role of the IMF', *IMF Survey*, 20 October (Washington, DC: IMF).

IMF (1998), *IMF Survey: Special Supplement*, 19 October (Washington, DC: IMF).

IMF (1999a), 'The Reforms of the Global Exchange and Financial Systems since the Eruption of the Asian Crisis', address by Shigemitsu Sugisaki, Deputy Managing Director of the IMF, at the International Conference on Central Banking Policies, Macau, 14 May (Washington, DC: IMF).

IMF (1999b), 'The International Financial Institutions: A View from the IMF', address by Alassane D. Ouattara, Deputy Managing Director of the IMF, at the Mid-winter Conference of the Bankers' Association for Foreign Trade, 3 February (Washington, DC: IMF).

IMF (2000a), *Annual Report* (Washington, DC: IMF)

IMF (2000b), 'The Role of International Financial Institutions in the International Monetary Fund', report of the Acting Managing Director to the International Monetary and Financial Committee on Progress in Reforming the IMF and Strengthening the Architecture of the International Financial System; available at www.imf.org/external/np/omd/2000/report.htm#11_F.

IMF (2000c), *Recovery from the Asian Crisis and the Role of the IMF*, IMF Staff Essays (Washington, DC: IMF).

IMF (2000d), *Capital Controls: Country Experiences with Their Use and Liberalization,* Occasional Essay 190, 17 May (Washington, DC: IMF).

IMF (2000e), *Recovery from the Asian Crisis and the Role of the IMF*, IMF Staff Essays (Washington, DC: IMF).

IMF (2000f), *Chile: Selected Issues*, IMF Staff Country Report (Washington, DC: IMF).

IMF (2001a), *IMF Survey*, 2 April (Washington, DC: IMF).

IMF and World Bank (2001b), 'Reports on the Observance of Standards and Codes (ROSCs) (Washington, DC: IMF); available at www.imf.org/external/np/rosc/2000/stand.htm.

IMF (2002), 'Reports on the Observances of Standards and Codes' (Washington, DC: IMF); available at www.imf.org/external/np/rosc/rosc.asp.

Jang Ha-sung (2001), 'Corporate Governance and Economic Development: The Korean Experience', in Farrukh Iqbal and Jong-Il You (eds), *Democracy, Market Economics and Development: An Asian Perspective* (Washington, DC: World Bank Group).

Jansen, K. (1997), *External Finance in Thailand's Development: An Interpretation of Thailand's Growth Boom* (London: Macmillan).

Jenkins, Barbara (1992), *The Paradox of Continental Production: National Investment Policies in North America* (Ithaca, NY: Cornell University Press).

Jessop, Bob (1983), 'Capitalism and Democracy: The Best Possible Political Shell', in David Held et al. (eds), *States and Societies* (Oxford: Martin Robertson), pp. 272–89.

Jessop, Bob (1999) 'Reflections on Globalization and its (Il)logics', in Peter Dicken, Philip Kelley, Kris Olds and Henry Yeung (eds), *Globalization and the Asia Pacific: Contested Territories* (London: Routledge), pp. 19–38.

Jessop, Bob (2000), 'The Dynamics of Partnership and Governance Failure', in Gerry Stoker, ed., *The New Politics of Local Governance in Britain* (London: Macmillan), pp. 11–32.

Johnson, S., et al. (2000), 'Corporate Governance in the Asian Financial Crisis', *Journal of Financial Economics* 58(1/2): 141–86.

Johnston, Barry K. (1998), 'Sequencing Capital Account Liberalization and Financial Sector Reform', IMF Paper on Policy Analysis and Assessment (Washington, DC: IMF); available at www.imf.org/external/pubs/ft/ppaa/ppaa9808.pdf.

Johnston, Chalmers (1999), 'The Developmental State: Odyssey of a Concept', in Meredith Woo-Cumings (ed.), *The Developmental State* (Ithaca: Cornell University Press), pp. 32–60.

Jomo K.S. (ed.) (1998) *Tigers in Trouble: Financial Governance, Liberalisation and Crises in East Asia* (London: Zed Books).

Jomo K.S. (2001a), 'From Currency Crisis to Recession', in Jomo K.S. (ed.), *Malaysian Eclipse: Economic Crisis and Recovery* (London: Zed Books), pp. 1–46.

Jomo K.S. (2001b), 'Capital Flows', in Jomo K.S. (ed.), *Malaysian Eclipse: Economic Crisis and Recovery* (London: Zed Books), pp. 134–73.

Kahler, Miles (ed.) (1998), *Capital Flows and Financial Crises* (Ithaca, NY: Cornell University Press).

Kapstein, E.B. (1994), *Governing the Global Economy: International Finance and the State* (Cambridge, MA: Harvard University Press).

Kapur, Devesh (1998), 'The IMF: A Cure or a Curse?', *Foreign Policy*, Summer: 114–29.

Keasey, Kevin, et al. (1997), 'Introduction: The Corporate Governance Problem – Competing Diagnoses and Solutions', in Kevin Keasey et al. (eds), *Corporate Governance: Economic and Financial Issues* (Oxford: Oxford University Press), pp. 36–50.

Kenen, Peter B. (2001), *The International Financial Architecture: What's New? What's Missing?* (Washington, DC: Institute for International Economics).

Kirton, John K., and George M. von Furstenberg (eds) (2001), *New Directions in Global Economic Governance: Managing Globalisation in the Twenty-First Century* (Aldershot: Ashgate).

Kopinak, Kathryn (1994) 'The Maquiladorization of the Mexican Economy', in R. Grinspun and M.A. Cameron (eds), *The Political Economy of North American Free Trade* (New York: St Martin's Press), pp. 141–61.

Körner, Peter et al. (eds) (1984), *The IMF and the Debt Crisis: A Guide to the Third World's Dilemmas* (London: Zed Books).

Lamfalussy, Alexandre (2000), *Financial Crises in Emerging Markets* (New Haven, CT: Yale University Press).

Lane, Timothy D., et al. (1999), *IMF-Supported Programs in Indonesia, Korea, and Thailand: A Preliminary Assessment*, IMF Occasional Essay 178 (Washington, DC: IMF).

Lannoo, Karel (1999), 'A European Perspective on Corporate Governance', *Journal of Common Market Studies* 37(2): 269–96.

La Porta, R., et al. (1999) 'Corporate Ownership around the World', *Journal of Finance* 54(2): 471–517.

Lazonick, William, and Mary O'Sullivan (2000), 'Maximizing Shareholder Value: A New Ideology for Corporate Governance', *Economy and Society* 29(1): 13–35.

Lerrick, Adam, and Allan H. Melzter (2002), 'Grants: A Better Way to Deliver Aid', *Quarterly International Economics Report* (Carnegie Mellon: Gailliot Center for Public Policy).

Lustig, Nora (1995), 'The Mexican Peso Crisis: The Foreseeable and the Surprise' (Washington, DC: Brookings Institution); available at www.brook.edu/dybdocroot/views/papers/bdp/bdp114/bdp114.pdf.

MacEwan, Arthur (1990), *Debt and Disorder: International Economic Instability and U.S. Imperial Decline* (New York: Monthly Review Press).

Magdoff, Harry, et al. (2002), 'The New Face of Capitalism: Slow Growth, Excess Capital, and a Mountain of Debt', *Monthly Review* 53(11); available at www.monthlyreview.org/0402editr.htm.

Mahon, James E., Jr. (1999), 'Economic Crisis in Latin America: Global Contagion, Local Pain', *Current History* (March): 105–10.

Marx, Karl (1991), *Capital,* Volume 3 (London: Penguin).

Masson, Paul R., et al. (1996), 'The Mexican Peso Crisis – Overview and Analysis of Credibility Factors', Working Paper No. 96/6 (Washington, DC: IMF).

Maxfield, Sylvia (1990), *Governing Capital: International Finance and Mexican Politics* (Ithaca, NY: Cornell University Press).

Maxfield, Sylvia (1996), *Gatekeepers of Growth: The International Political Economy of Central Banking in Developing Countries* (Princeton, NJ: Princeton University Press).

Méndez, J. Silvestre (1994), *Problemas Económicos de México*, 3rd edn (México: McGraw-Hill).

McConnell, James, and Alan MacPherson (1994), 'The North American Free Trade Area: An Overview of Issues and Prospects', in Richard Gibb and Michalak Wieslaw (eds), *Continental Trading Blocs: The Growth of Regionalism in the World Economy* (Chichester: John Wiley), pp. 163–88.

Miller, Marcus (2002), 'Sovereign Debt Restructuring: New Articles, New Contracts – or No Change?', *International Economics Policy Briefs,* No. PB02–3, April.

Mittelman, James (2000) *The Globalization Syndrome* (Princeton: Princeton University Press).

Monks, R.A.G., and N. Minow (1996), *Watching the Watchers: Corporate Governance for the 21st Century* (London: Blackwell Publishers).

Mutume, Gumisai (2001), 'US Congressional Commission Pushes for Deeper IMF, World Bank Reforms'; available at www.probeinternational.org/pi/wb/index.cfm?DSP=content&ContentID=2008.

Naim, Moises (1995), 'Mexico's Larger Story', *Foreign Policy* 99: 112–31.

Naim, Moises (1999), 'Fads and Fashion in Economic Reforms: Washington Consenus or Washington Confusion?', working draft of a paper prepared for the IMF Conference on Second Generation Reforms, Washington, DC; available at www.imf.org/external/pubs/ft/seminar/1999/reforms/Naim. htm.

Ocampo, José Antonio (2000), 'A Broad Agenda for International Financial Reform', in J.A. Ocampo et al. (eds), *Financial Globalization and the Emerging Economies* (Santiago: United Nations Economic Commission for Latin America and the Caribbean), pp. 41–62.

Ocampo, José Antonio (2001), 'A Broad Agenda for International Financial Reform', American Economic Association Annual Meeting, New Orleans, 5–7 January, mimeo.

Ocampo, José Antonio (2002), 'Rethinking the Development Agenda', *Cambridge Journal of Economics* 26(3): 393–407; available at www.eclac.org/noticias/ articulos/4/5784/rethinking3.pdf.

OECD (1997), *The World in 2020: Towards a New Global Age* (Paris: OECD).

OECD (1998), *OECD Corporate Governance Guidelines* (Paris: OECD).

OECD (1999), *OECD Principles of Corporate Governance*, SG/CG (99)5 (Paris: OECD).

Palan, Ronen (2000), 'New Trends in Global Political Economy', in R. Palan (ed.), *Global Political Economy: Contemporary Theories* (London: Routledge), pp. 1–18.

Panitch, Leo (1994), 'Rethinking the Role of the State in an Era of Globalization', in Ralph Miliband and Leo Panitch (eds), *Socialist Register 1994* (London: Merlin Press), pp. 60–93.

Panitch, Leo (2000), 'The New Imperial State', *New Left Review* 2: 5–20.

Panitch, Leo (2001), 'Reflections on Strategy for Labour', in Leo Panitch et al. (eds), *Socialist Register 2001* (London: Merlin Press); available at www.yorku. ca/socreg/panitch01.html.

Pastor, Manuel, Jr. (1999), 'Globalization, Sovereignty, and Policy Choice: Lessons from the Mexican Peso Crisis', in David A. Smith et al. (eds), *States and Sovereignty in the Global Economy* (London: Routledge), pp. 210–29.

Patomäki, Heikki (2001), *Democratising Globalisation: The Leverage of the Tobin Tax* (London and New York: Zed Books).

Pauly, Louis W. (1997), *Who Elected the Bankers? Surveillance and Control in the World Economy* (Ithaca: Cornell University Press).

Pauly, Louis W. (1999), 'Good Governance and Bad Policy: The Perils of International Organization Overextension', *Review of International Political Economy* 6(4): 401–24.

Pender, John (2001), 'From "Structural Adjustment" to "Comprehensive Development Framework": Conditionality Transformed?', *Third World Quarterly* 2(3): 397–411.

Petras, James, et al. (1994), *Democracy and Poverty in Chile: The Limits to Electoral Politics* (Boulder, CO: Westview Press).

Petras, James, and Henry Veltmeyer with Steve Vieux (1997), *Neoliberalism and Class Conflict in Latin America: A Comparative Perspective on the Political Economy of Structural Adjustment* (New York: St Martin's Press).

Phongpaichit, P., and C. Baker (1995), *Thailand: Economy and Politics* (Kuala Lumpur: Oxford University Press).

Poulantzas, Nicos (1974), *Classes in Contemporary Capitalism* (London: New Left Books).

Pound, John (1995), 'The Promise of Governed Corporation', *Harvard Business Review* 73: 89–98.

Porter, Tony (1997), 'NAFTA, North American Financial Integration and Regulatory Cooperation in Banking and Securities', in Geoffrey R.D. Underhill (ed.), *The New World Order in International Finance* (New York: St Martin's Press), pp. 174–92.

Prebisch, Raúl (1971) *Change and Development: Latin America's Great Task. Report Submitted to the Inter-American Development Bank* (New York: Praeger).

Raghavan, Chakravarthi (1998), 'Institutional Funds – The Main Channel for Market Turbulence', *Third World Economics* 187/188 (16 June–15 July); also published in the *South–North Development Monitor*, www.twnside.org.sg/title/main-cn.htm.

Rajan, Ramkishen S. (2000), 'Examining the Case for an Asian Monetary Fund', Visiting Researchers Series 3 (Singapore: Institute for Southeast Asian Studies); available at www.iseas.edu.sg/vr32000.pdf.

Randel, J. et al. (eds) (2002) *An Independent Review of Poverty Reduction and International Development Assistance: The Reality of Aid* (Manila: IBON).

Report of the President's Working Group on Financial Markets (1999), *Hedge Funds, Leverage, and the Lessons of Long Term Credit Management* (Washington, DC: US Treasury Department); available at www.treas.gov/press/releases/reports/hedgfund.pdf.

Ricketts, M. (1998), *The Many Ways of Governance* (London: Special Affairs Unit).

Rodrick, Dani (1998), 'Who Needs Capital Account Convertibility?', *Essays in International Finance* 207 (Department of Economics, Princeton University); available at http://ksghome.harvard.edu/~.drodrik.academic.ksg/essay.pdf.

Roman, Richard and Edur Velasco Arregui (2001), 'Neoliberalism, Labor Market Transformation, and Working-Class Responses: Social and Historical Roots of Accommodation and Protest', *Latin American Perspectives* 28(4): 52–71.

Rosenau, James N. (1995), 'Governance in the Twenty-first Century', *Global Governance* 1(1): 13–43.

Rupert, Mark (1997), 'Globalization and the Reconstruction of Common Sense in the US', in S. Gill and J. Mittelman (eds), *Innovation and Transformation in International Studies* (Cambridge: Cambridge University Press); also available at www.maxwell.syr.edu/maxpages/faculty/merupert/Research/cox.htm

Sachs, Jeffrey (1998), 'The IMF and the Asian Flu', *The American Prospect* 37; available at http://epn.org/prospect/37/37sachf.html.

Saxton, Jim (2000), 'International Dimensions to U.S. Monetary Policy' (Washington, DC: Joint Economic Committee of the United States Congress).

Schleifer, A., and R. Vishny (1997), 'A Survey of Corporate Governance', *Journal of Finance* 52(3): 737–83.

SEDESOL (Secretaría de Desarrollo Social) (1999), *Programme to Overcome Poverty 1995–2000*; available at www.sedesol.gob.mx/html2/over/sistesis.htm.

Sen, Amartya (1999), *Development as Freedom* (New York: Anchor Books).

Shelley, Mary (1988), *Frankenstein* (New York: Tom Doherty Associates).

Shiller, Robert J. (2000), *Irrational Exuberance* (New York: Random House).

Showstack-Sassoon, Anne (1982), *Approaches to Gramsci* (London: Writers & Readers).

Sinclair, Timothy J. (1994), 'Passing Judgement: Credit Rating Processes as Regulatory Mechanisms of Governance in the Emerging World Order', *Review of International Political Economy* 1(1): 133–59.

Sinclair, Timothy J. (1996), 'Beyond International Relations Theory: Robert W. Cox and Approaches to World Order', in Robert W. Cox with Timothy J. Sinclair, *Approaches to World Order* (Cambridge: Cambridge University Press), pp. 3–18.

Sklair, Leslie, and Peter T. Robbins (2002), 'Global Capitalism and Major Corporations from the Third World', *Third World Quarterly* 23(1): 81–100.

Smith, John Grieve (1999), 'A New Bretton Woods: Reforming the Global Financial System', in Jonathan Michie and John Grieve Smith (eds), *Global Instability: The Political Economy of World Economic Governance* (London: Routledge), pp. 227–50.

Soederberg, Susanne (2001a), 'The New International Financial Architecture', Guest Editor, *Global Governance* 7(4): 453–67.

Soederberg, Susanne (2001b), 'From Neoliberalism to Social Liberalism: Situating the National Solidarity Program within Mexico's Passive Revolutions', *Latin American Perspectives* 28(3): 104–23.

Soederberg, Susanne (2002), 'A Historical Materialist Account of the Chilean Capital Control: Prototype Policy for Whom?', *Review of International Political Economy* 9(3): 490–512.

Soros, George (1998), 'Capitalism's Last Chance?', *Foreign Policy* 113: 55–66.

Sternberg, Elaine (1999), *The Stakeholder Concept: A Mistaken Doctrine* (London: Foundation for Business Responsibilities).

Stiglitz, Joseph (1998a), 'More Instruments and Broader Goals: Moving Toward the Post-Washington Consensus', 1998 WIDER Annual Lecture, Helsinki; available at www.worldbank.org/html/extdr/extme/js-010798/wider.pdf.

Stiglitz, Joseph (1998b), 'The Role of International Financial Institutions in the Current Global Economy', address to the Chicago Council on Foreign Relations by Joseph Stiglitz, Senior Vice President and Chief Economist, the World Bank, Chicago, 27 February; available at www.worldbank.org/html/extdr/extme/jssp022/98.htm.

Stiglitz, Joseph (1998c), Foreword to *Global Economic Prospects 1998/99 Report* (Washington, DC: World Bank); available at www.worldbank.org/prospects/gep98–99/foreword.htm.

Stiglitz, Joseph (2002), *Globalization and its Discontents* (New York: W.W. Norton).

Story, Dale (1986), *The Mexican Ruling Party: Stability and Authority* (New York: Praeger).

Strange, Susan (1986), *Casino Capitalism* (Oxford: Oxford University Press).

Strange, S. (1994), *States and Markets*, 2nd edn (London: Pinter).

Strange, S. (1998a), 'The New World of Debt', *New Left Review* 230 (July–August): 91–114.

Strange, Susan (1998b), *Mad Money* (Manchester: Manchester University Press).

Stremlau, John (1994/95), 'Clinton's Dollar Diplomacy', *Foreign Policy* 97: 18–36.

Sugisaki, Shigemitsu (1999), 'The Reforms of the Global Exchange and Financial Systems since the Eruption of the Asian Crisis', 14 May (Washington, DC: IMF).

Taylor, Marcus (2002), 'An Historical Materialist Critique of Neoliberalism in Chile', *Historical Materialism* 10(2): 45–76.

Taylor, Marcus (2003), 'The Reformulation of Social Policy in Chile, 1973–2001: Questioning a Neoliberal Model', *Global Social Policy* 3(1): 21–44.

Taylor, Marcus (2004) 'Responding to Neoliberalism in Crisis: Discipline and Empowerment in the World Bank's New Development Agenda', in P. Zarembka and S. Soederberg (eds), *Research in Political Economy* 21, forthcoming.

Teichmann, Judith (2002), 'Private Sector Power and Market Reform: Exploring the Domestic Origins of Argentina's Meltdown and Mexico's Policy Failures', *Third World Quarterly* 23(3): 491–512.

Tobin, James (1978), 'A Proposal for International Monetary Reform', *Eastern Economic Journal* 4(3–4): 153–9.

Tooze, Roger, and Craig N. Murphy (1991), 'Getting Beyond the "Common Sense" of the IPE Orthodoxy', in R. Tooze and C.N. Murphy (eds), *The New International Political Economy* (Boulder, CO: Lynne Rienner), pp. 9–31.

Tooze, Roger (1999), 'International Political Economy in the Age of Globalization', in John Baylis and Steve Smith (eds), *The Globalization of World Politics: An Introduction to International Relations* (Oxford: Oxford University Press), pp. 212–30.

Trejo, Raúl Delarbre (1991) 'El movimiento obrero: situación y perspectivas', in Pablo Casanova González et al. (eds), *México Hoy* (México: Siglo XXI), pp. 128–41.

Ugarteche, Oscar (2000), *The False Dilemma, Globalization: Opportunity or Threat?* (London: Zed Books).

Underhill, Geoffrey R.D. (1997), 'Private Markets and Public Responsibility in a Global System: Conflict and Co-operation in Transnational Banking and Securities Regulation', in Geoffrey R.D. Underhill (ed.), *The New World Order in International Finance* (London: Macmillan), pp. 17–49.

United Nations (2002) 'Final Outcome of the International Conference on Financing for Development', A/CONF.198/3 (New York: United Nations); available at www.un.org/esa/ffd/0302finalMonterreyConsensus.pdf.

UNDP (United Nations Development Programme) (1999), *Human Development Report 1999* (New York: Oxford University Press).

UNDP (United Nations Development Programme) (2000), *Human Development Report 2000* (New York: Oxford University Press).

UNDP (United Nations Development Programme) (2002), *Human Development 2002* (New York: Oxford University Press).

Van der Pijl, Kees (1993), 'The Sovereignty of Capital Impaired: Social Forces and Codes of Conduct for Multinational Corporations', in Henk Overbeek (ed.), *Restructuring Hegemony in the Global Political Economy* (London: Routledge), pp. 28–57.

Van der Pijl, Kees (1998), *Transnational Classes and International Relations* (London: Routledge).

Veltmeyer, Henry, et al. (2000), *Neoliberalism and Class Conflict in Latin America: A Comparative Perspective on the Political Economy of Structural Adjustment* (New York: St Martin's Press).

Veltmeyer, Henry, James Petras and Steve Vieux (1996), *Neoliberalism and Class Conflict in Latin America: A Comparative Perspective on the Political Economy of Structural Adjustment* (London: Macmillan).

Van Den Berghe, L., and L. De Ridder (1999), *International Standardisation of Good Corporate Governance: Best Practices for the Board of Directors* (Boston: Kluwer).

Vives, Xavier (2000) 'Corporate Governance: Does it Matter?', in Xavier Vives (ed.), *Corporate Governance: Theoretical and Empirical Perspectives* (Cambridge: Cambridge University Press), pp. 1–22.

Von Braunmühl, Claudia (1978), 'On the Analysis of the Bourgeois Nation State within the World Market Context: An Attempt to Develop a Methodological and Theoretical Approach', in John Holloway and Sol Picciotto (eds), *State and Capital: A Marxist Debate* (London: Edward Arnold), pp. 160–77.

Wade, Robert and Frank Veneroso (1998a), 'The Asian Crisis: The High Debt Model versus the Wall Street–Treasury–IMF Complex', *New Left Review* 228 (March–April): 3–24.

Wade, Robert, and Frank Veneroso (1998b), 'The Gathering World Slump and the Battle over Capital Controls', *New Left Review* 231 (September–October): 13–43.

Walker G., and M. Fox (2000), 'Corporate Governance Reform in East Asia', *Corporate Governance* 2(1): 4–9.

Weber, Heloise (2002), 'Imposing a global development architecture', *Review of International Studies* 28(3): 537–55.

Weintraub, Sidney (2000), *Financial Decision-Making in Mexico: To Bet a Nation* (Pittsburgh: University of Pittsburgh Press).

Williamson, John (1990), *Latin American Adjustment: How Much Has Happened?* (Washington, DC: Institute for International Economics).

Williamson, John (1993), 'Democracy and the Washington Consensus', *World Development* 21(8): 1329–36.

Williamson, John (1997), 'Orthodoxy is Right: Liberalize the Capital Account Last', in Christine P. Ries and Richard J. Sweeney (eds), *Capital Controls in Emerging Economies* (Boulder, CO: Westview Press), pp. 13–16.

Wolfensohn, James D. (1999), 'A Proposal for a Comprehensive Development Framework', memo to the board, management and staff of the World Bank Group, Washington, DC.

Wolff, Richard D. (2002), 'The U.S. Economic Crisis: A Marxian Analysis', *Rethinking Marxism* 14(1): 118–31.

World Bank (1998), *Financial Vulnerability, Spill-over Effects, and Contagion: Lessons from the Asian Crises for Latin America – World Bank Latin American and Caribbean Studies: Viewpoints* (Washington, DC: World Bank).

World Bank (2000a), *World Development Report 2000/01 Attacking Poverty* (New York: Oxford University Press).

World Bank (2000b), *World Development Report 2002: Building Institutions for Markets* (New York: Oxford University Press).

World Bank (2001), *Global Development Finance: Building Coalitions for Effective Development Finance* (Washington, DC: World Bank).

World Bank (2002), *Global Development Finance: Financing the Poorest Countries* (Washington, DC: World Bank).

World Bank (2003), *Global Development Finance: Striving for Stability in Development Finance* (Washington, DC: World Bank).

Zhuang Juzhong et al. (2000), *Corporate Governance and Finance in East Asia: A Study of Indonesia, Republic of Korea, Malaysia, Philippines, and Thailand* (Manila: Asian Development Bank).

Zysman, John (1983), *Governments, Markets, and Growth: Financial Systems and the Politics of Industrial Change* (Ithaca: Cornell University Press).

Index

Reports on the Observances of Standards and Codes (ROSCs), 1–2, 4, 23, 25, 131–2, 136–8, 141–2, 153–5, 174, 179; transparency module, 139

ringitt devaluation, 117

Rio de Janeiro, Earth Summit 1992, 'Agenda 21', 180

Rivero, Oswaldo de, 183, 188

rogue states, notion of, 176

Rosenau, James, 140

Rubin, Robert, 10, 78

Rupert, Mark, 3

Russia, 112, 125; bail-out, 71; financial crisis, 15, 117

Sader, Emir, 18, 20

Salinas de Gortari, Carlos, 37, 42–3, 46

Saudi Arabia, 2, 81

savings: East Asia domestic high rates, 16, 86, 107, 123, 133; US rates, 77, 98

Schiller, Robert J., 156

second generation reforms (SGRs), 19, 164, 172–4, 198

securitization, 98–100, 153

Sen, Amartya, 174

shareholder rights: activism, 150–53, minority shareholders, 136, 145–6; 'value', 132; voting, 147

Shelley, Mary, 8

Silva, Luíz Inacio 'Lula' da, 21

Singapore, 2, 137, 183; FSF meeting 2000, 82

Somalia, 179

Soros, George, 64, 86

sound fundamentals, 156

South Africa, 2, 81

South Korea, 2, 64, 81, 89, 125, 183, 185, 191; financial crisis, 15; fiscal transparency level, 154; IMF bail-out, 71, 135; IMF leverage, 137

South, the: accumulation conditions, 22; capital account liberalization, 7, 15; crisis of authority/legitimacy, 7, 15, 17–18, 20, 97, 109, 169; definition of, 163, 169; high interest rates, 20, 79; income inequality, 171; market credibility, 17; Northern investment, 100; over-lending to, 31; policy autonomy constraints, 15, 79; political elites, 97, 109; poverty, *see* poverty; 'Third Way' politics, 90; US interference, 73; US structural power, 8

sovereign bankruptcy procedures, 164, 167, 193–4, 197; SDRM-2, 195–6

sovereign debt management, 166

Spain, Mexican bank ownership, 19

Special Data Dissemination Standard (SDDS), IMF, 56–7

Sri Lanka, portfolio investment, 105

Standard & Poor's, 131, 139, 142–4, 153; coercive power, 140; corporate governance definition, 145; index, 48; Japan downgrading, 141

state intervention, economic, 148

Stiglitz, Joseph, 33, 64, 124, 136, 175, 186

Strange, Susan, 4, 8, 15–16, 22, 46, 52, 78, 100–101, 194

structural adjustment policies (SAPs), 33, 73, 78, 83, 88, 139, 165–6, 171, 173; depoliticization aim, 32; Mexico, 34–5; neoliberal-led, 37

Suharto, ex-President, downfall, 120

Sweden: aid target fulfilment, 180; corporate governance model, 148

'systematically important' emerging markets, 1–2, 5, 23, 81, 84, 125

Taiwan, 86, 123, 126, 183, 185; companies, 154; outsourcing, 188

tax avoidance, 186

Taylor, John, 177, 195

Taylor, Marcus, 112, 174

Teichmann, Judith, 35

Telmex, Mexican telephone company, 46

'Tequila Effect', 52